Also by Philip Hamburger

THE OBLONG BLUR AND OTHER ODYSSEYS
J. P. MARQUAND, ESQUIRE
MAYOR WATCHING AND OTHER PLEASURES
OUR MAN STANLEY
AN AMERICAN NOTEBOOK

PHILIP HAMBURGER

Curious

World

A NEW YORKER AT LARGE

NORTH POINT PRESS
San Francisco *1987*

FOR ANNA

Contents

Introduction: A Personal Note

While putting together this selection of almost fifty years of work I have allowed my mind to wander, somewhat freely, over many of the experiences and personalities encountered during this particular, and exhilarating, personal journey. Since all of the stories in this book first appeared in the *New Yorker*, most of my memories deal with life at that singular and exceptionally humane publication. I have had the privilege of being permitted to write as I pleased—minus diktat or interference, and always with patient support—by two of the most remarkable editors of my time: Harold W. Ross and William Shawn. Indefinable and magical qualities somehow got hold of both of these men, and they in turn transmitted glimpses of their strange alchemy to those fortunate enough to work for them. Their message to the writer (at least, to *this* writer) was both immensely simple and immensely complex: Be yourself. Be unafraid. Stretch your imagination. Above all, seek the truth, as you see the truth. Don't fret about the possibility of offending someone if what you write is what you know to be correct. We are presenting you with that most precious elixir—freedom. The rest is up to you.

I went to work for the *New Yorker* in February 1939, the fifteenth year of the magazine's existence. I was twenty-five years old. Through the good offices of Henry F. Pringle, who had been a teacher of mine at the Graduate School of Journalism at Columbia University, who had written many of the early *New Yorker* Profiles, and whose biography of Theodore Roosevelt had won the Pulitzer Prize, I was given a letter of introduction to St. Clair McKelway, then the *New Yorker*'s managing editor. McKelway was not only a superb editor, but was one of the truly beautiful prose writers of his day, and it is typical of the fickle spotlight that catches literary celebrities in its glare that he has never been properly recognized for the master literary craftsman that he was.

McKelway read Pringle's letter and asked me to come to his office at 25 West Forty-third Street. McKelway was tall, suave, strikingly handsome, and given to tugging at a rather distinguished blond mustache. "Try your hand at some of these 'Talk of the Town' assignments," he said, almost apologetically. "Try to make the stories funny. And you might remember that one can be serious without being solemn." It was quite evident that he was not given to small talk. The interview was over. I had been too excited to notice much about the office. I was too anxious to get on with the assignments he had handed me. I do not recall exactly what they were about, but for the next week I went to Queens, to Staten Island, into the turbulent tide (on a boat) of the East River, wrote my stories, and took them back to McKelway. McKelway read the stories while I sat at his desk. I was calmer now, and some impressions of the office became etched in my memory. There was nothing remotely grand about his office, or for that matter about any of the other spaces that constituted the *New Yorker*. The premises—they are still occupied by the magazine—were so undistinguished and unglamorous that they reached a plateau of genuine elegance and honesty unmatched anywhere else in my experience. The bare white walls, the somewhat battered wooden desk, the swivel chair with tattered green leather backing, the stacks of proofs piled high on McKelway's desk, gave me a feeling of the deepest comfort. I recall being especially impressed by an ordinary Big Ben alarm clock that ticked loudly, and by a marmalade jar crammed with extraordinarily sharp, thick brown pencils. McKelway finished reading what I had given to him, tugged at that mustache, and mumbled something that I took to be neither encouragement nor its opposite, and I left.

For the next few days, I sat at home pondering what appeared to be a dark future. The phone rang. It was McKelway.

"Where are you?" he said.

"What do you mean?"

"I hired you last week. You haven't showed up."

"When do you want me?"

"Now," he said, and hung up.

I reached the office in World Class time, and was directed to a cubicle roughly the size of a hotel icebox, containing three desks. "That's yours," said McKelway, pointing to the desk in the middle. On the desk was a typewriter, a telephone, a tall pile of yellow copy paper, and an ordinary water glass, filled with the brand of sharp pencils I had seen in McKelway's office. "We're a bit crowded here," said McKelway. "Your companions in this room are Brendan Gill and David Lardner. They would seem to be out at the moment. I'll be in touch."

I was a happy man. I sat a while and just stared across the next desk and out the window. The view was north, toward the imposing monolithic slab of the RCA Building in Rockefeller Center, over a group of relatively low structures. (Incidentally, my office today, forty-eight years later, although one floor above the original, looks out upon the same striking cityscape; those low buildings are among the few not destroyed by real estate's inexorable midtown march.) My reverie was interrupted by a knock on the door. A man with the most direct and honest features I have ever seen entered volcanically. The terrain of his face was rugged. There were gaps between his teeth. Humor played all over his face. His dark hair stood straight up, porcupine-style. His wrists did not seem permanently attached either to his hands or his arms. They revolved in private orbits. "Hamburger," he said, in a deep, resounding voice that I continue to hear down through the years, "I'm Ross. Welcome, and God bless." And he was gone.

It dawned on me that I had become a member of the staff. There had been no mention of salary, and no forms had been filled out. Some sort of celebration seemed in order. I telephoned a young woman of my acquaintance, met her in front of the New York Public Library (one block from the office), took her to a Times Square restaurant, where we demolished a seven-course dinner for one dollar twenty-five cents each, walked over to the nearby St. James Theatre, purchased two seats in the second balcony for one dollar ten cents each, and saw Maurice Evans as Falstaff in *Henry IV, part I*. The day had been a perfect one. Thinking back now, I find myself drawn to the words of the poet Czeslaw Milosz: "How could I have expected that after a long life I would understand no more than to wake up at night and to repeat: strange, strange, strange. . . . O how funny and strange."

Work began in earnest the next morning. The *New Yorker* does not officially open until ten o'clock (a civilized hour), but Brendan Gill, a slim man with jet black hair, was already at his desk by the window when I arrived. He was extremely pleasant. "I'm glad I got here first," he said, "as it was necessary to climb over your desk in order to reach mine." Brendan is an early riser and to this day (although now occupying an office entirely to himself) is reputed to arrive at the crack of dawn. Our friendship has been a close one for many years, and for reasons obscured by the mists of time we invariably address one another as Uncle Brendan and Uncle Phil. McKelway had left some assignments on my desk, and I was out of the office until later in the day. When I returned a young man was occupying the first desk, and I had to scramble unceremoniously across his desk to gain mine. He was amused by the procedure. "Welcome to our cozy little nest," he said. It was David Lardner, the youngest son of Ring Lardner. My all-fours entrance was the beginning of another close friendship. We spent a great deal of after-hours time together in the semi-official watering holes of the *New Yorker*, Bleeck's Artist & Writers Restaurant (Formerly Club), on West Fortieth Street, and at Tim Costello's celebrated saloon on Third Avenue. David and I were constant moviegoers, with special attention to the films of the Marx Brothers and W. C. Fields. David loved to laugh. He always sat in the first or second row (his eyes were wretched) and laughed and laughed. He went overseas for the *New Yorker* as a war correspondent, and this brilliant man was silenced forever by an exploding mine at Aachen on October 18, 1944.

Time spent with Harold W. Ross: He has often been presented to the public in what I consider misleading terms, as a diamond in the rough, basically uneducated, and given to wondering whether Moby Dick was the man or the whale. This is a form of blasphemy. How can one define genius? (It is true that he had little formal education, and had never been near a college. Neither had Wolcott Gibbs nor McKelway. Lardner had found Yale wanting, and walked away. Joseph Mitchell had attended the University of North Carolina at Chapel Hill, but had failed mathematics. A. J. Liebling had flunked out of Dartmouth by failing to rise in time for morning chapel. Shawn had attended the University of Michigan at a tender age, but dropped out. Thurber came from Ohio State, John McNulty from the back of a candy store in Massachusetts, E. B. White from Cornell, Bainbridge from Northwestern. I had graduated from Johns Hopkins, almost, as I look back, by accident. Gill *had* graduated from Yale, and Kahn from Harvard. And so it went.) But back to Ross. He had a custom in those days of calling in, one by one, the young persons who had turned in "Talk" stories for that week, and going over them line by line and point by point. This provided an unmatched and unparalleled education. I still find it hard to believe that a fledgling writer could have so direct, clear, understanding, and rewarding a relationship with the editor in chief. His questions were deeply penetrating. "Facts," he would say, "give me the facts." Detail fascinated him. The human comedy fascinated him. From time to time, looking up from the copy on his desk, he would say, "Never go cosmic on me, Hamburger," or "Circulation is rising too fast— a very dangerous business," or "Don't expect literary fame—it's like lightning, either it'll strike or it won't." Hardly a word left his lips that was not hugely colloquial, wise and funny. I have no idea where the notion of Ross as an ill-mannered ogre arose. He had a deep concern for other people. "I saw your wife on the street today, Hamburger," he said to me one early evening in his office. "For Christ sake, she's pregnant. You have one child already, where in hell you going to put the next one? *Writers!* I called your landlord, and I think he'll give you a larger apartment." The next day, my landlord, Vincent Astor, telephoned me. "My friend Ross tells me you need larger quarters," said Captain Astor. "I'm going to knock down a wall to the next apartment for you." Some ogre!

The *New Yorker* family in those days was relatively small. The great E. B. White was in a corner office, turning out incomparable "Notes and Comment" pieces for the "Talk of the Town." A handful of us wrote the "Talk" pieces that followed "Comment" in the book: Bainbridge, Kahn, Charles Cooke, Eugene Kinkead, Lardner, and myself, among others. Russell Maloney would rewrite the "Talk" notes of new reporters. Within a week or two, McKelway told me that my notes were of sufficient quality that no rewriting was necessary, and that I was on my own. "By the way," he said, "your salary will be twenty-five dollars a week."

I kept hearing stories about a remarkably intelligent, shy, remote man named William Shawn, who had an office somewhere down the hall near Ross. Between them, he and Ross were reputed to turn out dozens of ideas for the magazine each day. I caught my first glimpse of him one bright, warm day, waiting for an elevator on the nineteenth floor. He was carrying a bulging briefcase and a furled umbrella, and he was tightly bundled in a dark greatcoat with wraparound scarf. He politely tipped his hat to me as he stepped into the elevator. I did have time, though, sailing down that corridor, to be struck by the delicacy of his features, the kindness of his face, and the all-encompassing look with which he took me in. Soon thereafter, McKelway went off to South America to write some pieces and was replaced as managing editor by Shawn. Now I worked directly with him as well as Ross. Once again, I was blessed. Here was a man of seemingly boundless intellectual capacity, warm, considerate, and, above all, open to almost any idea. His mind worked with such swiftness that I often said no more than one or two words about a projected idea for a piece before he would nod vigorously, and say, "Fine. Of course. Go ahead." And then he would leave me alone—often for achingly long periods—while I wrote the piece. He made it clear that he had complete confidence in me. How could I ever do less than my best for such a person? Although Shawn and Ross were almost completely different physically, they shared the same clear views. They had the deepest respect for writing and writers. They were passionately devoted to the truth. They fervently believed that the editorial functions of a magazine must be kept strictly separate from the business end of things, and that the editorial department must have the final word if excellence and survival are the desired goals.

So many friends, so many years. Lunch was regularly held at a number of restaurants (all gone now) in the neighborhood of the office. Liebling, Mitchell, S. J. Perelman and I ate together a great deal, and the friendships deepened, as did those with Geoffrey Hellman, John Bainbridge, William Maxwell and Milton Greenstein. I recall weekends with Perelman on his farm in Erwinna, Pennsylvania, with his wife, Laura, when Sid would bring out the Ouija board (Sid believed in the Ouija board) and try to reach Harold Ross, who had died in late 1951. "I want to ask Ross about the future of humor," he would say. He sounded dismal as he said it. Through great good fortune, I came to know Janet Flanner when she returned to New York at the start of the war, and the closeness continued until her death. No one could have been more supportive of a younger person's work than Flanner, and I found myself, in the early days, like a homing pigeon, turning up in her office when I came back from a story, and acting out for her *everything* that had taken place during an interview. "Keep going!" she would say. "Tell me more!"

I return for a moment to Shawn, who had become editor in early 1952. He is difficult to write about, since he is such a private person, but scenes come to mind and will not dislodge. Shawn late one night, in his office, going over proofs with me of an Argentine piece, and insisting that a hyphen was grammatically required in a certain word at the end of the article. I argued forcibly that the hyphen—the mere presence of the hyphen—would destroy the sentence. "That's a ruinous hyphen," I said. I wanted two separate words, and no hyphen. I was quite worked up over the hyphen. Shawn was calm and cool. "Perhaps you had better sit outside my office and think it over," he said. From time to time he would pop his head out. "Have you changed your mind?" he asked. This continued from about ten at night until close to two-thirty the next morning. Shawn finally said, sadly, "All right. No hyphen. But you are wrong." And I will never forget the many evenings when, after supper with his family and a few friends, he would sit down at his Steinway and play memorable jazz for us, invariably ending the evening with a rousing "When the Saints Go Marching In." A strange crimson flush would then rise into his face. He would leave the piano and sink into a chair at a far corner of the room and give the impression that he wished that he had played better.

I have travelled widely, at home and abroad, but headquarters have been a red brick building that lies between Forty-third and Forty-fourth Streets, and between Fifth and Sixth Avenues, on the island of Manhattan. I have moved all over the *New Yorker*—writing "Talk of the Town" pieces, "Reporter at Large" articles, "Profiles," all fifty-five "Notes for a Gazetteer," "Onward and Upward with the Arts," "Our Far-Flung Correspondents," "Notes and Comment," "Casuals," parodies, Letters from Foreign Places, the first television columns, even movie and music criticism. The place has been truly a home, both mentally and spiritually, but a home without boundaries. For this book, I have selected stories that interested me most as I read them over. They represent no point of view but my own. They are not confined to any one area of human endeavor, as I am by nature inquisitive, and in love with the diversity of the world. They are presented neither chronologically, nor by subject matter, but in an intuitive arrangement that strikes my fancy. In writing them, I moved around in much the same unhampered, free-flowing way, it being a curious world.

CURIOUS WORLD

We Have Nothing to Fear . . .

Fifty years ago, on March 4, 1933, Franklin Delano Roosevelt was inaugurated president of the United States for the first time, and I was there, in the crowd. (This was the last of the March 4 Inaugurations; ever since, they have taken place on January 20.) I was eighteen, and I drove from college in Baltimore to Washington in a battered Ford owned by a classmate; the mere fact that he owned a four-wheeled vehicle gave him the appearance of being exceedingly rich. The times were desperate. Thirteen million Americans were out of work (including my own father); thousands of families were living in makeshift shacks in our greatest cities; farmers were rioting to prevent foreclosure of their land and homes; hunger was commonplace; and every bank in the nation was about to be closed. I was lucky: I had a scholarship that credited so many hours of work in the library against so much tuition. I was young and healthy and had my share of dreams.

The day was ominously overcast, and became more so as we approached Washington, forty miles south. Thick dark clouds hung over us; I was certain it would rain, and rain heavily. We had no tickets or credentials. The idea was to get as close as possible to the Capitol's East Front, within sight of the Inaugural stand, and find a citizen's perch for the ceremonies. My friend at the wheel knew nothing of the complexities of Washington traffic, and we drove around the city's circles and broad boulevards trying to find a place to park. Soldiers and policemen were everywhere; flags and bunting hung from every lamppost. But there was no hint of festivity in the air. Small knots of people had begun to line the sidewalks (it was late morning), but for the most part they appeared dispirited and sullen. We parked not very far from the Capitol, on a quiet, tree-lined street with neat, clean row houses with white stoops. It was a poor, black neighborhood. I was dressed for the day in the clothes of the time: a dark-blue vested suit (no jeans, of course), a long dark winter overcoat, and a snappy gray fedora with a huge brim. (The suit, as I recall, was a hideous shade of blue, and had come with two pairs of pants, for thirty-two dollars.) In my pocket I carried binoculars.

We worked our way fairly close to the Capitol before being stopped by a Marine guard. With extreme amiability, he asked for our tickets. He then gave us a friendly wink and pointed at a nearby icicle-laden, leafless tree. My friend and I scrambled into the tree and surveyed the special nexus of the nation that spread out before us. The white dome of the Capitol was gray, partly obscured by wisps of fog. The official grandstand was filling up with top-hatted dignitaries, all bundled up against the expected downpour. There must have been a hundred thousand people spread out over the vast Capitol grounds. For the first time, I examined my neighbors in our particular tree, each on a separate bare limb: an elderly gentleman in rumpled and ancient green tweeds, with patches; a beautiful redheaded young woman wrapped in a skimpy coat of rabbit, or of some other unfortunate domestic animal; a woman of indeterminate age who can best be described as dressed in rags, and whose face was lined with worry and pain. For the moment, at least, we were precariously snug in our tree house, waiting for a president to be inaugurated. President or no president, I had a hard time taking my eyes off the redhead; we subsequently became close friends.

The ceremonies were scheduled to start at noon. Noon came and went. The crowd was strangely silent. One could sense the unease. Rumors began to spread through the crowd, called up to the tree people by the less fortunate groundlings. Rumor: A mob somewhere along Pennsylvania Avenue had broken through police lines and surrounded the car containing President Hoover and President-elect Roosevelt. Rumor: Machine guns had been spotted along the route of the cavalcade from the White House to the Capitol. Rumor: Roosevelt had been wounded by an assassin's bullet, perhaps fatally. The lady in rags prayed quietly in the tree:

"No more trouble, please, God. No more trouble." The man in the patched tweeds said that he had known all along that something terrible was going to happen on this day, and that one man's leaving office and another man's taking over would have no effect: only revolution would turn things right side up, once and for all. Nonsense, said the redhead; have a little faith, and don't fall out of the tree. Suddenly, there was a stirring in the crowd. The red-coated Marine band directly in front of the grandstand began to play. I pulled out my binoculars and focused straight ahead. President Hoover, glum and downcast, appeared and took a seat in a leather armchair to the left of the rostrum. A sound like the rustling of otherworldly leaves went through the crowd. Far away, through the giant center doors of the Capitol, appeared the president-elect. His face was totally without color. He made his way, painfully and slowly, along the ramp leading to the rostrum, leaning heavily on the arm of his son James. He seemed to be drawing on bottomless reservoirs of physical and mental strength to make the short journey to the rostrum and the presidency. The crowd held its collective breath. I doubt whether anybody, at that moment, knew that he was carrying ten pounds of heavy steel around his crippled and wasted legs.

I spotted the white-bearded chief justice, Charles Evans Hughes. He was wearing an odd black skullcap. As he delivered the oath of office, Roosevelt repeated every word of it in frighteningly solemn tones. Once power had passed into his hands, he seized it kinetically, with a vigor and force that stunned the throng. Both hands firmly gripped the rostrum. "This is preeminently the time to speak the truth, the whole truth, frankly and boldly," he said, in a clear and unforgettable voice. "This great Nation will endure as it has endured, will revive and will prosper. So, first of all, let me assert my firm belief that the only thing we have to fear is fear itself—nameless, unreasoning, unjustified terror which paralyzes needed efforts to convert retreat into advance. In every dark hour of our national life a leadership of frankness and vigor has met with that understanding and support of the people themselves which is essential to victory. . . . Yet our distress comes from no failure of substance. We are stricken by no plague of locusts. . . . Plenty is at our doorstep, but a generous use of it languishes in the very sight of the supply. Primarily this is because rulers of the exchange of mankind's goods have failed through their own stubbornness and their own incompetence, have admitted their failure, and have abdicated. . . . The money changers have fled from their high seats in the temple of our civilization. We may now restore that temple to the ancient truths. . . . Happiness lies not in the mere possession of money; it lies in the joy of achievement, in the thrill of creative effort. . . . Restoration calls, however, not for changes in ethics alone. This Nation asks for action, and action now. Our greatest primary task is to put people to work. This is no unsolvable problem if we face it wisely and courageously. . . . We do not distrust the future of essential democracy. The people of the United States have not failed. . . . They have asked for discipline and direction under leadership. They have made me the present instrument of their wishes. In the spirit of the gift, I take it."

The crowd had come to life. It shouted approval. Roosevelt, still holding tightly to the rostrum, gave no sign of satisfaction. His expression was as grim as when he had started to speak. The ceremony was over. "I think we'll live," said the redhead as we climbed down from the tree. The man in tweeds burst into tears. "You know something?" said my college friend. "It never rained."

For many years, I have kept a tattered bulletin board in the kitchen, every inch covered with tacked-up addresses, memos, cards from loved ones, stray quotations from Shakespeare and Yeats (life-sustaining forces). Among them is an old, pockmarked newspaper photograph of F.D.R. leaning on a cane and listening intently to two ragged men who appear to have stopped him somewhere. I have no idea where the picture came from, but it is one of my priceless treasures. One of the men is small and scrappy-looking. His hands are in his pockets, and he is leaning into Roosevelt's face. The other man, larger and older, is wearing an ancient greatcoat, and is unshaved. Roosevelt's gray hat is somewhat smashed. He is being attentive to every word that is being said to him. The caption reads, "He knew how to listen."

Since that far-off inauguration, I have learned that the family Bible on which Franklin Roosevelt took the oath of office lay open to the thirteenth chapter of I Corinthians—to "And now abideth faith, hope, charity, these three; but the greatest of these is charity."

(1983)

The Perfect Glow

Oscar Hammerstein II, the lyricist, librettist, and producer, went to the theatre for the first time when he was four years old. He considers the preceding years of his life a total loss. Now a robustly successful showman of fifty-five, Hammerstein recalls his initial glimpse of the mysteries and enticements of the stage with the mixed clarity and fuzziness of the possessed. For the better part of a year, he had been badgering his father, William, or Willie, Hammerstein, to take him downtown from the Hammerstein home, near Mount Morris Park, to see a show. Willie Hammerstein was firmly opposed to the notion. Oscar, he said, should stay home and play with his velocipede. Willie spoke with more than parental authority. He was managing Hammerstein's Victoria Theatre, at Forty-second Street and Seventh Avenue, for *his* father, Oscar Hammerstein I, and he had turned it into the leading variety house of its day. There was no business like show business, Willie conceded, but he was dead set against any offspring of his getting a taste of it. Oscar persisted, however, and one afternoon, in a moment of weakness, Willie succumbed. He took Oscar, by means of a series of trolley cars, to the Victoria to see a matinee performance of a vaudeville show. When Oscar and his father walked into the lobby of the Victoria, his grandfather, a short, squat, determined-looking man with a goatee, was standing beside the box office, scanning the line of ticket buyers. He was wearing a black silk top hat and a black jacket. He had a cigar in his mouth. Willie took Oscar II over to say hello. Oscar I glanced down at him, shook his head two or three times, made an odd clucking sound, and turned away. "I don't know what the old man had on his mind," Oscar II said recently. "I don't know whether he meant, 'What's my grandson doing down here?' or 'What a silly-looking boy,' or 'Good God, here's another generation of Hammersteins inside a theatre.'"

In any event, within a matter of minutes, Oscar II was alone in a box overlooking the stage. The auditorium was crowded. As the houselights were lowered, a hush came over the audience. The orchestra began to play, and the curtain went up. Oscar broke out in a cold sweat. His legs trembled. His stomach quivered. His excitement was so acute that he could barely see what was happening onstage. Actually, nothing much *was* happening. Several young ladies were posed around a large, tangled fish net. A bright, golden haze filled the stage. The girls, it seemed, were drying the net. One of them, disengaging herself from the others, stepped to the footlights and sang what he remembers as:

> "Oh, I am a water maiden,
> I live on the water,
> A fisherman's daughter."

Oscar was transported. The mist before his eyes was like a London fog. After the maidens performed a short dance, other acts came on, but Oscar recalls nothing more until intermission, when his father fetched him from the box and said, "Now we'll go backstage." He was led down some narrow stairs, through a dark doorway, and up a few steps; he then found himself backstage, and face-to-face with a large cage. The cage was occupied by a lion. The lion was prowling up and down, and did not look especially happy. As Oscar was watching it, the cage began to roll toward him. He was too stunned to move. The lion let out a roar, and Oscar was snatched to safety by a stagehand. Other stagehands rushed forward to stop the cage. Oscar felt that he just might get sick to his stomach, and asked his father to take him home. When he reached home, his mother put him to bed. He slept for fourteen hours, and when he awoke, he announced that the theatre would be his lifework.

Hammerstein has spectacularly stuck to his word. He has been associated with more notable musicals than any other showman in the history of the American theatre. He has either written the book and lyrics or collaborated on the book and lyrics for some forty musicals, including *Rose-Marie*, *The Desert Song*, *Sunny*, *Show Boat*, *Oklahoma!*, *Carousel*, *Allegro*, *South Pacific*, and *The King and I*. Of these, at least three—*Show Boat*, *Oklahoma!*, and *South Pacific*—have been called classics of the American musical stage so many times and in so many places that today they can categorically be described as classics of the American musical stage. *South Pacific* and *The King and I*, two shows on which he collaborated with Richard Rodgers, the composer and producer, are now playing across from each other, on Forty-fourth Street, and neither one has had an empty seat since it opened. Together, the two shows gross more than a hundred thousand dollars a week. Hammerstein has written the words to almost a thousand songs, including "Ol' Man River," "Who?," "Oh, What a Beautiful Mornin'!," "People Will Say We're in Love," "Some Enchanted Evening," "We Kiss in a Shadow," and "The Last Time I Saw Paris." His songs are distinguished by such lucid wording, such unabashed sentimentality, such a gentle, even noble, view of life, and such an attachment to love, home, small children, his native country, nature, and dreams come true that he has been called the Bobbie Burns of the American musical stage. He has been called this so many times and in so many places that today he can categorically be described as the Bobbie Burns of the American musical stage. Since Hammerstein became professionally associated with the theatre, more than thirty years ago, he has earned more than five million dollars—royalties, profits as a producer, and receipts from the sale of sheet music and phonograph records—and he now enjoys an income that ranges exuberantly between a half and two-thirds of a million dollars a year, before taxes. (The government permits him to keep approximately one dollar out of every seven.) Not the least phenomenal aspect of his career is the affectionate regard in which he is held by his fellow showmen. By and large, whenever a producer or writer on Broadway has a hit, other producers or writers turn up the collars of their coats and wander off alone, to drink quietly. When a venture with which Hammerstein is connected is pronounced successful by the press and the public, his competitors often appear as exhilarated as they would be if they owned the property themselves. "The only trouble with Oscar," a fellow producer said not long ago, after the opening of *The King and I*, "is there's no trouble with Oscar. You have to love the fellow. He works hard, he's true-blue to his friends, he never speaks harshly to an actor, he's modest, he drinks sparingly, he keeps out of the niteries, he's in bed by midnight, he doesn't fool around with dames, he has no visible quirks, he's got a sense of humor and he's talented. He doesn't sound human; he sounds like a stuffed shirt. Hell, he's the most human man I know."

Invisible as his quirks may be, Hammerstein is a major eccentric. "I am in love with a wonderful theatre," he often says. It is one of the monumental love affairs of history. He cannot enter a theatre without experiencing that acute aesthetic dizziness reported by travellers when they gaze for the first time upon the Taj Mahal. Hammerstein is six feet one and a half inches tall, weighs slightly less than two hundred pounds, and has the broad, hunched shoulders, the long, easy gait, and the ready, comforting, it's-going-to-be-all-right-fellows smile of a popular football coach, but passing through a stage door makes him feel weak and helpless. The sight of a bare stage illuminated by a single glaring rehearsal light sends sharp pains up and down his back. These sensations are nothing compared to the exquisite paralysis that comes over him when he stands at the rear of a packed theatre and observes an audience enjoying one of his own shows. Outwardly, he is calm, even indifferent, on such an occasion. Standing quietly, with his arms resting on the rail, he could easily be mistaken for a theatre manager. The only hint that the Furies are raging within is a slight droop at the corners of his mouth, which gives him the look of a man who fears, as Hammerstein feared at the Victoria when he was four, that he might any moment get sick to his stomach. Often, while one of his songs is being sung, he walks swiftly into the empty lobby and bursts into tears. Hammerstein has listened to "The Surrey with the Fringe on Top" at least five hundred times, but every time he has been reduced to weeping. "It's so beautiful that it makes a man want to cry," he explains.

Hammerstein's overpowering devotion to the theatre includes not only an intense appreciation of his own lyrics but an equally intense appreciation of the music composed for them by his partner, Richard Rodgers. Rodgers is sometimes able to sit down at a piano and turn out a hit tune in a few minutes. His head is filled with an extraordinary collection of whistleable airs that require only a set of lyrics to bring them out into the open.

Hammerstein is a slow and tortured writer. He often labors for weeks to produce a refrain of fifty words or so. He worked for five weeks, for example, over the lyrics of "Hello, Young Lovers!," in *The King and I*, and finally threw all his previous efforts aside and wrote the song, in a frenzy of creation, in two days. Once he has completed the lyrics for a song, he is spiritually and physically exhausted. As a result, he is exceedingly attached to what he writes, and when he listens to the words he has a tendency to recall the suffering he underwent while putting them together. Hammerstein is a tolerant man, but his tolerance stops short of letting anyone tamper with so much as a word of his lyrics. Some years ago, a radio singer, not quite sure of "Oh, What a Beautiful Mornin'!," inadvertently substituted "An' a li'l ol' willer is laughin' at me" for "An' a ol' weepin' willer is laughin' at me." Hammerstein was tuned to the program, his eyes full of tears. Shocked by the alteration, he switched off the radio, and swore that *that* particular singer would have a pretty hard time ever getting into one of *his* shows.

Although Hammerstein is sentimental about the theatre, his affection has a pragmatic base. "Oscar is a very careful dreamer," one of his oldest friends says. In Oscar's estimation, the public is the final judge of what is and what is not a work of art, and he has small patience with the experimental theatre. The test of a good play, for Hammerstein, is the length of the line at the box office on a rainy morning. "With my shows," he says, "I don't want to wake up in the morning and have to worry about whether or not the weather will affect the size of the house." In spite of his firm faith in the judgment of audiences, Hammerstein has been engaged for years in a strange personal struggle with them. "It's a matter of love and hate," he explains. He has evolved a method of evaluating an audience's reactions to a show, which he uses during the out-of-town tryouts of his productions. He stands at the rear rail and observes the backs of the heads of the audience. He believes he can pretty well figure out what is going on inside the heads. "There's a silent criticism felt by all actors, and everybody else who knows the theatre," he says, "but my method goes beyond that. And I don't pay any attention to coughs, either. They don't mean a thing. But if the heads are motionless, we're OK. If they move either up or down or from side to side, we're in trouble. If people start rustling through the programs, we're in *real* trouble." Hammerstein does not confine his researches to the backs of heads. He often goes into a box and peers down at the faces of the audience. If the customers are enjoying a show, he feels, an indefinable glow comes over their faces. "I can't describe it, I just know it when I see it," he says. He may concentrate on one face and, crouched low in the box, await the arrival of the glow. If, instead of the glow, the face reveals dislike or, what is even worse in Hammerstein's opinion, no expression at all, the muscles of his stomach become even tighter. "There are faces that rise to haunt me," he says. "Years ago, a man sat in the third row in a tryout in Trenton, a big, fat, red-faced, snorey fellow, everybody around him laughing and laughing, and he just sat there, no expression, no nothing. I remember every line of that face. I would recognize him anywhere. My dislike is still quite active. I remember, too, a young woman once in Baltimore. What a glow! The perfect glow! A lovely, sweet face, responsive to everything!"

Hammerstein feels that the severest test of how a show is working out comes the moment the first-act curtain falls. Just before this moment, Hammerstein leans forward and cups a hand to one ear, then stiffens like a bird dog. "If that curtain drops and there is silence followed by silence— oh, we're in trouble!" he says. "If that curtain falls and there is silence followed swiftly by an excited buzz of conversation, a sort of ground swell of buzzy talk, we're probably safe." After only a minute or two of such listening, he rushes into the lobby. There, head down, he mixes in with the crowd. "I concentrate on a man and woman who spy another man and woman they know," he says. "If one pair approaches the other and says a few quick words about the play, and then there's general conversation about the play, we're OK. If they merely say, 'Pretty good first act. When are you and Mary coming over for bridge?' we're in *real* trouble!" Hammerstein slips back into the theatre after the intermission and again is on the alert for the glow. He thinks that the glow is even more important during the second act. "If they glow when they get back into their seats," he says, "the chances are that the glow is permanent and we have 'em for good." Hammerstein feels that the glow induced by *Oklahoma!* may never be duplicated within his lifetime or anybody else's. "People returned to their seats for the second act and the glow was like the light from a thousand lanterns," he says. "You could *feel* the glow, it was that bright."

Hammerstein has put all his adult years into inducing the glow. In what is perhaps his second most glowing triumph, *South Pacific*, the glow begins to spread across the faces of the audience soon after the curtain is up. Hammerstein has given a good deal of thought to the effect that *South Pacific* exerts upon audiences, and he is sure that he has pinned down some of the reasons for its phenomenal success, and glow. "The curtain rises," he recently told a friend, "and we are on an island in the Pacific with luxuriant foliage. A native boy and girl are singing a little song in French. The audience says, 'What's this?' Then, before they have even settled in their seats—bang!—you're off to the races with a complication. The hero and heroine come onstage—the curtain has been up a bare few minutes—and an honest approach to a love story has been placed before you. There is Emile de Becque, fifty-odd, a planter, cultured, a Frenchman, and a highly romantic figure. There is Nellie Forbush, in her twenties, American, fresh, young, beautiful, a nurse. Two people who have nothing whatsoever in common are in love. No lecherous stuff, you understand. Emile de Becque *loves* Nellie Forbush. There is nothing underhanded about it. She is ashamed to admit her love—afraid, really, for fear of its not being reciprocated. It's too good to be true, it's unbelievable. They express their love and we have the audience in a death grip; we jump on them, we beat them up. Then, suddenly—bang!—the scene changes and there's a fat old thing, a native woman, selling grass skirts. That's Bloody Mary, and she is unlike anything the audience has ever seen before. The change of pace is terrific. The audience is still in the death grip! They're caught, they're helpless, they can't breathe. We never let go!"

Hammerstein is a gentle person, with a genuine affection for his fellow man, and he takes extreme pains in his writing to avoid hurting anybody's feelings. While working on *The King and I*, he was acutely and almost constantly fearful that he might, in some way or other, offend the people of Siam, whose king is the "King" of the title. "I did not want to tread on any Oriental toes," he said recently. "I had to be careful about gags about the huge number of wives in the royal family. You know, I think we are crude in the West compared to the East. What was required was the Eastern sense of dignity and pageantry—and none of this business of girls dressed in Oriental costumes dancing out onto the stage and singing 'ching-a-ling-a-ling-ling' with their fingers in the air." For the most part, during the construction of a book for a musical, Hammerstein does not attempt to pry too deeply into any of the subtle and complex aspects of human relationships. He is content to stay close to what he considers the fundamentals—love, jealousy, death, and so on. A great many observers of his career regard this simplified attitude toward life as evidence of almost surpassing wisdom. "Oscar has pinned down the verities," a friend of his says. "He knows precisely what audiences want, their saturation point on any one emotion, and he gives them just that and no more. It's uncanny, it's wizardry." To another group of observers, equally fond of Hammerstein, the limitations of his plots indicate the boundaries of his experience. "Oscar has a beautiful and unsullied view of life," a man who has known him since childhood declares. "He's an anomaly in this ugly world. He believes that love conquers all, that virtue triumphs, and that dreams come true."

While he is working on lyrics, Hammerstein relies almost entirely upon flights of fancy, even when he is dealing with what would appear to be matters of fact. He does not feel that research adds materially to the value of his lyrics, so he rarely dips into a reference work. On the few occasions when he has undertaken research, it has been of an uncomplicated nature, and he early discovered that it raised more questions than it settled. While writing *Carousel*, he decided to compose a lyric about a clambake. He had never been to a clambake, but he had heard of them, and they sounded like fun. He found himself putting down the words "This was a real nice clambake," and they sounded like real nice words. He felt that in the second stanza he should describe the clambake in detail, and he tried to recall clambakes he had heard of or read of. He wrote about codfish chowder "cooked in iron kettles, onions floatin' on the top, curlin' up in petals," ribbons of salt pork, and so on, and he felt certain that he was on safe clambake ground. He was aware that lobsters often turn up at clambakes, but when he began to think about the lobsters, he ran into a snag. He assumed that they "sizzled and crackled and sputtered a song, fitten fer an angels' choir. Fitten fer an angels', fitten fer an angels', fitten fer an angels' choir!," but a pang of conscience struck him when he came to describing what happened to the lobsters after they were pulled out of the fire. He wrote, "We slit 'em down the front." Then he wrote, "We slit 'em down the back." Then he began to wonder just where in hell you do slit a lobster. He dropped in one day at an obscure seafood restaurant and asked the chef there how he slit his lobsters. The man said down the back, and Hammerstein wrote it that way, adding, in the flush of creation, "and peppered 'em good, and doused 'em in melted butter." After *Carousel* opened, a disconcerting number of complaints poured in to Hammerstein. "HOW DARE YOU SAY THAT LOBSTERS EMPLOYED IN CLAMBAKE BE SPLIT DOWN BACK?" one telegram read. "ANY FOOL KNOWS LOBSTERS SPLIT DOWN FRONT. THAT WAS NO CLAMBAKE." "Shame on you for lack of facts re lobster split," read a sample letter. Hammerstein decided that thenceforth he would trust his intuitions. Since that unfortunate experience, he has done little research, but he did make an effort to gather background for *South Pacific* by glancing at some maps of the Pacific area and speaking to several people who had been out there during the war.

A man's lyrics, Hammerstein feels, are a reflection of his attitude toward life. "I couldn't write a sophisticated or sharp lyric, or something terribly, terribly clever, like some lyric writers," he once told a friend. "I couldn't, because I don't see things that way. To me, one of the most beautiful and expressive lyrics of all time is Irving Berlin's simple 'All alone, by the telephone.' Examine those words. Think about them. They tell an entire story. Nothing more needs to be said. You see the picture, complete and whole. All alone by the telephone—the girl jilted perhaps, lonely, unhappy, waiting for the phone to ring. I envy those who can write tricky words, but they are a different sort of man." Hammerstein feels, too, that if his lyrics display a certain simplicity and wholesomeness, it is largely because he tries to live a simple and wholesome life. His habits are a source of wonder along Broadway, and many of his colleagues regard the regularity of his life as dangerously close to heresy. "The fellow breaks all the rules," a producer said to a colleague in Lindy's early one morning. "Why, he's home now, sleeping like a baby. Isn't that horrible?" Hammerstein has a real dislike of nightlife, and he rarely turns up at nightclubs. He does his best to avoid large parties, too, and when he is persuaded to attend one, he departs quietly about midnight. He sleeps a full eight hours each night, eats a large hot breakfast, works until one, eats a large hot lunch, works all afternoon, eats a large hot supper, and then, unless he goes to the theatre (he makes a point of seeing practically every show that comes to New York), pokes around in his study, either watching television or reading.

He owns an imposing five-story house on East Sixty-third Street and an eighty-acre Bucks County farm near Doylestown, Pennsylvania, eighty-five miles from New York. In both town house and farmhouse, he has large, impressively furnished studies, and he spends a great deal of time in them, sometimes, for days at a stretch, emerging only to eat and sleep. Hammerstein's family life is a warm and affectionate one. He is married to the former Dorothy Blanchard, an attractive, redheaded woman who was understudy to Beatrice Lillie in *Charlot's Revue of 1924*. It is the second marriage for each of them, and each has two children by the previous marriage. The Hammersteins also have a twenty-year-old son, James, who works for Leland Hayward, the producer and agent.

When working on his lyrics, Hammerstein prefers to be on his farm. He's convinced that the muse has little chance of flowering among the fleshpots of New York. When he begins to write, he broods, and when he broods, he becomes unapproachable and sullen. He writes standing up, and in one corner of his Bucks County study there is a high writing desk, like a lectern. For hours at a time, clasping and unclasping his hands behind his back, he paces up and down the study, occasionally stopping before the desk to jot down a word or two on a sheet of yellow foolscap. The countryside around Doylestown nourishes his spirit, he claims, and he often walks along the roads, alone and brooding, his head down almost inside his coat collar. "Oscar meditating on a country road looks like something out of Thomas Hardy on a heath," a friend of his said not long ago. On rainy days when he feels the need for communion with nature, he tramps back and forth on the porch of his house. As soon as he hits upon a line for a lyric, he sets it to a dummy tune of his own and sings it to Mrs. Hammerstein. "Oscar's dummy tunes are so terrible they make you want to cry," she has declared, "but he has perfect rhythm."

Until he worked with Joshua Logan on the book of *South Pacific*, Hammerstein wrote his dialogue in longhand. Logan, a man who cannot utter a simple "Thank you" without making it sound like a second-act denouement, had long been addicted to recording dialogue on a dictaphone. Hammerstein ridiculed the notion, but Logan persuaded him to speak a few of Emile de Becque's lines in *South Pacific* into his machine. "In peacetime, the boat from America comes once a month," said Hammerstein tentatively. "The ladies—the wives of the planters—often go to Australia during the hot months. It can get very hot here." Hammerstein listened to the playback and was somewhat bowled over by his performance. Throughout the writing of the book, all of which was done at the Hammerstein farm, the two men used Logan's dictaphone. They would speak several lines, passing the mouthpiece back and forth, and then listen with deep appreciation to their work. The writing of *South Pacific* accomplished another change in Hammerstein's habits. Logan is a nocturnal animal, and he does some of his best work during what are known as the small hours. He suffers from a chronic inability to fall asleep until nearly dawn, the time of day Hammerstein is usually leaping out of bed, ready for a day's work. The two men compromised by working until two in the morning. Hammerstein then retired, yawning. Logan went upstairs and alternately read poetry and took hot baths until four or five. He slept until noon, when he and Hammerstein would start revising a typed transcript of their dialogue of the previous evening. By the time this began, Hammerstein would have been up for hours, pacing his study, writing lyrics. "It was a real sacrifice for Oscar, working past midnight," Logan told a friend. "I am very grateful."

In recent years, Hammerstein is convinced, books and lyrics have come into their own, and their contribution to a musical show is no longer taken for granted. Writing about his early days in show business, in an introduction to a collection of his lyrics, Hammerstein said, "The librettist was a kind of stable boy. If the race was won, he was seldom mentioned. If the race was lost, he was blamed for giving the horse the wrong feed." These days, he feels, words are as important as music, and the score of a musical comedy will not be successful if the lyrics lack interest, do not advance the plot, or are not carefully integrated with the music. In fact, Rodgers and Hammerstein have developed a new popular art form that is neither musical comedy nor opera but something in between. The most common question put to Hammerstein by people he meets is whether the words or the music come first. Hammerstein is a reasonable man, and doesn't mind answering the question, weary as he is of it. Until he began collaborating with Richard Rodgers, Hammerstein wrote his lyrics after the composer had written the music, but today, as a rule, his lyrics are done first. He considers this a sensible arrangement, far more favorable to the writing of good lyrics. Most scores, however, are done the other way. The music-first method, Hammerstein thinks, developed from the fact that during the first years of the century a good many musical shows were imported from the Continent, notably from Vienna, so that the American lyric writers had to fit their lines to the music. Some of the foreign composers subsequently were themselves imported to the United States. Lyric writers working with them discovered that if the words were written before the music, they sounded weird, and were sometimes completely unsingable, because of the composers' unfamiliarity with English. Hammerstein believes, too, that the rise of jazz and the fondness for dancing placed the emphasis on the music of a song, and that the lot of the lyricist was made easier if he performed his stint after the music had been composed.

Uppermost in Hammerstein's mind while he is writing a lyric is the larynx of the performer who will have to stand on a stage and sing the thing. "The larynxes of singers are limited," he has remarked. He tries to provide convenient breathing places in his lyrics, and to avoid climaxes in which a singer will be straining at a word that closes the larynx. "A word like 'sweet' would be a very bad word on which to sing a high note," he says. "The *e* sound closes the larynx, and the singer cannot let go with his full voice. Furthermore, the *t* ending the word is a hard consonant, which would cut the singer off and thwart his and the composer's desire to sustain the note." Hammerstein worries a good deal about closed larynxes, and he is inclined to brood morbidly over the times he has permitted his affection for a word to outweigh his concern over a closed larynx. For example, he often berates himself for ending the refrain of "What's the Use of Wond'rin'?," in *Carousel*, with "You're his girl and he's your feller, And all the rest is talk." He feels that if he were to write this song again, his last line would go something like "And that's all you need to know." "The singer could have hit the *o* vowel and held it as long as she wanted to, eventually pulling applause," he says. The song was not a distinguished success as sheet music or on records, and Hammerstein is convinced that the word "talk," which closed the singer's larynx at the finish, was responsible for this. The majority of his last lines are, he feels, forceful larynx-openers, conducive to applause-pulling, such as "Oh, what a beautiful day!," "Once you have found her, never let her go!," "Ol' man river, he jes keeps rollin' along," and "Bali Ha'i, Bali Ha'i, Bali Ha'i."

Hammerstein recalls with painful poignancy the problems he faced during the creation of certain lyrics. To a person who does not write lyrics, many of his dilemmas might seem elementary, but to Hammerstein they represent heroic struggles with the muse. "The problem of a duet for the lovers in *Oklahoma!* seemed insurmountable," he says. His leading characters—Curly, the cowboy, and Laurey, the young girl—are very much attracted to each other, but Laurey, who is shy, tries to hide her feelings. Curly does not like her attitude, and assumes a fairly belligerent one of his own. Instead of expressing their love, they take to bickering and squabbling. Since both Hammerstein and Rodgers wished to maintain the atmosphere of crackle and snap until at least the second act, it was impossible for Hammerstein to write a simple song in which Curly and Laurey said, out loud and with their larynxes open, "I love you." Hammerstein talked his dilemma over with Rodgers at great length. Together they hit upon the solution of having the two young people caution each other against demonstrating any warmth, since this might be construed by outsiders as an expression of affection. "People Will Say We're in Love" was the successful result. Hammerstein had another problem when he collaborated with Rodgers on the musical film *State Fair*. In the story, a young girl has the blues, for no particular reason, since her family is about to treat her to a visit to a state fair. Hammerstein wanted a song for her mood—it was time for a song, anyway—and it occurred to him, while he was pondering, that her melancholy condition bore a resemblance to spring fever. This thought made Hammerstein even more melancholy than the girl, since state fairs are held in the fall, not the spring. "I toyed with the notion of having her say, in effect, it's autumn but I have spring fever, so it might as well be spring," Hammerstein has said. He casually mentioned this possible solution to Rodgers. "That's it!" cried Rodgers. "All my doubts were gone," Hammerstein says. "I had a partner behind me." Out of this came the well-known "It Might as Well Be Spring."

Hammerstein thinks that one reason for his success as a lyricist is that his vocabulary is not enormous. A huge vocabulary, he is convinced, hampers a lyric writer; it might persuade him to substitute "fantasy," "reverie," "nothingness," "chimera," "figment," or even "air-drawn dagger" for the simple word "dream." He has discovered that a lyric writer seems always to have a supply of the word "dream" on hand, much as a housewife keeps salt in the house. Before composing the lyrics for *South Pacific*, he decided that he would avoid "dream." He felt that it had been turning up too often in his lyrics. When he had finished the *South Pacific* lyrics, he found that "dream" appeared with frightening regularity. "Bali Ha'i" speaks of "Your own special hopes, your own special dreams." "Some Enchanted Evening" says, "Then fly to her side, and make her your own, or all through your life you may dream all alone" and "The sound of her laughter will sing in your dreams." "Happy Talk" declares that "You gotta have a dream; if you don't have a dream, how you gonna have a dream come true? If you don't talk happy an' you never had a dream, den you'll never have a dream come true." Even one of the songs withdrawn from *South Pacific* during the pre-Broadway tryout said, "The sky is a bright canary yellow . . . you will dream about the view." Hammerstein lost his dream of the view but retained the view itself—the bright canary-yellow sky in "A Cockeyed Optimist."

The word "dream" has worried Hammerstein in more ways than one. Not only has it turned up uninvited in his lyrics but its meaning, he feels, is not precisely clear to him. He is certain that he has never written a word in which he did not believe, which did not spring from the heart, and he is therefore disturbed by the fact that he and the word "dream" don't entirely understand each other. "The most important ingredient of a good song is sincerity," he has often remarked. "Let the song be yours and yours alone." He can put down such words as "love," "ain't," "feelin'," "rain," "yes," "forget," "home," "blue," "bird," "star," "believe," "arms," "nice," "little," "moon," "trees," "kiss," "sky," "dame," "beautiful," "baby," again and again, and he has been doing so for thirty years, and his only concern is whether they belong in a lyric, or at that particular point in a lyric. These words do not trouble him at all. The word "love" poses no problems for him, and he has no qualms about using it all the time. He will write down, "I'm in love, I'm in love, I'm in love, I'm in love, I'm in love with a wonderful guy" or "Dat's love! Dat's love! Dat's love! Dat's love!" without hesitation. He will even dwell upon the idea—"Love is quite a simple thing, and nothing so bewildering, no matter what the poets sing, in words and phrases lyrical. Birds find bliss in every tree, and fishes kiss beneath the sea, so when love comes to you and me, it really ain't no miracle"—eat a large supper, sleep eight hours, and rise the next morning to write another lyric about love. But the word "dream" perplexes him, even though he once went so far into dreamland in "Music in the Air" as to write, "There's a dream beyond a dream beyond a dream beyond a dream." It first made a real nuisance of itself seventeen years ago, while he was working with Sigmund Romberg on a motion picture. Romberg had turned out a waltz tune, and Hammerstein took it home to compose the lyrics. The moment he finished looking over the music, the first line, which he also thought would make a good title, popped into his head: "When I grow too old to dream." A moment later, a second line miraculously popped into his head, below the first: "I'll have you to remember." "I have it!" he recalls crying out loud. "'When I grow too old to dream, I'll have you to remember.'" Suddenly, and for perhaps the first time in his life, he was afflicted with a curious sensation that something was wrong with his words. He realized that he didn't understand what he had written. He remembers that he said to himself, "Too old for what kind of dreams? As a matter of fact, when you're old, aren't you likely to dream more than at any other time in your life, don't you look back and dream about the past?" For three weeks, he struggled with other words, but he kept returning to the original ones. "I loved to sing it to myself, alone in my study," he says. He decided to stick to these lines, and the song became a big hit, but its triumph shook Hammerstein deeply, since innumerable colleagues asked—and ask to this day—what the words meant. Before writing "When I grow too old to dream, I'll have you to remember," Hammerstein had religiously believed in simple, unambiguous lyrics. If he wanted to ask, "Why do I love you? Why do you love me?," he went ahead and asked it. Here, however, was a mysterious, perhaps meaningless combination of words, and they were commercially successful. The more Hammerstein brooded over the lyric, the more he felt that he had stumbled onto something bigger than himself. A year or so ago, still brooding, he brought the matter up in the introduction to his collection of lyrics. "Gertrude Stein has, of course, this unspecific approach to the use of words," he wrote, "and Edith Sitwell, in her group of songs entitled 'Façade,' has made a deliberate attempt to write words with special emphasis on sound and very little attention to meaning or clarity. I do not believe that the future of good lyric writing lies in this direction, but my experience with 'When I grow too old to dream' forces me to admit that there is something in the idea. It belongs with the general flight from literalism in all art expression—notably painting—which characterizes the creative works of this century."

Oscar Hammerstein II, considered by many students of the Broadway stage the outstanding theatrical figure of his day, has spent a good part of his life running after and trying to overtake the ghost of his grandfather, Oscar Hammerstein I. The chase has been a long, hard one, but Oscar II feels that he is justified in thinking he may have caught up. "People are just now beginning to refer to Oscar I as the grandfather of Oscar II, after years of referring to Oscar II as the grandson of Oscar I," Oscar II said recently. When Oscar II was a boy, Oscar I was the most celebrated showman in America, if not in the entire civilized world. His short, round figure, goatee, black topper, and cigar were as familiar to the public as the broad grin and gleaming teeth of Theodore Roosevelt, his contemporary. Records of the period reveal that when it came to getting publicity, the Rough Rider and Hammerstein were just about neck and neck, with Hammerstein occasionally slightly out in front. Old Oscar had the knack of getting his name in the papers wherever he happened to be, and he became a legend in his own lifetime. All literate people knew that he had ordered the King of Portugal tossed out of his opera house in London because the King persisted in talking during a performance. They knew, too, of his encounter with King George V of England. One night, His Majesty attended a Hammerstein operatic production in London and, spying Oscar in the lobby, his hat on his head and his cigar in his mouth, walked over to greet him. Hammerstein listened impassively to the royal hello, and, without removing either his hat or his cigar, grunted, "Glad you could come, King." It was common knowledge that Hammerstein once kept a cow on the roof of his highly successful variety house, Hammerstein's Victoria, at Forty-second Street and Seventh Avenue, on the site now occupied by the Rialto Theatre; that he lived above the lobby, in a room crowded with miniature opera sets and odd-looking machines for the manufacture of cigars, holdovers from his days as a cigar maker; that although his income was derived from vaudeville, his heart belonged to opera; and that when he wanted to snatch a famous soprano from the Metropolitan opera, he would think twice, but no more, before throwing thousand-dollar bills at the lady's feet.

Opera was a sickness with Oscar Hammerstein I. He built variety houses all over Manhattan and installed in their lobbies busts of Beethoven, Verdi, Gounod, and Mozart, to remind himself to turn them into opera houses if and when he could raise the money. He once came so close to forcing the Metropolitan to close its doors with his rival Manhattan Opera House that the trustees of the Metropolitan bought him out for a million dollars, with the understanding that he would not produce another opera in the United States for ten years. He took the money, sailed to England, produced operas there, went broke, returned to the United States, built an opera house at Lexington Avenue and Fifty-first Street, put on excerpts from operas as part of a vaudeville show, and went broke again. "When I was young, opera was a bad word around our house," Oscar Hammerstein II said recently. Oscar II rarely came into contact with Oscar I, meeting him, in all, perhaps half a dozen times, but the old man's influence pervaded the home in which Oscar II was brought up. Oscar II's father, William, or Willie, Hammerstein, managed variety houses for Oscar I and was a famous showman in his own right. Oscar II recalls that he could tell by the look on his father's face when Grandfather Hammerstein had got himself in trouble with an opera again. "My father would put on a variety bill that played to sold-out houses, and Grandfather would come along and take great hunks of the receipts and invest them in his opera ventures," Hammerstein has said. "There was no question of our starving, or anything like that, but it *was* discouraging."

Willie Hammerstein looked upon show business purely as a way of earning a living and was determined that he and his brother Arthur, a producer, would be the last of the Hammersteins to be connected with the theatre. He vowed that his two sons, Oscar II and Reginald, who was a year and a half Oscar's junior, would never be involved with it. He had little use for actors outside the theatre and practically never invited one to his home. As far as he was concerned, there was nothing even remotely glamorous about chorus girls, either, and Oscar II didn't meet one, socially or otherwise, until he was an undergraduate at Columbia. At the Hammerstein home, any discussions of the theatre were pretty much confined to questions of box-office receipts. Willie Hammerstein, who was of German-Jewish descent, and his wife, who was of Scottish-Protestant descent, maintained a genteel, bourgeois household in an apartment building near Mount Morris Park. Mr. Hammerstein insisted upon large, hot dinners and almost always got home from the theatre by mealtime. He went to bed early. He hardly ever went to a play, and never went to any variety house but the Victoria, on the theory that if an act was any good, he had already seen it. For a reason that escapes him, Oscar II, when he was four, was moved one flight downstairs to an apartment occupied by his maternal grandfather, James Nimmo, a tall, twinkly Scotsman who looked rather like Mark Twain. For four years, Oscar slept in his grandfather's apartment, but he ate his meals upstairs with his family. Grandfather Hammerstein was for Oscar a shadowy, distant, somewhat frightening figure—he never visited his grandchildren, and his grandchildren were never taken to visit him—but Grandfather Nimmo was young Oscar's idol and companion. He was a carefree retired insurance man, who rose at six each morning and prepared a milk punch spiced with Scotch for himself and a milk punch spiced with Scotch for Oscar. He would then give Oscar half a dozen sour balls from a candy jar. Oscar would shove two or three in his mouth, put the rest in his pocket, and the two of them would head for Mount Morris Park. Mr. Nimmo and Oscar always arrived at a bell tower in the park a few minutes before seven. In those days, an attendant climbed the winding staircase to the bell tower and, at seven, rang the bell seven times. Grandfather Nimmo told Oscar that the Devil climbed the stairs and rang the bell, and that the Devil was a little old man whose heart was filled with kindness and whose pockets were filled with sour, or "devil," balls. Today, Hammerstein feels that the old saying "You can't get away from your grandfather" has in his case a double application. He suspects that his love of the theatre can be traced to Grandfather Hammerstein, and that his healthy point of view toward life, expressed in the thousand lyrics he has composed, springs from his pleasant experiences in Mount Morris Park with the Devil and Grandfather Nimmo.

No matter how hard Willie Hammerstein tried, he could not keep his son Oscar out of the theatre. The more he told Oscar that show business was not for him, the more enticing the boy found the inside of a theatre. When Oscar, aged four, was taken by his father, against his better judgment, down to the Victoria to watch a variety show, the die was cast. From that day forward, vaudeville was the central jewel of Oscar's existence, and each Saturday afternoon found him, his pockets stuffed with devil balls, at a vaudeville show. For a period, baseball was a rival for his affections, but this period was brief. By the time Oscar was nine, his fascination with vaudeville was almost suffocating. He never ceased to wonder at the showmanship of the old-time vaudevillians. When he was sitting in the audience at the Victoria, he felt that he was living life to the hilt. He could listen to Irene Franklin sing "Let me whisper gently in your large Lynnhaven ear" twenty times and feel transported each time. When Princess Rajah stepped onto the Victoria's stage, her neck entwined with snakes, and swung a kitchen chair around and around by her teeth, young Oscar considered himself the luckiest mortal alive just to be under the same roof. He began to roar the moment Ed Blondell, the father of Joan Blondell, walked out of the wings, and by the time Blondell, a fat man who simply stood on the stage and cried and cried and cried, had really got into his act, which was called "The Lost Boy," Oscar was helpless. Frank Fogarty had the same effect on him. Mr. Fogarty's stock in trade was the song "You Can't Bunko Me!" It was about a man who spied his wife drinking beer in a tavern with another man but pretended not to notice them. After they had gone, the man walked over to their table, drained their glasses of whatever beer remained, and remarked, "You can't bunko me!"—a line that always threw Oscar into convulsions.

Aside from these excursions, Hammerstein had a routine upper–middle-class boyhood. For a few years, he attended P.S.9, on West End Avenue at Eighty-second Street, and he helped plant a tree in nearby Riverside Park. When he was ten, his parents entered him, as a day pupil, in the Hamilton Institute, on Eighty-first Street near Central Park West. Hamilton Institute made a slight pretense of military training, and Oscar, a gangly, extremely thin boy, would sometimes drill, in an ill-fitting uniform, at the Twenty-second Regiment Armory, at Sixty-eighth Street and Broadway. After school, he would often walk up to the Columbia campus, at 116th Street, and wander around the grounds. "I had a feeling of awe about Columbia," he says, "and I resolved I would go there." He spent several summers at a boys' camp at Highmount, New York, and is convinced that his intense appreciation of nature—as expressed in such lines as "There's a bright golden haze on the meadow," "All the sounds of the earth are like music," "I can see the stars gittin' blurry," and "June is bustin' out all over"—is a result of this experience. The camp opened up new vistas. Hills and water were in abundance at Highmount; crickets chirped at night; the wind blew, sometimes gently, sometimes fiercely. "I would lie on the grass in wonderment," Hammerstein says. "I fell in love with nature at camp. I was nuts about the country."

In 1912, Hammerstein entered Columbia. On the campus there were a number of bright and eager young men who have made what is known as their mark in the world: Bennett Cerf, the anecdote-teller and publisher; M. Lincoln Schuster, of Simon & Schuster; Morrie Ryskind, the librettist; and Howard Dietz, the lyricist and press agent. Hammerstein mingled quietly with this group of incipient celebrities. He was inordinately shy. Columbia provided him with a certain amount of intellectual stimulation, and his marks ranged from B to B-plus, but his true interest was the Varsity Show, an enterprise that began rehearsals for its annual April production in January. The Varsity Show was of transcendent importance to everyone connected with it, and between January and April those involved had little time to crack a book. The performances were major social events in the world of Morningside Heights. They were put on in the ballroom of the Hotel Astor, usually for a week's run, and the audience wore evening clothes. Dr. Nicholas Murray Butler attended one performance of each show; on that night, all smudgy jokes and bits of innuendo were removed. Willie Hammerstein died in 1914; on his deathbed, he made his brother Arthur promise to keep Oscar from the evils of the theatre. Uncle Arthur tried to dissuade Oscar from Varsity Show activities, but Oscar said that these theatrical adventures were merely extracurricular and that he intended to be a lawyer, that he'd enter law school after his junior year, which he did.

Hammerstein's contributions to the drama at Columbia were no better, and no worse, than those of his classmates. In the 1916 production, *The Peace Pirates*, he wore a leopard-skin costume, and at one point had to leap across the stage. While making his exit, he would pretend to barely miss cracking his head against one side of the proscenium arch, and this invariably drew a big laugh. (He received his Bachelor of Arts degree in 1916, Columbia accepting a year of law as the equivalent of the fourth college year.) In 1917, he collaborated with a student named Herman Axelrod, now a real-estate man, on the lyrics for a song for *Home, James*, the varsity production of that year, entitled "Annie McGinnis Pavlova." The joint creation read, in part:

> Annie McGinnis Pavlova,
> I'll stop you from puttin' one over.
> 'Twas in Hogan's back alley
> You learned the bacchanale . . .

While still in law school, Hammerstein took a part-time job with the New York law firm of Blumenstiel and Blumenstiel. His father had left him some securities, which brought him in approximately fifty dollars a week, and Blumenstiel and Blumenstiel paid him five dollars a week for his legal efforts, which consisted of serving summonses, a form of endeavor for which he was not temperamentally fitted. His first summons-serving assignment took him to Jersey City, where, in response to his ring, a man came to the door of a run-down building, said, "The fellow you're looking for is out," and slammed the door in his face. His second assignment took him to a bar on Third Avenue. Nobody there had ever heard of the proprietor, the person to whom the summons was addressed, and once again Hammerstein quietly departed. Blumenstiel and Blumenstiel then shifted him to indoor work.

Had the financial rewards been more attractive, it is possible that Hammerstein would have continued at law school. However, he had fallen in love with a young woman he had met some years before at Highmount, where the young woman's family summered, and he was eager to get married, so, in the spring of 1917, he decided to quit. He paid a call on his Uncle Arthur, a flamboyantly successful producer of musical comedies, and said that he wanted to be a playwright. Arthur was horrified to learn that his nephew wanted to enter the theatre. "I told your father on his deathbed that I would never permit it!" he cried. "It's in my blood," Oscar said, "and, furthermore, I need the money." "How can I face the memory of your father?" said Arthur. Oscar replied that it would be criminal if he, a Hammerstein, were to be denied entrance to the profession that was his heritage and the compelling interest of his life. Arthur mumbled something more about the solemn necessity of keeping one's word, but it was evident that he was weakening, and the interview ended with Oscar's being hired by his uncle at twenty dollars a week, as assistant stage manager for a musical entitled *You're in Love*. Oscar II was at last launched on one of the more remarkable theatrical careers of history. Thirty years later, half an hour after the New York opening performance of *South Pacific* Arthur Hammerstein, then in his seventies, turned up in an excited state at the home of an old friend. "What's wrong, Arthur?" his friend asked. "Show no good?" "Tonight I have seen the perfect show," the aging producer said. "My decision to take Oscar into show business years back has been justified. Tonight I know that I did right by Willie after all, even though I broke my word. I am a happy man."

Shortly after the Rodgers-and-Hammerstein musical play *The King and I* opened a few weeks ago, a writer with a biographical interest in Hammerstein spent a day with him at his farm near Doylestown, Pennsylvania. When Hammerstein greeted the visitor, he was wearing a pair of gray flannel slacks and a robin's-egg-blue house jacket with gold buttons. "Let's walk around the place," he said. For the next fifteen minutes, he showed the visitor his rolling acres, on which he grows corn, alfalfa, and an impressive assortment of vegetables; his tennis court, which has a cork surface; and his herd of purebred Black Angus cattle, which were standing around in a large fenced-in enclosure beside a handsome white barn. A bucolic expression came over Hammerstein's face as he placed his elbows on the fence, put his chin in his hands, and stared at the cattle. The cattle stared back. "I just like to come out here and stare at the Black Angus," he said. "It's a habit with me to look at things. I once told George Kaufman that I loved to sit on my porch and look out over the fields at twilight and not think about anything, and George said, 'Anybody can sit and think of nothing; the trick is to think of *something*!' We raise turkeys and chickens, hang bacon in the smokehouse, and have a deep freeze here and one in Doylestown. Let's go inside."

Hammerstein led his guest into a comfortably remodelled two-hundred-year-old farmhouse. His wife's touch—she is a professional decorator—could, he said, be seen in every room. The two men walked up to Hammerstein's second-floor study, a large room the width of the house. The room was restful. Hanging at the windows were soft turquoise curtains. There was a fireplace in one wall. Another wall was lined with bookcases, containing, among other things, scripts of his musical shows, bound in bright red leather. In a corner, near a window, stood a high writing desk, resembling a lectern, on which, Hammerstein said, he composes most of his lyrics. On a small table near the desk was a framed card reading "Department of Public Instruction, City of New York. A GOOD BOY. Primary School 9" and signed by the principal. Hammerstein is proud of the card, which he says has brought him a good deal of luck. One wall was covered with all sorts of framed awards, including a Pulitzer Prize for his part in the writing of *South Pacific*. He flopped into an easy chair and suggested that his visitor sit behind an old-fashioned, highly polished cherrywood desk, ornamented by a lamp with a green glass shade and a silver inkstand. Hammerstein unbuttoned his jacket and stretched his legs out before him.

"Times have changed in show business," he said. "Back in the old days, when my Uncle Arthur was putting on musicals—why, somebody would come to him with an idea for a startling scenic effect and he'd build a whole show around it. Take *Rose-Marie*, for which I collaborated on the book and lyrics with Otto Harbach, the librettist, who is one of my dearest friends in all the world. Somebody told Uncle Arthur that up in Quebec there was an annual ice carnival—a grandiose business, with an ice palace high on a hill overlooking the city—and that at the close of the week's festivities the festival folk would climb the hill, all on snowshoes or something, and, torches in hand, melt down the ice palace. 'What an idea for a musical!' cried Arthur. 'What a finish!' He told me and Otto Harbach to go to Quebec and do some research. We went up there and found out, right off, that the ice-palace thing was nonsense. Nothing of the kind happened. Anyway, how could you melt down a palace every night on the stage? Uncle Arthur might have been able to do it, though. He produced *Tickle Me* just because a fellow turned up with a reducing-glass effect that was supposed to make the actors look small—a sort of reverse magnifying-glass idea. 'We'll put it on,' said Arthur, and he did, in Hartford, and the reducing-glass effect made the actors damn near invisible. *Tickle Me* was all about the White Lama of Tibet, and a girl was sacrificed onstage with a bubble-bath effect. But to get back to Quebec, Otto Harbach and I went to the Château Frontenac. We saw Eskimos and dog races and went on a toboggan ride, but no melting ice palace could be found. Somebody told us about an Indian-moccasin factory, and off we went, on nature's coldest day, and got frostbitten, and when we arrived, the Indians were taking a half day off. The whole trip yielded one scene in *Rose-Marie*, a scene in a novelty shop with colorful Indian costumes. We had seen such a shop up there. The words to 'The Indian Love Call' in *Rose-Marie* were written in a taxicab during rehearsals, and so were most of the other songs. The thing ran forever and netted Uncle Arthur three million. It made us all famous."

Hammerstein shifted in his chair. "I remember the night before *Rose-Marie* opened in London," he went on. "An assistant stage manager came up to me—it was raining outside, and foggy—and he told me there was a little old lady sitting on a campstool in front of the theatre, waiting to see the show the next day. 'Bring her in and let her see the dress rehearsal,' I said. The man went outside, and the little old lady said, 'Oh, I couldn't do *that*. It would spoil things for me!' That's the British. I love London. I love the hotels, and the courtesy, and the sea trips over. I'd rather write on a boat than anywhere. I can get more done. I like teatime, at four-thirty, come hell or high water, rehearsal or no rehearsal. England! I wish I'd gone to the opening of *Oklahoma!* over there, but I *was* in London, as I've said, for the *Rose-Marie* opening. We didn't think anybody was going to like it. There it was, dying right in front of my eyes. I sat in a box with Arthur, and the audience was strangely silent. 'Wait until the Mounties come on. They'll love the Mounties,' I whispered to Arthur. No sign of enthusiasm when the Mounties came on. 'Wait for the totem-pole dance,' I whispered to Arthur. We had outfitted a bunch of girls in totem-pole costumes—quite an effect, since they fell down on the stage one by one like a row of wooden soldiers. We outfitted forty people for the totem-pole sequence for twenty-four hundred dollars—that's sixty dollars a costume. Today the same thing would cost four hundred dollars a girl—sixteen thousand dollars. Well, the totem-pole dance came and went, and no response. However, the play ran two years at the Drury Lane and broke every record until *Oklahoma!* came along, at the same theatre. I love the English. *Rose-Marie* put me in the hundred-thousand-a-year class. I made big money every year from the time I was twenty-nine until my flop period, about ten years later. During the twenties, six of my shows ran for more than a year. Things went well after *Rose-Marie*."

Getting up, Hammerstein began to pace back and forth. "The old-time producers were funny fellows, all right," he said. "They didn't care much about the book for a musical. If it was good, nobody noticed it; if it was bad, *you* got blamed. You think Charles Dillingham cared about the book? He threw in the kitchen sink for *Sunny*, for which I collaborated with Otto Harbach on the book and lyrics. He engaged George Olsen and his band, Marilyn Miller, Jack Donahue, Clifton Webb, and Ukulele Ike. Ukulele Ike said he had to come on between ten and ten-thirty, thought this the best time to appear, and Dillingham said to me, 'Work it into the book.' I've never liked the story of *Sunny*—it was about a girl marrying a fellow in order to get to America to marry somebody else—but it was my first show with Jerome Kern. It brought us together. I loved Jerry Kern. I first saw him at the funeral of Victor Herbert, a rainy day at Woodlawn Cemetery. Everybody told me to watch out for Jerry Kern, that he was a son of a bitch. I loved him. We always said the way we ought to spend our declining years was acting out our own shows for ourselves and spending the rest of our time attending other people's dress rehearsals. I'm ahead of myself, though. Moss and Fontana were to be in *Sunny*, too. They were choice dancers of the period. Said that they couldn't join us until the second week in Philadelphia, and that they wanted to be met at the station by a brass band, so Dillingham met them at the station with a brass band. This was in the fall of 1925. I sat down with Marilyn Miller one afternoon and outlined to her the whole story of *Sunny*, every step of the way. She never opened her mouth throughout the exposition. I told her everything—gave her dialogue, acted out scenes, ran through tentative lyrics—and when I was through, she looked at me and said, 'Mr. Hammerstein, when do I do my tap specialty?'"

Hammerstein walked over and leaned on the writing desk, then looked out the window for a moment before he spoke again. "Ziegfeld was the same as Dillingham," he said. "Ruthless about everything but the public. Jerry Kern and I made a radical revision in the second act of *Show Boat* and asked him to come see it, and he sat all through the radical revision, and when the scene was over, he cried out to a chorus girl, 'You've changed the way you do your hair!' When we worked on *Show Boat*, Kern lived in Bronxville and I lived in Great Neck—I was married to my first wife then, and the house cost a hundred and eighty thousand dollars, and the taxes on it were twenty-four hundred a year—and Jerry would phone me every morning from Bronxville and put the phone on top of the piano and play the music. He was a warmhearted fellow, Jerry. When we were out on the road, throwing a show together, the minute we'd check in at the hotel, we'd run out and buy a bottle of Worcestershire sauce. Jerry would stick it in the piano. We liked steaks in our rooms after working hard, and no hotel ever had Worcestershire when you wanted it. Jerry had a yacht and a yachting cap and liked to be called Commodore, but he never took the yacht to sea, never pulled up anchor, because he was afraid of getting seasick.

"When we went to work on *Show Boat*, we heard about an old show boat down on the Eastern Shore, in Maryland, and decided to travel down there and pick up some local color. Incidentally, when Kern first called me about *Show Boat*, I was working on *Golden Dawn*, a musical about the Tanganyika Territory. To get back to *Show Boat*, Edna Ferber said there was no real reason to go to Maryland—everything was in her book anyway—but we wanted to see an old show boat for ourselves. You never met such fine people as the actors on that show boat. Sweet, gentle, and kind, and they treated us like royalty and invited us for supper. We ate with them, and joked, and got on fine, and I said to Jerry, 'These are real people, these are show people, these are our kind of people.' After supper, we went upstairs to the auditorium and watched the show. Oh, God, what a performance! I began to hate those people. They weren't show people at all, they didn't give a hoot about the theatre, they just ran through their lines as though they were butchers or something. It wasn't that they were bad—I can forgive bad acting—it was just that they didn't care. They read their lines mechanically—one performance, I'm sure, like another, and to hell with it. Jerry and I sneaked away before it was over, without saying good-bye. We were heartsick. They were almost as bad as amateurs. How I hate amateurs! I put my feelings down in some lines in *Music in the Air*, and I meant every word of it. I had a character say, 'That's what I hate about beginners. They have the conceit to think they can start at the top of the ladder, and when they fall off, they blame everybody else.' "

Hammerstein moved over to the mantelpiece and began toying with a miniature metal surrey with a cloth fringe on top. "Dorothy Stickney and Howard Lindsay sent me this after *Oklahoma!* opened," he said. "A strange thing. Lots of people like to talk about the good old days in the theatre and tear down the present. Actually, everybody has more humility these days, and works harder. It would have been unthinkable in the old days to hold auditions for the leading parts in a musical. The big stars would have been mortally insulted. You hired a star, and if she didn't work out, there'd be a blowup in Baltimore or Philadelphia and you'd have to run around at the last minute and corral another one. Times have changed with respect to treating minorities decently on the stage, too. The stage Irishman is gone, d the stage Jew, and the stage Negro, and it's all to the good. The Irishman was always drunk, the Jewish fellow always wore a derby, the Negro was always treated with disrespect. We can't afford that sort of thing now. People who wrote parts for those characters were engaging in lazy writing, stereotype writing.

"The twenties were golden for me—*The Desert Song*, *Show Boat*, *Sunny*, *The New Moon*—but the thirties were black. I was in Hollywood a good deal of the time in the thirties, always making seventeen hundred and fifty or two thousand or twenty-five hundred a week, but there isn't much to look back on—pictures like *Champagne and Orchids* or *High, Wide and Handsome*. Why, I remember right after the preview of *High, Wide and Handsome*, a party was held at the Riviera Country Club, in Hollywood, and Adolph Zukor walked across the polished floor, like an archduke, and wrung my hand and said, 'That's the greatest picture we ever made.' A couple of months later, when the picture had opened and gone sour, I walked past him in a restaurant and he stared through me as though he had never seen me before in his life. I had a bad time. I've had my option not renewed—some of the pictures got so bad that Warner's paid me to stop writing them—and I've gone from studio to studio. I'd alternate Hollywood with fast trips to New York, to see the shows, and fast trips to England, to see more shows. I went to England once and saw nine shows in a week, I was that hungry for the theatre. Nothing seemed to work out. I came back East at one point and tried three shows, and within five weeks all had opened and all had closed. People were beginning to say that the parade had passed Oscar by. I suppose I was using the old formulas, and they didn't work out anymore."

Hammerstein walked over to a map of Scandinavia standing on a book-case shelf. Small pins with paper pennants had been stuck into it. "Touring companies of *Oklahoma!*, *The Desert Song*, and *Carousel*," he said. He smiled and sat down again in the easy chair. "The deluge came after Jerry Kern and I opened our musical *Very Warm for May*. Mrs. Hammerstein and I came in from Great Neck, and we took a room at the Weylin for the opening, and the next morning I got up to read the notices. I remember that I'd left my dressing gown back home, and I put my overcoat on over my pajamas and went down to the lobby for the papers. Then I went back to the room. 'How are they, Oscar?' Mrs. Hammerstein asked. 'The worst notices I've ever had in my life,' I said, and we got dressed and went to an early movie at the Music Hall. Then we went down to Palm Beach, and I lay on the beach and thought a lot. Things just weren't working out. This was just too many failures. My spirits picked up a bit when the 'Hit Parade' began to play 'All the Things You Are' from *Very Warm for May*. I went out to Hollywood again for a while, and all I could get was twelve hundred and fifty a week. I had an income from ASCAP—eighteen, twenty thousand a year, from performing rights—but it wasn't the money I used to make. In 1940, I came East, bought the farm here, then went back to Hollywood, and my price was down to twelve hundred a week. In 1941, I wrote *Sunny River* and it was produced in New York, and the critics said, '*Sunny River* stay 'way from my door.' I was pretty blue. I just wanted to come down here to the farm and sit around and be alone and think. It's not easy to hear people say that the parade has passed you by. When you come right down to it, Broadway is charitable, the street is forgiving, but I wanted to keep the confidence I had in myself. I did a funny thing, down here alone. My wife spent the weekdays in New York, handling her decorating business, and I went out and bought myself a complete La Scala recording of *Carmen*. To me, *Carmen* has always been the perfect story. It's like *Hamlet*; it has everything. It's a great story of a good boy and a good girl. Even the bad girl has a courageous heart, and I admire her. In her own way, she is utterly honest. There are inevitable things, too—the shift to the toreador, the devoted mother. There is a Greek inevitability about *Carmen*. Another deep interest in *Carmen* is that boy. He's a good boy, but when he falls—oh, he falls hard. I guess it's the best libretto ever written. Well, I'd take those records and play them by the hour, over and over again, until I knew every bar by heart. I would get up early every morning and play my records. And then I got to work to fashion a modern *Carmen*. I called it *Carmen Jones*, and when it was produced, people stopped saying that the parade had passed Oscar by. At first, I thought I would keep *Carmen Jones* small and modest, and produce it myself, but I ran into Billy Rose one night at the Diamond Horseshoe and told him the idea, and he said he wanted to do it.

"Dick Rodgers phoned me one day, just after I'd finished working on *Carmen Jones*, and said he wanted to lunch with me, he had something to talk over. I knew him, but not too well. I knew his older brother, Mortimer, better; we had been contemporaries at Columbia. I met Dick at the Barberry Room, and he said, 'Oscar, the Theatre Guild wants to make Lynn Riggs' *Green Grow the Lilacs* into a musical. I'm not too familiar with it, but I wonder if we could get together.' He needed a lyricist, I needed a composer. We were both at loose ends. He was having his troubles with Larry Hart—poor fellow, always wandering off and leaving Dick stranded without lyrics. I told Dick I was crazy about the play, and we went to work. Did I struggle with the comic lyrics! I knew I had the ballad field licked, all right, but comic lyrics frightened me. When we finished, we didn't know what we had on our hands, and nobody else did, either. The Guild had a hell of a time raising money. People would ask who the stars were going to be; they thought in terms of big musicals, with Gaxton, Moore, and Merman, and when we said there would be no stars, they would say, 'No, thank you.' Dick took a room in Steinway Hall, and we were there day after day, singing the songs and trying to raise a few dollars. I always sang 'Poor Jud Is Daid.' I remember one swanky fund-raising party; there was a lot of money in that room, and about fifty people heard us run through the show, champagne and caviar were served, and nobody put up a nickel. One fellow there had already put up a thousand, and he didn't withdraw it, but he didn't add anything, either. We were pretty discouraged. At this time, Arthur Freed came along with a Hollywood offer—a thousand dollars a week for a hundred and four weeks. I sat down with my lawyer and figured things out. I considered the tax on the salary, the agent's fee, the expenses of moving, and so on, against staying here, taking in my royalties, and gambling on *Oklahoma!* being a big hit. I decided to stay East. It opened in New Haven, and lots of people didn't like it one bit. Up in Boston, the critics found something to it, but too many people would come up in the lobby and say, 'It's fun' or 'Nice little show you have there,' and we were nervous."

Hammerstein slouched down in his chair. "I don't have to tell you what happened to *Oklahoma!*," he said. "Dick and I have worked together ever since, and it's a perfect partnership. He likes to handle the business end of things, and he goes down to the office every day and has a good time at it. I enjoy staying at home in my study when I'm in town and watching the world come through. I enjoy it not from any sense of power but because I think I'm in my prime and I'm functioning well. Dick and I have worked so well together it's hard to believe. We think alike. When I mailed him some of the lyrics for *Allegro*, from Australia—I had gone there with Mrs. Hammerstein on a vacation—he cabled back instantly, 'YES, YES, A THOUSAND TIMES YES.' *Allegro* didn't go over with the critics, it wasn't an artistic success, but it ran for nine months in New York and seven months on the road, and was the biggest grosser of the year. I still have faith in *Allegro*. Many a dinner party was broken up that year over it. It was an original story, and I had a great many things to say, but they didn't come off, I guess. I wanted to write a large, universal story, and I think I over-estimated the psychological ability of the audience to identify itself with the leading character. We told the thing in the second person, saying 'you' to the audience, and having the 'you' onstage, as a baby. This was confusing. I was concerned in *Allegro* with the integrity of doctors, too—a big subject. These days, 'integrity' has taken on almost a double meaning; in some instances, it's a screen for failure. We were pretty severely criticized for what was taken as censure of rich city doctors. We never understood that. Why, I even had a line in the play that went, 'There's nothing wrong with people just because they have money or live in the city—nothing wrong with being a city doctor.' But just the same, people said we were rich city boys and had no business criticizing rich city doctors. I'm going back to the *Allegro* idea someday—the idea of writing a story about a man from the cradle to the grave. It's still churning inside me."

Hammerstein got up again and went over and stood by a window. "The Theatre Guild had the idea for *Carousel*," he said. "I resisted it at first. I had read *Liliom* and liked it, but it seemed too serious for musical adaptation. It struck me that I myself wouldn't enjoy seeing a show about Central Europe—and that's a big test for me. Theresa Helburn, of the Guild, suggested we put it in New Orleans, with lots of French atmosphere. Creole lyrics, and the like. I knew that all those 'zisses' and 'zoses' wouldn't work. We puzzled a long time over this one. In those days, we met every Thursday at Sardi's for lunch—Dick, Helburn, and Lawrence Langner, of the Guild. We were sitting there one Thursday, just thinking about where to put *Liliom*, when Dick suddenly said, 'New England!' I saw it instantly. It was perfect! I think in terms of ensembles and ensemble problems. I've always thought in terms of ensembles. You can't just have them leap in from the wings. They have to be indigenous—the Mounties in *Rose-Marie*, for example, or the Riffs in *The Desert Song*. New England was perfect—the mill hands and the mill girls in a New England town, and the fisherfolk and the fishing life. Gosh, I love *Carousel*! I saw a revival at the City Center a year or so ago, and I cried all night. I was grateful for having written it. We had a little trouble with it on the road. I had written a scene with a New England cottage where Mr. and Mrs. God lived, but it didn't go over, and we changed it to the one in Heaven where there's a clothesline hanging out and stars hang from the clothesline."

Linking his hands behind his head, Hammerstein settled down comfortably in his chair. He seemed to be in almost complete repose. "I've never been so happy as I've been since *The King and I* opened," he said. "It's a *real* hit, but it was a hard one. We tell a real story to music—it's truly a musical drama, with every song advancing the plot—and we ask the audience to believe that those people onstage, who face many serious problems of life, will suddenly stop talking and burst into song. We had to avoid destroying the reality by the singing, and the singing by the reality. In New Haven, it ran forty-five minutes too long, but that never worries me. The flops always end on time, but when you start cutting out things you love, you're down to a pretty high standard. You know, these days I feel like a delicious bum. If I saw a rhyme, I'd run a mile. I'm reading for pleasure. I'm spending a lot of time down here at the farm, puttering around and pasting photographs of the place and pictures of myself at different ages into albums." Hammerstein suddenly leaned forward, and his eyes took on a faraway look. "I was looking at those pictures of myself the other day, and I figured that I've absorbed a good deal in my time about show business," he said. "I learned a lot about timing from watching Ed Wynn, and Otto Harbach taught me a great lesson, too. He used to say, 'When you write a song, think of a boy and a girl dancing together and try to express what the boy is trying to express to the girl.' And Max Gordon taught me a valuable truth. He always says, 'The curtain goes up and two people are out on the stage, and somebody better say something pretty damn fast!' Oh, I love life and I'm in great shape and my mind is blooming, but I know that the life span is still threescore and ten. I'm only temperamental about writing lyrics, nothing else, and it hurts that here I am, fifty-five, and I'm just learning my craft."

(1951)

Costumes

Theoni V. Aldredge is chief costume designer for Joseph Papp's Public
Theatre and New York Shakespeare Festival, and has been for twelve years.
We have long admired her work (the costumes of several current productions, including *That Championship Season* and *Two Gentlemen of Verona*,
were designed by Mrs. Aldredge, and the richly embroidered tapestries of
the costumes in last summer's *Hamlet* in the Park keep running through
our dreams), and last week we went down to Lafayette Street to have a talk
with her. We found her in the throes of moving the costume shop from a
building on one side of the street, housing a compound of Papp's theatres,
to larger quarters in a loft building on the other side. All around us were
what appeared to be millions of spools of restless, jumping thread and
thousands of yards of excited fabrics, but Mrs. Aldredge was calm, even
serene. She is tall, slim, beautiful, and in her early forties, has patrician
high cheekbones, and was wearing an unadorned muted-brown sweater
and a gray skirt. "Soft colors," she said. "I love soft colors, and very simple,
understated things. I own half a dozen skirts and blouses, and keep chang-
ing them, and I look pretty good. Fabric is a passion. I love to touch fabric. Taffeta, brocade, silk, cotton, wool. Velvet, velveteen, moire. Chiffon.
Crêpe. I have a passion for fabric. I was born in Salonika, and we moved to
Athens when I was a year old, and I was brought up there. My mother died
when I was very young. My father, Athanasios V. Vachliotis, was surgeon
general of the Greek Army and a member of Parliament. He died a few

years ago. I considered him a great friend, a very great friend. I was brought up in a house with three brothers, and you can imagine the cars and bicycles and assorted hardware, so when I got off by myself and dressed a doll, there was a special satisfaction. My dolls are still part of me. I have a large collection. Wherever I go, I head for the native section and buy native dolls—not the tourist stuff. Many of them are in costumes of my own making, of course, but some, from Russia and Poland, are in their original dresses. I never had a dollhouse, but I needed the dolls around me. They still sit around my room and on top of a trunk, looking at me. I consider them my friends. I look at them. They are never covered. They sit there, and we have something important between us."

Mrs. Aldredge paused for a few moments. "Back in 1950, when I was quite young, I had some vague ideas about the theatre," she went on. "I really knew nothing about it. I was mysteriously drawn to it. I mentioned to my father that I might want to try my hand at theatre in the United States. 'Why, you come from the country where theatre was born,' he said. I tentatively mentioned costumes. 'Why, you are living right next door to Rome,' he said. 'The fabrics are in Rome. Rome has the goods.' I went to the American Embassy in Athens and discussed American academic theatrical experience. They suggested that I try the Pasadena Playhouse, the Drama Department of Carnegie Tech (now Carnegie-Mellon), or the Goodman Theatre, in Chicago. I chose the Goodman. When I arrived in New York, after a thirty-six-hour flight from Greece—thirty-six hours!—I went to a movie called *Caesar and Cleopatra*, with Vivien Leigh and Claude Rains. A strange thing happened. I was overwhelmed by the beauty of the flowing garments worn by Vivien Leigh. They were very tight-fitting, very form-fitting. They flowed with an exquisite grace. They had a rhythm of their own. I learned later that they were a special pleated Egyptian fabric, and that they fitted so snugly because they were soaking wet and clung to Miss Leigh. I also learned that she had become ill from being wrapped in them. But the vision was one of loveliness. 'People can look so beautiful in clothes,' I said to myself. 'There is a mystery to costumes.' And that's where it started. At Goodman, I taught costume, and met Tom Aldredge, the actor, who was teaching makeup. I admire him so much! I think he is a great actor. We have been married now for nineteen years, and it looks like a good thing, I must say. We have our own interests; we never interfere with each other. My first Broadway costume was for Geraldine Page in *Sweet Bird of Youth*. We had been friends at Goodman, and she wanted me to design her costume. I still have my Geraldine Page doll, wearing the proper costume. Then I walked in on Joe Papp one day, when his headquarters were at the old Heckscher Theatre, on Fifth Avenue, and he said, 'Let me see what you've got,' and I've been with him ever since. I do a great deal of outside work, and an occasional movie, and sometimes I will design a wedding dress for a friend, but when the marriage ends up in divorce it makes me sad, and I don't like that work. When I work for Papp, I feel I am working for my family. He even worries about actors' *feet*! I am doing about twenty shows a year now, and work closely with Milo Morrow, the costume-shop master at the Public. A fantastic man! We have worked together so long he knows exactly what I have in mind, exactly where I am heading. He has a sixth sense—of color, of fabrics in the light, of material."

She leaned forward. "One tells oneself one wants to do something, and one does it," she said. "I start out with a costume plot—a detailed description of every single character in the play, every garment, every accessory. I plot the changes in character. I do watercolor sketches of the characters. We decide on a color scheme for a given show. The costume shop fans out all over the city, to every fabric house in town. New York City is *the* center of the fabric industry. We hunt up velvets, silks, cottons, prints, moires. We find leather. We find man-made fabrics. Morrow's people pour back with thousands of swatches for us to order from. We have trouble finding real silk and real wool these days, by the way. We dye our own costumes and perform miracles. We have five whole armies downstairs in the storeroom—*all* those Wars of the Roses—and they can be used again by dyeing and painting. Richness is achieved in many ways. We embroider a great deal. In any one garment, there may be as many as fifteen different velvets, woollens, silks. In *Hamlet*, there were different browns turning black—taffeta, brocade, and silk all mixed up together. There was red woven underneath the fabric. And there may be four or five *layers*, with different colors. The texture changes on the stage. The colors change. The change is almost palpable. Queen Gertrude had a huge heavy red velvet gown laced with metal brocade. Claudius was in heavy brown of velveteen, moire, brocades, all sewn together and heavily embroidered—a royal extravagance. The light catches these things. The audience should be aware of them but not too aware. They are to help the actor, help the audience. You should look at them and forget them. But a tone is set. We make everything but shoes. We make period purses and gloves. Period pieces are easy for me, comparatively. I can go to the books. I pore over the art books, mostly for mood. The colors of Velázquez, Fragonard, El Greco! Imagine a Lear with that lean, drained El Greco look, and those *colors*."

Mrs. Aldredge stared into space for a few moments. "I am thinking of a visit I once paid to the Old Palace in Krakow," she said, "where they have exhibited the tents of Polish warriors—room after room of them. Pitched tents, tapestries, even the slippers laid out, and always color. I wandered through in great excitement. The colors had me feverish. And yet I seem to stay with subdued colors in my costumes. Perhaps I am afraid of colors. I may be playing it safe; the bright colors frighten me. Not, of course, the bright, whitewashed glaring white of the Greek rocks, or the living lavender, the positive lavender, of Greece, or the olive color. I can close my eyes now and see the olive color and the gleaming white. But then I open my eyes and know that we are no longer a laughing people. We thought everything would be over in a few months. It is now six years. But the rocks are still washed with white, and we will be a laughing people again."

(1973)

All in the Artist's Head

Robert Beverly Hale is a beloved teacher. He is a tall, spare, somewhat rumpled patrician of seventy-six, with black-rimmed glasses and an El Greco face. He teaches two courses, Artistic Anatomy and Elements of Drawing, at the Art Students League, on West Fifty-seventh Street, and his classes are a continual, and almost legendary, celebration not only of the beauty and wonder of the human form but of Hale himself. Many people consider Hale the foremost teacher of artistic anatomy in the country, and perhaps the world. His classes are always oversubscribed, and students return year after year. When Hale enters a lecture hall or a studio, his students burst into applause. They do the same thing as he leaves. Hale is a modest, philosophical man, with a long view of history and of life, but he does not attempt to hide his pleasure at these tributes. "I have a flair for teaching," he often says. "The role of teacher fits me, and I play it. I never empty a lecture room." He does not attempt to hide his pleasure, either, at having recently received, at Alice Tully Hall, one of the Mayor's Awards of Honor for Arts and Culture, the citation for which reads, "Artist, poet, and teacher, he has inspired generations of ardent disciples at the Art Students League."

"Subtle and elemental forces are at work inside Hale," a former student told me not long ago. "There's an encyclopedic knowledge of art and artists, extraordinary humor, and the ability to make anatomical drawings with a piece of charcoal attached to a long stick which are miracles of precision and art." The young man paused for breath, but not very long. "I get extremely excited when I talk about Hale and his classes," he said. "So does everybody I know who works with him. There's a magic to the man as he stands up there drawing and talking. He's generous. He holds nothing back. He puts down everything he considers essential. Unlike some teachers, who assert themselves, he eliminates himself and concentrates on reverence for art and artists. There are no sly, arcane corners with Hale. He tells you what he knows. And in some inexplicable way it is always allied with the earth and with human beings, and with their survival as human beings on this planet."

Hale and I are friends. His company invigorates me and gives me a sense of purpose. I like to hear him talk, either formally, in front of a class or at some public function, or informally, at home. Hale enjoys talking. He talks quietly, in a dry, clipped tone, and each word emerges as though it had been leading a detached, private, educated life of its own. As he talks, his mind gracefully unfolds, and a landscape is dotted not with the delicate bridges, willows, houses, and carp-filled streams of a Chinese scroll but with ideas, fancies, memories—precise and embroidered—and technical details, wrapped in poetry, his own and others'. (His poem "The Big Nasturtiums" has appeared in anthologies all over the world; in addition to poetry, he has written critical essays, short stories, a children's book, and a celebrated and widely used text, *Drawing Lessons from the Great Masters*, and has translated for the first time from French into English Dr. Paul Richer's classic nineteenth-century work *Artistic Anatomy*.)

I close my eyes and see Hale at different times and in different places. Hale was at the hundredth-anniversary dinner of the Art Students League at the Waldorf. By the time he rose to his feet to speak, the audience—artists, students, former students, patrons of the League—had worked their way through avocado caprice, cream of wild-mushroom soup, roast prime rib of beef, and crown of raspberry sherbet. They had listened to extensive reminiscences from another longtime teacher at the League, some hard-nosed money talk from a foundation chief (Matching Grant Country), and the remarks of a local critic. And now, Hale. Guests who had been idly making fork tracks on napkins and tablecloths put down their forks and listened. Hale, it appeared, wished to discuss fundamentals. He recalled that some years earlier a technical school in the neighborhood of the League had sent a group of its students to the League to "teach them about art." Hale was asked to conduct the initial lecture. "I intimated that the artist doesn't see things as they are, he sees things as he is," he said. "I warned them that there was nothing more dreadful than imagination without taste. I also told them that the life of the artist was desolate and dangerous, and finally I told them, in the words of Camus, that I was convinced that a man's work was nothing but the long journey through life to recover, through the detours of art, the two or three great and simple images that first gained access to his heart." Hale and his colleagues at the League struggled painstakingly, he said, with their young technical-school visitors. "We told them, for instance, that science had actually sprung from art, and that it had developed in those great periods when artists looked at nature very closely and carefully and tried to record exactly what they saw," he said. "That, we explained, was what scientists have been doing ever since, but, we took great pains to point out, the artist, unlike the scientist, has always felt that the things he couldn't see were just as important as the things he could see." After a few months, Hale felt that a slight but perceptible change had come over the technical people. He would occasionally overhear them discussing "such invisible entities as the grace of Raphael, the compassion of Rembrandt." He continued, "So it would appear that we artists have a job on our hands. Especially now that the scientists are almost capable of exterminating, in a flash, not only us but all other living matter on this planet. They can't quite do this yet, but they are hoping that through earnest sweat and total dedication they can reach this goal by lilac time, 1978." Hale offered a highly personal solution. "I've got two very nice color photographs at home that were taken shortly after the bombing of Hiroshima and Nagasaki," he said. "In the middle of each is a brilliant orange spot—a nuclear ember dying, no doubt—and around each spot is a massive cloud of rising dust. I'm going to hang these photographs on my wall and between them paste up a poem by Emily Dickinson. Then, next week, I'm going to ask a scientist I know home for supper. He's a very nice man. He has two little children. I'm sure that as soon as he comes in, his professional curiosity will attract him to the photographs, and undoubtedly he will glance at the poem. It reads:

> This quiet Dust was Gentlemen and Ladies,
> And Lads and Girls;
> Was laughter and ability and sighing,
> And frocks and curls."

I close my eyes and see Hale in his apartment. He lives in a comfortable old building on Sixty-seventh Street, just off Central Park West, with his second wife, Niké, an art historian, who is considerably younger than he, and their two children, Alexander Curzon Hale, thirteen, and Evelyn Everett Hale, four. Mrs. Hale is small, dark, and vibrant. She was born in Greece and educated at Vassar. She has a long, mobile face, recalling many strong women painted by Picasso in his classic period. The apartment has an austere, somewhat unsettled look, as though the Hales were just about to move in or move out. Quite obviously, it is the home of people who disdain material possessions. A few scatter rugs, designed and handmade by Mrs. Hale, lend splashes of color to the living room and increase the singular independence of a large, spidery free-flowing ink abstraction, painted by Hale, that dominates one side of the room.

On this day, Hale was dressed in a pair of unpressed gray flannel trousers, an old bluish-gray sports jacket, and gray Wallabees. He sat in a small rattan chair, I opposite him on a sofa. He was in a talkative mood. "My life has been a considerable struggle to find out what I am best suited for, and the Art Students League has been a true friend, a true home," he said. "I went to teach there in 1943, broken in spirit, and in a depression. I have terrible depressions. My mornings are especially terrible. I often don't think I'm going to get through. I've had a great many advantages. I come from quite a family, really. Sometimes when I think of it I am astonished. My grandfather Edward Everett Hale was a Unitarian minister, and he wrote *The Man without a Country*. When he was eighty-one years old, he was made chaplain of the United States Senate. Someone said to him, 'In your capacity as chaplain, do you pray for the Senate?' and Edward Everett Hale said, 'My friend, I look at the Senate and I pray for the country.' My grandfather's uncle Edward Everett was president of Harvard and a celebrated classical speaker of the old school, and he shared a platform with Abraham Lincoln at Gettysburg on the day that Lincoln delivered the address that begins, 'Fourscore and seven . . .' Everett spoke for two hours and Lincoln for two minutes, and it is generally accepted that Lincoln's remarks were not only shorter but better. Somewhere along the line, Harriet Beecher Stowe is involved with my family tree, and also that ghastly man Henry Ward Beecher, but I'm fuzzy about details. It seems that Harriet was my grandmother's aunt. In any event, my beautiful mother was

born on East Thirty-ninth Street, in Manhattan. She was lovely and gracious. Father was Herbert Dudley Hale, a partner in Hale and Rogers, ar-
chitects. When my father was forty-two and I was seven, in 1908, he died.
The next year, my mother married another architect, John Oakman.
When my parents were in New York, they were at the center of what might
be called upper bohemia. That's where I was at. Artists, writers—they all
came around at five o'clock for drinks or tea. The Americans influenced by
the Barbizon school—my parents knew 'em. My mother and father knew
Whistler intimately. Whistler once painted my mother on top of an oil of
Anthony Eden's mother. A complicated story, with a complicated lawsuit
between Sir William Eden and Whistler, but the upshot was that my
mother's picture was painted on top of the face of Lady Eden by Whistler,
in Paris, and that somehow Whistler walked off with my mother's mink
coat. A mixup, of course, but the coat was *gone*. The picture is now in the
University of Glasgow museum.

"Let's talk about another age. Around the time of the Armory Show and
the First World War, my family lived on West Sixteenth Street. From
1920 or 1921 on, they went to Paris in the summers. I went along. I was at
the moveable feast with a vengeance. In some ways, Waldo Peirce, the
painter, was the head of the clan. Six feet six, huge beard, knew everybody.
Picasso, Matisse—you name 'em. I often stayed in an attic in his apartment, at 77, rue de Lille. Joyce would come to the parties—and, incidentally, if there was anything Joyce's wife couldn't stand, it was Joyce's
drinking." There was a solemn, frightening parlor game that Joyce would
play, Hale said. It began with placing several small bowls on a table. Water
would be put in one bowl; that signified a trip somewhere by water. Some
laurel leaves would be put in another; that signified fame. Still another
would contain earth; that meant death. One at a time, the participants
would be blindfolded, go forward to the table, and grope for one of the
bowls. One evening when Hale was playing, he was solemnly blindfolded,
and just as he was about to plunge his hand into the bowl filled with earth,
Joyce, moving swiftly as a cat, switched bowls, and Hale's hand went
down into the bowl of laurel leaves. "A lovely gesture," said Hale.

"But I am ahead of myself in the evolution of an anatomist. I was born
in Boston and spent the first months of my life there. But I cannot make
any memory of it come true. I try to get back to the recollection, but I

cannot. A few years ago, when I had an operation, under anesthesia I saw the most beautiful swirling patterns and the most interesting colors and shapes, and I remember saying to myself later, 'Beautiful paintings these, if I can ever see them again, but they are gone.' So are whatever pictures I may have had of the earliest, Boston days. In general, I had a hard time finding myself. I first went to Columbia when I was fifteen—that would have been around 1916—leaving, coming back, leaving, studying, travelling, moving around until 1931. I took every course in biology I could get my hands on. My stepfather had said to me, 'This is a scientific century,' and I took him seriously. I studied physics. I studied geology. I studied with John Dewey and Irwin Edman and Franz Boas and John Erskine. You name it, I studied it. I didn't take all those courses for credit—I just wanted to see how the world was put together. I also wanted to write fiction, like my first cousin J. P. Marquand. I studied architecture at Fontainebleau, but I discovered that I wanted something looser than architecture. The galleries everywhere fascinated me, and the Art Students League fascinated me. I actually first attended classes there as far back as 1922, and I am one of the few artists left with the full technical training. I am damn pessimistic. I don't know who will die first, me or the world. My rigorous scientific training contributes to the pessimism. The reality of today—not a fantasy—is that someone could blow us all up tonight. Grand Central, the Empire State Building—you name it. The power that has been unleashed by man is unimaginable, except that I can imagine it."

Hale stood up and moved slowly into an adjoining long, narrow corridor and took a photograph from a hook on the wall. He moved back into the living room, handed me the photograph, and began pacing. The photograph was of a fine-looking innocent, bright-eyed boy. "My son, Alexander," said Hale, with an admiration that was at once both deeply felt and oddly detached. He sounded as though he had studied Alexander's face many times—bone structure, eyes, formation of the nose—and had decided that, objectively viewed, it was, son or no son, a beautiful face. "My friend Walker Evans took this one evening several years ago," he said. "Just happened by the apartment as Alexander was getting ready for bed. Evans had a few aboard—far too many, really—but he whipped out his camera, glanced somewhat foggily at Alexander across the room, snapped the shutter once, and put away the camera. A great artist, a sympathetic subject, and a moment in time. I doubt there will ever be a greater picture of Alexander, one with more understanding or communication. That was Evans for you. Wonderful man! Wonderful wild man! Many years ago, down at East Hampton, I was going through quite a depressed period, and for therapy I built myself a wooden tower some twenty feet high. Working with all that wood quieted me down, and I loved fashioning the ladder that took one to the top of my tower. Walker showed up one evening and instantly raced up the ladder, like a child, and then raced back down. Next morning, at breakfast, he looked out and saw the tower. 'What in God's name is *that?*' he said. I told him it was my therapeutic tower. 'Well,' he said, 'one thing's certain. I could never get up those rungs.' "

Hale went back to his chair. "I have an almost mystical feeling about the teaching of anatomy," he said. "There is continuity in the teaching, and you can always see the roots. I teach a special course, ten weeks each year, in anatomy, but I also teach, throughout the academic year, a straightforward class in drawing and draftsmanship, light and shade, perspective and proportion. Once a month, I go down to Broad and Cherry Streets in Philadelphia to teach anatomy at the Pennsylvania Academy of the Fine Arts—the oldest art school in the country, housed in a Victorian Gothic jewel, with beautiful tiled floors. Two hundred to five hundred take my course there. Standing room only, sometimes. Anatomy is one of the elements of drawing—only one. Wrapped up, you see, with all the elements of draftsmanship." Hale had a strange smile on his face. "The teaching of anatomy," he said slowly, "is almost like a laying on of hands. Someone has studied with Gérôme, who studied with someone who studied with David, and so on down the years. For almost forty years, George B. Bridgman taught anatomy at the Art Students League. I studied with Bridgman, and I inherited his sticks—both about three and a half feet long. One has a chamois cloth at the end—that's for cleaning the board. And one has charcoal at the end—that's for drawing. These sticks have their own mystique at the Art Students League. The chamois cloth at the end of the erasing one is quite venerable, limp and dusty—a part of me. My classes have almost as deep a feeling for the sticks as I have. They also know that this teaching is much like a father-son relationship, a tradition transmitted by a turn of the brush, generation after generation. Margaretta Salinger, at the Metropolitan, once traced me back, as an anatomy teacher, in a direct line until she reached Titian. Very flattering, but I only wish she had managed to get me back to Leonardo! How can I possibly know how much I owe to having studied at the League with William C. McNulty? McNulty was a fellow who could draw anything out of his head, anything at all. It was all in his head. When you come down to it, as I keep telling my classes, it's *all* in the artist's head. Artists are in the metaphysical world. They may be drawing reality, but the reality is a convention. The artist's reality is an illusion. When he draws a line, it's an illusion, and where lines meet, the planes don't exist, but the artist puts a line down and builds up perspective. I make my students write on their drawings, 'This light was provided by the artist, not by Consolidated Edison.' There is nothing more difficult for an artist than to create his own light. The light is in his head. He must learn to still the light. Someone once asked me, 'What time do you think it is in Vermeer's *View of Delft*? Is that morning light? Is that evening light?' I told him that the exquisite light was Vermeer Time—that the light was in the artist's head. Basically, there is no such thing as progress in art—just in science. Nobody can draw as well, anyway, as those cave artists of sixteen thousand years ago. When it came to anatomy, they knew what they were doing. After all, they cut up their own dinners. They knew what they were eating! You can't imagine the silent fun I have at dinner parties while eating my food and dissecting a beautiful muscle. How I enjoy the *spinalis dorsi*—largely constituting a lamb chop. And I get almost sensual pleasure from skillfully dissecting a harmless pineapple, cutting all around the hard core. Takes lots of time."

Hale lit a cigarette. "I keep bumping into strange bones in strange places," he said. "I was visiting a doctor friend once and saw a vertebra hanging in his office. Someone had given it to him as a gift. I took one look and said, 'That's the seventh cervical vertebra of a zebra.' Just one of those things, but the doctor was astonished." Hale dropped a shower of ashes over his jacket. "The modern tradition is to flout the rules, but I do have certain feelings about basic training. It's my feeling that all the great artists knew all the rules, even if they broke them. The Cubists, for instance, couldn't fracture perspective unless they knew perspective. There's nothing against breaking the rules. I'm all for it, if you know the rules. Picasso, Matisse, Duchamp—they knew what rules they were breaking. In my own paintings"—he pointed to the abstraction on the wall—"there are a thousand rules being broken. And there's no accounting for talent— none. No telling where it will pop up. In any class, I may have two or three talented people. Double the class and if I'm lucky I'll get four or six. When it comes to artists—and this is the cruel part—there are some who have it and some who don't. This has an aristocratic sound, and nobody wants to hear it. As for artists' being recognized or appreciated, that's another matter. Political and social forces beyond the artist's control must come together in some inexplicable way for him to be noticed. The *climate* must be right. The good old artists knew, unconsciously, all there was to know about bones. Degas knew all about bones. Rembrandt caught the whole thing. Reginald Marsh was one of the great draftsmen of America. He had it all in his head. He would go to a burlesque show with a sketch pad deep in his pocket, and a pencil, and, seated there in the dark theatre, he would draw perfect anatomical pictures in his pocket. Or he would criticize a student's work at the League while looking at the work upside down over the easel, and correct it upside down, and his drawing would be perfect. Matter of practice. On the order of playing the piano. The great artists are like the great pianists—they play unconsciously, one hand over the other. My own drawings in class are much better now than they were years ago. I've had lots of practice with Japanese ink drawings, and it contributes to what I draw on the board in class. I paint with my body and shoulder. My wrist and fingers are locked. I get my shoulder into it. No shortcuts here. The line requires enormous control."

Hale is a chain-smoker, and he had now filled several ashtrays. He started on another cigarette. "I went to the Metropolitan in 1948, when Francis Henry Taylor said that the trustees wanted an American Department at the museum. They had enormous funds—such as the George A. Hearn Fund—but not much taste for contemporary American art. The money was being spent on John Singer Sargents. Collectors hated contemporary American art. The trustees didn't think much of it, either, and the trustees held the purse strings. The market in modern American art had not yet started, and American paintings hung in the European galleries of the museum. Childe Hassam was with the French Impressionists. You could still buy a Mary Cassatt oil for five thousand, and a Winslow Homer watercolor for three thousand. I once took three Walt Kuhn pictures of clowns—*wonderful* pictures—into the boardroom and put them before the trustees. One of them flew into a rage and waved his arms around and shouted. 'If I couldn't paint better than that,' said this particular tycoon, 'I would shoot myself.' We did soon have three people on the board—Walter Baker, Elihu Root, Jr., and Sam Lewisohn—who appreciated contemporary American art, and Lewisohn, especially, was so taken aback by the attack on the Kuhns that he persuaded the board to buy all three of them. The only thing that could produce more palpitations, seizures, and hallucinations than American art was abstract art. I brought a lovely abstract seascape around one day and showed it to the trustees, and one of them remarked, 'I've had a yacht for forty years, and, by God, I've never seen waves like that.' I was in with the last of the Victorians. I always wore a dark suit to the Met, and a dark tie, so that I could duck out at a moment's notice to a funeral, but that was a slow process and didn't really solve my problem. My chance to indulge in a little education came when a trustee suddenly said to me, 'I don't know anything about these artists. I've never met one. Can you get some of them together to talk to the trustees?' He gathered together a group of tough old businessmen, and I got hold of Stewart Klonis, the executive director of the Art Students League, and I got Eugene Speicher, William Zorach, and Vaclav Vytlacil, and we met in a private dining room of a midtown club. We had a full, pleasant meal, and some good wines. One of the trustees then said to one of the artists, 'How can I tell a good picture when I see one?' There was a strange silence. One of the artists said, 'Well, my method is to go to a gallery, look at the pictures, and then say this one stinks or that one stinks. That's one way of doing it.' We were getting nowhere. Another artist spoke up quickly: 'Have you ever taken a walk by the sea and seen a wet and glistening stone that you particularly liked? Or perhaps a shell that you liked for its geometrical qualities? Or a piece of tattered seaweed that had taken on a certain shape? And you picked these up and put them in your hand. And sometimes you even took them home and put them on the mantelpiece to look at and admire and cherish. You have a feeling about their goodness. Have you ever done anything like that?' The trustee seemed quite bewildered. 'I don't believe I ever have,' he said.''

While Hale was telling me this story, a strange sensation came over me. I was peculiarly aware that the room in which I was sitting was quite deceptive, and that what had at first seemed somewhat threadbare was fairly bursting with a life of its own. I have often walked along a dark and wooded path at night and thought that I was entirely alone, in a soundless, remote limbo—concentrating on something else—when suddenly my ears were opened to hundreds upon hundreds of strange night sounds: whispers, rustles, cries, mysteries beyond mysteries. I had been listening closely to Hale. We had been talking so much that I had seen only a fragment of his room. Now I took a long look around, and intently observed the seashell or seaweed to which he had metaphorically referred. I noticed that the floor was tiled in white vinyl. The white vinyl had been there before, of course, but I had not seen it. A fire was blazing in the fireplace. The fireplace itself was capacious and baronial, of the outsize type still seen in some of the older, well-built West Side apartments. High on the mantelpiece stood a stuffed loon in winter plumage—a gift, Hale told me, from a friend. What appeared to be a medium-sized tree stood in a wooden tub not far from the fireplace. Hale could see that I was perplexed. "That's a Norfolk Island pine, from the Pacific," he said. "I brought it back from a store one Christmas Eve instead of the usual tree. I never thought it would last."

"How did you get that huge thing in here?" I asked.

Hale shrugged. "Took a bit of doing," he said. "Things are always popping up in this apartment. Alexander brought in a No Parking sign the other day. Pure whim. I pride myself on my decorative horse paintings. The horses are proud, elegant creatures, and I used to paint them in the calligraphic style, holding the ink brush vertically, directly above the paper. There are only a few of them left here. I have given a number away to friends. A few years back, there was a Japanese invasion, and Japanese collectors swarmed into town, took a shine to my horses, and almost cleaned me out."

I noticed a copy of *The Human Figure*, by Dürer, on a small table. "I love that book," said Hale. "And those"—he pointed to a tall wicker basket filled with objects of assorted shapes—"are bones. Every kind of bone is in that basket. I dip into that basket all the time when I need a bone to draw from. I buy them from the Clay-Adams medical-supply people, in Parsippany, New Jersey, and students are always adding to my collection. There are bones all over the place." He led me into the long hallway and showed me a small framed photograph of a young woman seated in a field of flowers, painting. She was wearing a big hat. "My pretty mother," he said.

"Painting watercolors. That's my grandfather, at about my own age. And that"—he pointed to still another small framed photograph—"is my pretty mother on top of an elegant carriage drawn by four horses. There she is, sitting way up there on the box." I could barely make out a tiny figure high on the box. The carriage was standing in front of a huge, rambling structure of the type one associates with European spas, long walks, mudpacks, and string ensembles playing in cavernous hotel lobbies after dinner. "Germany somewhere, I believe," said Hale.

We walked slowly back into the living room. The experience of the last few minutes had shaken me a bit. Once again, as so many times in my life, I had been made aware of the initial superficiality of one's impressions of things, of people, and of places. That room had been a comfortable, if somewhat alien, room when I first walked in. Now it had become a room of distinctive objects. And the scene and the leading character had merged and become one. I could never again look at the room without seeing Hale, or see Hale without thinking of the room. He was now speaking softly. "The beginner draws only what he knows exists," he was saying. "But there's an anatomy to everything—not just to the human body but to trees, for instance, and to all forms. What is required is detachment, the artist's detachment. A hard thing to learn. When someone bursts into tears is a prime time for acute observation. I say to my students, 'Observe. Observe the highlights on the tears as they course down the cheek.' And when some model faints at the League—the models range from eighteen to eighty, and someone periodically keels over—it isn't good enough just to rush forward to help, I tell them. 'Observe! Watch the changes in tone and value as the model changes position. Watch as the light on his or her face changes with the reflected light from the floor! Observe, as an artist must observe.' I have often thought how difficult it must be to remain non-human in one's sympathy after one has studied at the League and observed all those models. Young, old, tall, thin, and squat—all sizes, all shapes. Drawing from the nude is an enriching experience. Of course, the instant reaction of the square to the nude model is a sexual one. 'Aha,' he says. 'A naked body!' But this has to be unlearned by the student. A most important lesson. This is the true beginning of observation and detachment. The experience is not unlike that of the medical student when he first dissects a human body. A difficult business, looking objectively at the human body. The student's fear of death is either overcome or changed. He *becomes* changed. I suppose I'm a humanist because I teach the human body. Extraordinary how much interest there has been in anatomy since Hiroshima." Hale crossed the room and toyed with some bones in the wicker basket. One of his wife's rugs, which an hour before had seemed to me a mild orange, now appeared to be a deep, rich, vibrating rust red.

I close my eyes and see Hale at the Art Students League. Hale was on the ground floor of the League, in the administration offices, opening some mail before giving an anatomy lecture upstairs at 8:00 P.M. He still had a few minutes left. He was dressed almost exactly as he had been in his apartment; that is to say, he was casually but elegantly mussed. The life of the League swirled in the corridors outside—bluejeaned crowds moving back and forth with something of a holiday air. The exhilarating smell of paint and turpentine was all-pervasive. Hale was flexing and unflexing his hands. "I must do a good deal of drawing tonight, and I exercise my hands as though I were about to play the piano," he said. "There is a celebrated hand doctor who occasionally comes to the lectures, and we have long talks on the subject of hands. He says there are more industrial accidents to the hands than to any other part of the body. Speaking of playing the piano, back in the Depression I went to work for an antique dealer whose shop, on Sutton Place, backed right up to the East River—no East River Drive yet. There was mostly English eighteenth-century stuff in the place, and few customers, and I spent day and night in that shop looking out over the river and drawing anatomically correct nudes. I would stick them in every cubbyhole of the antique furniture. All of a sudden, there was a great fire on Sutton Place, not in the shop but nearby, and the fire chief set up command headquarters in the shop. There would be a hurried call for Engine Company No. 4 and then for Engine Company No. 6, and the chief sat near me and dispatched orders to his lieutenants. As the fire was brought under control, the chief looked around and said, 'What an elegant piano over there! Body is late Sheraton, legs are Regency.' It was Chief Kidney, a celebrated firefighter and antique hobbyist. I can't explain why I am thinking of this now, but I remember Chief Kidney saying to me, before he marched off to other conflagrations, large and small, 'Play something for me.' And I played some Mozart for Chief Kidney, and a piece by Chopin.

'What sweet music!' said the chief, and he departed. Incidentally, for my own funeral I want Bach's Prelude and Fugue in A Minor." A gloomy look crossed Hale's face. "There has been no real charcoal since the fall of France," he said, "but I use Grumbacher No. 17, and make out. I draw on a chalkboard—which you will see in the lecture room—of plywood painted with a white abrasive powder, similar to a substance used by dentists. This material gives tooth to the charcoal and holds the drawing to the board."

Hale suggested that I go upstairs and take a seat he had reserved for me. "You'll find Wash—that's Mr. Randolph Washington, the assistant superintendent at the League—expecting you." I went upstairs to a large, almost square room, whose walls were covered with portraits, landscapes, still lifes, charcoal sketches, oils, abstractions—a bright patchwork sample of work being done in various League classes. There were about two hundred people in the room. A quiet man, whom I took to be Mr. Washington, was standing by the door and noticed me glancing around for a seat. He recognized me, saying, "I was afraid you'd be late," and led me to a seat halfway back in the hall. "They start coming in for Mr. Hale's classes at about six-thirty, and just sit quietly sketching in their sketchbooks until the lecture starts." I sat down and glanced around. I was surprised at the number of middle-aged and elderly men and women seated among the bluejeans. The audience had a notably professional appearance, a high level of earnestness, and a palpable air of expectancy. A wall clock to the left showed three minutes to eight. In the front of the room, on a somewhat crudely constructed wooden platform, stood a small plaster cast of the human form, showing the muscles of the body. At the other end of the platform, a skeleton dangled from a metal stand, jiggling slightly with the vibrations in the room. The skeleton had such a youthful, relaxed quality, a sort of Bojangles looseness, that I almost forgot it was a skeleton. It seemed like a very happy skeleton. The chalkboard at the rear of the platform was covered with random sketched anatomical sections, apparently holdovers from a previous session. At one minute to eight, there was a distinct stir in the audience, and promptly at eight Hale moved slowly into the room, somewhat stooped and carrying his two long sticks, and went up onto the platform. The audience burst into applause.

On many evenings, I have sat and watched this tall, very distinguished, very fragile teacher deliver lectures on anatomy. The chalkboard, the barely dancing skeleton, the long sticks, and the lectures themselves— on, say, the upper arm, or the elbow, or the head, or the features, or the rib cage—have become transformed in my mind, and my mind's eye, into one continuous, quietly flowing lecture, during which time and space and subject matter dissolve and are mysteriously reformed into another entity, with a distinct life of its own, which I think of as The Lecture. Hence:

Hale is holding the stick with charcoal at one end. He pours himself a glass of water from a pitcher on a small table. He says something into the microphone, and a great growling sound comes out. "Oh, Wash, Wash, something is wrong with the machine again!" Mr. Washington patiently steps onto the platform and performs some mechanical magic, and when Hale speaks again his voice is clear and firm. He is talking about the arm, and his own arm moves gracefully and slowly as shapes begin to form on the chalkboard. The members of the class are doing two things at one time: looking at Hale's drawings and making sketches of their own. There is the silence of study in the room. Hale is drawing and erasing—shoulder blades, collarbones. "See how the arm is closed," he says. "It is done with the biceps and the rib cage. . . . The ulna. All the ulna can do is go up and down, up and down." Drawing, erasing, drawing, erasing. "Artists have certain ideas of the arm. You can think of the arm as a three-sided prism. Goya did a drawing of a woodman and broke the sleeve into planes, and for this he probably put his own arm up." Hale does so. "Watch out for a model who may be tired, for then you will get a tired arm. Raise your collarbone if you want vitality. 'I like to draw what I see,' said a man to Whistler. To which Whistler replied, 'Wait till you see what you draw.' And watch out for literary terms in relation to anatomy. Very misleading. Such as 'Her breasts were like two young roes feeding among the lilies,' or 'Her nose was like a tower in Lebanon,' or 'Her lips are like scarlet thread,' or Emerson's comparison of Thoreau's arm to the bough of an elm tree. Practice, practice! Take a look at the lower arm—the length of the hand is one-fifth of the length of the ulna above." He rolls up one sleeve. "So many muscles in this arm," he says. "Many students look at the muscles and give up anatomy forever. The hand! A miracle! You can pull corks out of bot-

tles, turn keys in doors. Your horse, however, is stuck. He can just go up
and down. Your cat is stuck. He can't do much, either. Practice contour
lines all the time." The stick crosses and recrosses the board. He is drawing
lines, some delicately shaded, some thick, some eerily thin. "You can't
draw a line unless you know where it's coming from and where it's going."
Cylinders appear on the board, and cubes, rectangles and squares. The
chamois cloth erases, and new drawings appear. "The positioning of the
thumb is very difficult. Watch the planes and lines where they meet and
change. A wrist is a block going in a certain direction. It's all in my mind.
The artist watches the flow from place to place—the tendons that carry the
flow, grasping and handling. It's all in the unconscious. Hang your baby
on a gas jet at home and he'll automatically hang on. You can begin to see
how subtle the body is. Hands can be as flat as the horizon"—he holds a
hand out flat—"or they can stretch out to the horizon." He stretches his
hand, making it look as though it were about to grasp the horizon. "Or it
can look like a bird, with wings on both sides. Keep drawing, keep drawing. You'll do better if you have real bones to work with. Not too difficult
these days. There were eleven murders yesterday in New York City." The
board is filled up with the front of the hand, the palm, a side view, pha-
langes, wrists, thumbs. "Practice, practice—it's all hard work. But why
should you think it would be easy? Remember Eliot," he continues:

> And so each venture
> Is a new beginning, a raid on the inarticulate
> With shabby equipment always deteriorating
> In the general mess of imprecision of feeling . . .

Hale briskly wipes the board clean and walks from the room. The class
applauds again. Intermission. Students gather around the skeleton with
their sketchbooks and continue to draw.

Hale reenters. A nose begins to take shape on the chalkboard, eyes begin
to form. "The eye is a Ping-Pong ball. You run your lines over the forms
you can see. Draw lines where planes meet." He discusses the muscles of
the face. "Through time, gravity just pulls everything down, down into
the grave. There are muscles of shape and muscles of expression. For

shape, you have the temporalis in the head, and you can feel it by placing your fingers on your temples and chewing. The expressions are limitless, depending on the muscles used. Artists know these things. For a real smile—not an airline-hostess smile—you employ the zygomaticus major, the smiling muscle. The circular muscles of the eye must act for a sincere smile. Pain and grief—the muscles of the mouth operate as the mouth opens more and more in relation to the pain. For torture, you cease employing the muscles of the forehead—they are for attention—and open the mouth more for amazement. All these things artists know. Let's assume a banker receives a man in his office. 'Good morning,' says the banker. 'And your name, sir?' 'Getty,' says the stranger." Hale breaks into a broad and sickening smile. " 'Ah, Mr. Getty,' says the banker. 'Won't you have a seat? Please be comfortable. You must have a little oil business and many large problems to handle. Have a cigarette. Relax.' 'Well,' says the man, 'my name *is* Getty, but I'm on welfare, and I haven't worked in five years, and . . .' " Hale's expression changes to horror, to pain, to grief, to torture, to revulsion. "There is a muscle of irony and there is a muscle of anger," he says. "There is a muscle of sneering and a muscle of grief. There are expressions of sneering and of grief, and in New York they are often the same expression. Sculptors have a terrible time with eyelashes. Most of them cast them as shadows. The mouth itself goes over the cylinder of the teeth. Draftsmanship really resides in the mind." Hale is drawing a human head now, slowly, the features taking form as though they were emerging from a mist. I see a nose, a mouth. "The mouth is under the nose for a special reason—the smelling of food," he says. "Bridgman often speculated how inconvenient it would be if the nose were under the arm. Then we would have to put the food there and sniff before eating." Long hair is now flowing from the figure on the board. It is the face of an older man. The expression is sad and wise. Long, steady sweep of the charcoal. "Sausages pull down over old men's eyes as they grow older," Hale says. The class is intently leaning forward now, watching the drawing. "I'll put in sideburns, and a goatee," he says. "When I was a little boy, every doctor had a goatee, and they all made house calls. And I'll put in a mustache, and I'll make the beard longer, and fuzzier at the end. Everything is moving, always moving, in a perspective block, and finally into a block six feet under.

There's a song of Leadbelly's about his days on the Louisiana chain gang, and it haunts me." Very slowly, standing in front of the wild and ancient figure with the long, flowing beard, Hale recites:

> Take this hammer
> And carry it to the captain.
> You tell him I'm gone,
> You tell him I'm gone.
> If he asks you
> Was I laughin',
> You tell him I was cryin'.

The lecture is over. Hale steps off the platform and heads for the door. There is a long moment of silence, and then long applause. By now, Hale is gone, but the class seems unwilling to leave, and many students move toward the chalkboard and stare and stare at the drawing.

(1977)

Ntozake Shange

We have had a talk with Ntozake Shange, the twenty-seven-year-old poet whose unclassifiable creation *For Colored Girls Who Have Considered Suicide: When the Rainbow Is Enuf*—made up of poetry, music, dancing, and light—is playing to somewhat stunned audiences at Joseph Papp's Public Theatre, on Lafayette Street. Ntozake Shange's poetry is mordantly witty, unpredictable, and disciplined. It has to do with love and death and the deepest feelings of young women—in particular, black young women. We met her last week in a restaurant near the theatre, on whose stage she herself appears as one of the seven members of the all-black cast.

We ordered coffee. "In New York, ordinary human chores tend to interfere with living," she told us. "I want to explicate my reality, to live here with some grace, to avoid as much emotional turbulence as I can. I spent seven months in Harlem last year, toward the end of the year, and I was very depressed. Mostly, I remember not the staircase or the sofa or the toilet down the hall but the three locks on my door. Three locks! My mind drifts back to other places—happier places. St. Louis has a hold on me. I lived there from about age eight to age thirteen, and it has great meaning—the jumping-off place to the West, the place from which runaway slaves might reach freedom and Canada via the Underground Railroad, the place where Jesse James and his men hid out in the same caves used by the runaway slaves. And the river. The Mississippi River. I am deeply affected by that mighty river. The St. Louis Municipal Opera would perform

Tom Sawyer, and I was there, entranced, and can see it even today. I also used to see, in my mind's eye, Mark Twain as a river pilot, and places like Natchez. I've never been to Natchez, but I can picture the carny shows there. Above all, I wanted to be a Mississippi River gambler like Tyrone Power, done up with his fancy frock coat and his ruffled sleeves and his big hat—and, especially, that fan of his lady's, the *white* fan, the one she snapped open with a swift gesture, and then snapped shut."

She continued, "The sense of connection is missing in New York. For one thing, I have only about one-tenth of the writers and painters and poets to nourish me here in New York that I had when I lived around San Francisco and Oakland. I really lived in Oakland—a sort of fairyland, where I loved the three-story wooden houses, the picket fences, the man who sold fish from a truck, the man who sold vegetables from a horse-drawn wagon, the man who sold crabs, live crabs, in buckets, for six dollars a bucket, and the old ladies coming forth each day to pick their flowers in their front yards. Everything was unconstrained, uncongested. I could think. I could put things together. Most of the poems we're doing these nights were written during the last three years, and I would read them in bars and bookstores in San Francisco. Just the other night, someone came backstage and said he missed the intimacy of his first encounter with them, at a San Francisco bar. Trenton, where I was born, seems pretty far behind. But I love my daddy—after all, he is my daddy. He is a surgeon, and my mother was a psychiatric social worker and now teaches early-childhood development at Trenton State College, and I have an artist sister and a sister who just graduated from Yale and a brother at Columbia Law. And I've been to Barnard, and taken American Studies at the University of Southern California, in Los Angeles, and here and there. Growing up was all right—skipping rope, kissing boys, adolescence—but it was a double life, and the reading was the real life. I read all the Russians in English (my goal in life was to free Raskolnikov from his guilts) and the French in French and the Spaniards with the aid of dictionaries. Simone de Beauvoir, Melville, Carson McCullers, and Edna Millay. And Jean Genet. I would say to my mother that I didn't understand a word he was saying but I liked him. Faulkner has always been a trial—I have to pretend to be white to understand what he's saying about blacks. At Barnard, I was alienated, and had only four black friends, but I went back up there last year and told the black students to hold fast, to stick—that they wouldn't find anything more libertarian outside. I guess I've been in every black-nationalist movement in the country, and I found that the flaw in the nationalists' dream was that they didn't treat women right. Five years ago, I took an African name; my father is Dr. Paul T. Williams, and I was Paulette Williams—a slave name, really. I am filled with rhythm and blues. My daddy plays some percussion, knows Miles Davis, knows Dizzy Gillespie, knew Charlie Parker. I like to watch dancing, and have studied dancing for three years. And I like to wear silver jewelry, and look at people. It's the faces I like to watch. And I like to listen to the words. I've watched people being beat up, and people putting up fifty thousand dollars bail, and this movement and that movement. Black poets are always having to prove the right to their emancipation, but I approach poetry with a sense of discovery. In San Francisco, I gave out and I got back. I felt this need to keep on giving, because I was getting so much. I have loving friends, and we call each other up and read to one another—read poems—and talk."

Ntozake Shange wanted another cup of coffee. "I find that I have an attachment to people in New York, but I have really no tactile or sensuous connection to the city," she said. "I walk the city, and watch the faces, and try to remove the mask. My poems are deeply personal. Take the poem that begins 'Somebody almost walked off wid alla my stuff.' I like that poem: 'My stuff is the anonymous ripped-off treasure of this year/did you know somebody almost got away wif me/in plastic bag under their arm/me danglin on a string of personal carelessness.' I wanted to be very clear and very honest in these poems. That's why I used the word *colored* in the title. That's a word my grandmother would understand. It wouldn't put her off and turn her away. I wanted to get back to the brass tacks of myself as a child; I was a regular colored girl, with a family that was good to me."

Ntozake Shange finished her second cup of coffee. "By the way, I'm not living in Harlem these days," she said. "I'm in Chelsea, with *one* lock. I know that poetry must be refined over and over, be honed, get stronger. I listen to words, and when people can't say what they mean they are in trouble. I remember telling classes I taught at Sonoma State College, in Rohnert Park, California, that when they read a poem with the word 'cry' they mustn't rush through but try to understand that the word had depth, and implication, and that someone was *crying*—that it wasn't just a plot outline or a scenario. I'm relatively happy now, but I am impatient when I'm not writing. Just before the opening downtown, I was working on a story I had to finish. Everybody was excited and running around, and I just went across the street to this restaurant and sealed myself off at this table and finished my story, and then the play opened. I'm writing a novel, and in the book the options for a woman are to stay with one man, stay alone, or go to a free country. In this world, I have to know who has suffered; I write about pain. Apathy stops me up. I think I write choppy prose, but the very choppiness of the prose releases my poetry. I am relatively stable at the moment, but I know how shaky the foundation is, how fragile the path I'm walking." A grim look came over her face. "You know, one of these days I am going to go up to Saks Fifth Avenue and walk right through that store, door to door," she said. Then she looked away. "Just this morning," she said, "I saw a group of women going into a bar downtown at nine-thirty, and I studied those faces and I knew those faces would be there tomorrow morning at nine-thirty and the day after tomorrow at nine-thirty, and I thought about a poem."

(1976)

Searching for Gregorian

The New York Public Library houses many treasures, but few are as colorful, complex, enigmatic, civilized, and stimulating as Vartan Gregorian, its president and chief executive officer. I have been looking things up all my life in the monumental Beaux-Arts building at Fifth Avenue and Forty-second Street, and one Saturday noontime not long ago I went over there to look up Gregorian, who holds a Ph.D. in history and is generally known as Dr. Gregorian. I had read of his somewhat legendary and magical work in restoring the library to financial and intellectual vigor—the strenuous fund-raising, the spotlight of publicity, the exhibits, the lectures, the unprecedented gala dinners—but I knew very little about the man himself. In a library, one thing leads to another, and each point of reference becomes an act of discovery, an extension of one's own horizons. My pursuit of Dr. Gregorian began in his office, on the second floor of the library—a spacious, high-ceilinged room with walls of green damask and dominated by an immense oval yellow oak conference table, which almost completely eclipsed a large desk in one corner of the room. The oak table was piled high with neatly stacked papers and books. Bookshelves and eighteenth- and nineteenth-century portraits—John Jacob Astor; Benjamin Franklin; Shelley's parents, by Romney—lined the walls. Tall windows opened onto Fifth Avenue, but the city seemed far away. The room is scholarly and noble, like so many spaces throughout the library, which was built by Carrère and Hastings, opened in 1911, and is universally acknowledged to be a classic structure. When I entered the room, Dr. Gregorian was standing by the desk going through some papers, and he didn't walk over to greet me—he bounced over, rapidly, with short, rolling movements. He is in his eary fifties, of medium height, rumpled, and on the heavy side, with an anarchic clump of graying hair and an arresting short salt-and-pepper beard. I was immediately struck by his benign resemblance to the two sculptured lions, Patience and Fortitude, that guard the main steps to the library.

Dr. Gregorian whipped off the jacket of his suit and carefully hung it over the back of a broad-bottomed yellow oak chair that matched the big oak table. He beckoned to me to sit down in a similar chair, one of ten or so spread around the conference table. "We'll talk about library and Gregorian and have sandwich," he said to me. The prospect seemed to delight him. He speaks softly but quickly, with a pleasant Middle Eastern accent. "A library is a sacred place," he said. "My role is educator and teacher. For four thousand years, humanity has gone through dreadful horrors, dreadful turmoils, varied glories. How do we distill the past? How do we retain the memories? *Libraries*. The New York Public Library is one of the greatest in the entire world. Its research libraries contain some twenty-nine million items, and there are eighty-eight miles of stacks right here in this building. Millions of memories. We are a treasured repository of civilization. Sometimes I am overwhelmed when I realize what we mean to the city and to the world. Libraries keep the records on behalf of all humanity. We contain the unique and the absurd, the wise and fragments of stupidity. We mirror the world, in all its folly and wisdom. We serve the masses and the individual. A library must never be indifferent to the individual, must always protect him. Think of a lone person in one of our reading rooms, who has just read a book, a single book that has perhaps not been read in twenty years by another living soul, and from that reading comes an invention of incalculable importance to the human race. It makes a man tremble. Endless sources of knowledge are *here*. We have books in three thousand languages and dialects. I can take you through here from Balanchine to Tibet. There are esoterica on synthetic fuels, neglected maps of the Falklands that were suddenly in demand at the time of the Falklands War. And Warsaw telephone directories from the years of the Holocaust, often invaluable as the only source of documentation of who lived where, in order to substantiate claims for retribution. There will never be an end to this library. Never!" By now, I was quite aware that the Dr. Gregorian I was seeking was a vital, driving force, and I was happy that I had undertaken the journey.

Dr. Gregorian was still talking as he bounced again across the room and opened a door to an anteroom where a few people were working. "Sandwich and coffee for my friend, and sandwich and Diet Coke for me!" he called to someone just outside the door. He closed the door and sat down again. "I have the most extraordinary, loyal staff," he said. "They come in on Saturday. To *work*. You have noticed how quiet it is in my suite of offices, but we must not forget the hundreds of people spread all through this building who are reading, studying, digging into subjects, gaining knowledge. When I came here, in the spring of 1981, the library was in a crisis, the city was in a crisis. I was in a critical period of my own life. The city was under attack. I had been under attack. As it turned out, I was in the right place at the right time. New York is full of chutzpah. I am full of chutzpah. There has been an extraordinary revival."

The door to the anteroom opened, and a tall, energetic, and strikingly attractive young woman entered, carrying lunch. Dr. Gregorian introduced her to me as Maryann Jordan, his executive assistant. I could sense immediately that she must exercise a strong, calming influence on the president's office. She put lunch on the big table and quietly left the room. "Thank you, Maryann!" he called out to her. "When I first met the staff of the library, I was a total stranger to them," he said to me. "Naturally, they were somewhat suspicious of a man who had never been a librarian before, who had been provost of the University of Pennsylvania, who was a professor, who spoke with a foreign accent, who dropped his articles. I stood up in front of them, and my first words were 'Fellow educators.' This was appreciated. This gave people a sense of the dignity of their profession. I also told them I would go back later and pick up all the articles I had dropped. One of my greatest teachers was my maternal grandmother, a most remarkable woman, and one of the many things she taught me was that dignity is not negotiable. Dignity is the honor of the family. I have thought about it many times. She also taught me that envy is very bad. Envy will deform your character. 'You must not have a hole in your eye,' she would say. The hole in the eye was caused by envy. The hole would be insatiable and could never be filled."

We both eyed the sandwiches lying on the table. "I think it's time for lunch," said Dr. Gregorian. He handed me an egg-salad sandwich hermetically sealed in a plastic container. I began to struggle with it, attempting to find some chink in its armor, some vulnerable corner into which I could perhaps slide a nail to reach the sandwich. No luck. No luck whatever. Dr. Gregorian observed me closely. He seemed to understand my plight completely. "Some people have the knack of these things and some people don't," he said, with kindness. I realized that I was in warm and friendly hands. He took the package and, with a flick of a finger, had it open. We went on to other matters.

He said, "I am an Armenian, born in Tabriz, in Iran, in 1934. This was northwestern Iran, near the Russian border. My family had been in Iran for many years. I can trace Tabriz Armenians back some two thousand years. Where I was born was very cold—very high, very dry. Since I am a teacher, I like to talk about Armenia, and sometimes I like to use phrases like 'one, two, three,' and hold up fingers to prove points to the class. The capital of Armenia is Yerevan. Turkey is on the west, Azerbaijan on the east, Iran to the south, and Georgia to the north. Armenia is the oldest Christian state." He paused a moment, to take a bite of egg salad. "One learns only by learning about different cultures, different places, different peoples. A funny thing—I know a Soviet Armenian who has said that Christianity was founded in 300 B.C. There's history for you!

"We lived in a large house in what was known as the Armenian quarter of Tabriz. A middle-class section. The family was still speaking Armenian at home. I also spoke Turkish. Today, I can speak seven languages. Armenia was the first nation to accept Christianity as a state religion. There were two apostles who were said to have travelled in Armenia—St. Thaddaeus and St. Bartholomew—and thus the church was known as an apostolic church. My church, the Armenian Apostolic, is independent. The Russian Orthodox Church Outside of Russia remains czarist in its sympathies. As for my family, my grandfather was called Father, and my grandmother was called Mother. I called my father Samuel. He is still alive. He is seventy-eight and lives in Tehran. He telephones me occasionally, perhaps on a birthday, but we have never been close. How is that sandwich?"

I said that it was fine, now that he had found the way.

"Coffee for you," he said, opening a white plastic container. "I take diet cola. Back to Tabriz. It was in a Turkish-speaking province. They spoke an eastern Turkish. They also spoke Persian. Persian was the language of instruction, Turkish the language of population, Russian the language of occupation. One's early memories are vivid, yet scattered. My father's father had a caravansary—a sort of animal parking lot. No camels. Absolutely no camels. Mules and donkeys brought goods to the place where the animals were parked. I remember that my father's father had lost an eye—gored by a bull. A bad bull. When he died, my mother was determined that her father-in-law should have a Christian burial. She wanted to avoid his being buried in a Muslim shroud—the Muslims don't have coffins. My mother would have done anything to have her father-in-law buried in a coffin. The body had been brought home. Very important that the body come home before burial. My mother bribed the police chief and gave his wife all her needlework, and then my mother and I went to the bazaar and bought a coffin. She rented a phaeton and put the body in the coffin and the coffin on the phaeton and gave him a Christian burial. As they sprinkled water on the dead man, his good eye opened, and the people at the funeral cried out, 'Bala Beg is alive! Bala Beg is alive!'

"The house in which I lived in Iran, like other houses of the Armenian community, was designed for maximum privacy. They were interior houses—no display outside, small windows. Made of brick and mud." Dr. Gregorian suddenly stood up and moved briskly across the room. "There was a basement and a first floor. There would be a big knock on the door"—Dr. Gregorian knocked on the wall of his office—"Who is there?" he cried. "The answer would come from the street." He was back in his memories now, far from Fifth Avenue and Forty-second Street. He had a strange smile on his face, a smile of contentment touched with pride. "Then you would enter the house and descend to a courtyard and a basement with windows. On the right was the living room"—broad, sweeping gesture—"the Official Occasion Room. There was a rug here, and good china. This was, in essence, the foreign ministry. There was a huge kitchen—oh, a *huge* kitchen—with a huge oven. My parents' room was across from the kitchen. There was a large dining room, converted at night into a bedroom, with storage space for bedding. We slept on thick mattresses on the floor, under beautifully embroidered quilts. But the kitchen was the centerpiece—half the size of this big office of mine, which still makes it quite large. We cooked with charcoal. Bread was always being baked. The bread hung in the cellar on trays suspended from the beams by ropes. They were rounded loaves, drying there along the walls, and when bread was needed someone would sprinkle water on a loaf. My grandmother had a small room to the right of the kitchen. Her name was Vosky; it means 'gold.' It meant gold to me then, it means gold to me now. She was known as Vosky Baji—a term of endearment, 'Baji' meaning 'sister.'

"Her influence was tremendous. She had no formal education, but immensely valued it. She lived her life with consummate dignity. She struggled. She coped. She never lost faith, was never cynical. She did not speak ill of others. She insisted that one must do good without expectation of reward. She believed that to think ill of others is to diminish oneself. She was deeply respected all over town. When I went to the store for her, I never carried money. It was enough for me to say that Vosky Baji had sent me. I am not superstitious; she was dreadfully so. She knew about the evil eye and believed in it. *You do not show your baby to someone with the evil eye!'* " Dr. Gregorian was pacing up and down his office now, speaking in what can perhaps best be described as circular terms—never in a straight line. I sensed that I was experiencing a classic library phenomenon: search for one thing, and a moment later discover something new and beckoning.

Dr. Gregorian continued, "My mother died shortly after the death of my grandfather. She died in 1941. She was twenty-six or twenty-seven; I was seven. She died of pneumonia—the Russians were coming, and there were no medicines. There she was in her bed. Dead. But nobody explained it to me. They told me later that she had gone to America. Since she was very beautiful, I thought that America must be doubly beautiful—beautiful for itself, beautiful because my mother was there. But I find that I go back to my grandmother. When I went away as a young man, my grandmother sewed a blue bead inside my jacket for good luck. The color of lapis lazuli. When I think of her, I think of the strength of a wounded wolf. I still have some objects from my grandmother—for example, a piece of hair from my first haircut. She saved it, presented it to me. Also her picture—a woman with powerful eyes. A letter I wrote when I was eight or nine. She stopped going to church after one of her sons died. She felt that her children had been taken away from her—he was the seventh child she had lost.

"I must tell you that I was a choirboy. I felt very important, because I could look down from the altar. *I was on high ground.* And when a rich man died you carried the unlit candles and banners through the streets from his home to the church. It was Christ being resurrected. You walked around, but never across, the Muslim section of town. I was one of two candle bearers. I had a certain unity with the priests, a feeling of belonging to some metaphysical order. You know, I actually got involved with street gangs. Nothing serious, you understand, but there was trafficking in cigarettes when I was growing up. You would buy something for nine dollars and ninety cents and sell it for ten dollars and eighty cents. Big deal. But there was another road, and I took it. I landed in the local Armenian library, on top of the local archbishop's residence. Another big room. I *like* big rooms. I like working in them. My office when I was provost of the University of Pennsylvania was big, too—Victorian Gothic, a room as big as this one, with the trustees' big room next door and a large suite of offices outside for my assistants.

"But I am ahead of myself. I was a page in the Armenian library, with freedom to read and roam. Almost all the books were in Armenian, and there were translations of the classics. There were two Armenian monasteries that translated Shakespeare. I read Shakespeare. I read Dumas, *père* and *fils*. I read Victor Hugo. I was especially impressed by *Les Misérables* and the character of Jean Valjean, a man whose soul was touched. My own soul was touched. I also read Tolstoy, and didn't understand him. Another place in which I would read was a street bookstore, a sort of rental library. More books and still more books. There was the real world to face. So-called reality. Two events brought it home to me. On the streets of Tabriz, there was a madwoman who kept cats in her bosom. She would walk up and down the streets with those cats in her bosom, singing, singing, singing. It was a dreadful sight. One Sunday when she came to the church, the priests did not like her looks, or her madness, and they refused her Communion. This shocked me. Another important experience in coming face-to-face with reality took place when I saw my priest emerging one day from a men's room. Until that moment, I had felt that priests were a special breed, a higher order of humanity, which under no circumstances engaged in normal human functions. I went to an Armenian-Russian school. Russian soldiers were all over the place, but there was no massacre, no looting, no resistance. I remember going down to the main street to see the tanks. There was a tremendous wooden map in the center of the city—with arrows and illustrated military campaigns. I learned a good deal in Turkish about Russian subjects. One of the teachers in this school was an ignorant wise man. We treated this fellow very badly. He wasn't really qualified to teach Persian history, and we teased him unmercifully—sent up a dreadful humming that must have driven him to distraction. He would call us animals, but we kept on humming. He would punch two holes in his newspaper and pretend to be reading while we were studying, but all the time he was peeping at us through the holes. Corporal punishment followed upon infraction of the rules—whippings on the palm of the hand, where it hurt, with a whip carrying a ball bearing at the end. But this ignorant wise man taught us several important lessons I have never forgotten: One [finger in the air], if you see a donkey carrying gold, it is not a golden donkey. Two [two fingers in the air], if you see a donkey carrying a diploma, it is just a donkey carrying a diploma. And, three [three fingers in the air], if you see a donkey in Jerusalem, it is not a holy donkey. Useful information for later life. I was very bright, no question about that—straight A's all over the place. But once I hit the principal with a snowball that was intended, believe me, for someone else, and got a spanking. My grandmother instantly came to my rescue and defense. Down to the principal she went. She didn't know the word 'principal,' or what it meant, but she said to him, 'Have you fed him? Have you taken care of him?' And then she slapped him in the face."

Dr. Gregorian bustled over to the anteroom door, disappeared, and returned a moment later with another can of Diet Coke. "A key to my character was my physical smallness," he said. "I was very thin. I was not physically strong. But my survival instinct told me to go after the bullies in the school. This was my way of showing my strength of character, my sense of self. I was bloodied from time to time, but people said, 'Keep away from this fellow, he is somebody to be careful of.' I put up a curtain between myself and others."

Dr. Gregorian paused to take a sip of soda, then continued. "A bit more about childhood," he said. "My father worked for the Anglo-Iranian Oil Company. He was an office worker, a functionary. He knew English, Persian, and accounting. He was a soldier in the Second World War, and I remember when he went off to the war, seated on a white horse. Of course, there was fear of the evil eye, so before he left everybody sat down and then stood up together, so that the evil eye would not know which one was the traveller. And water was thrown on the horse and on the ground where the horse stood, so that the evil eye could not trace the traveller's path. Within a few days of his leaving, everything collapsed on the front. First, we heard he was a deserter, had gone AWOL, and we thought that meant he was dead. So there was mourning and weeping. My father had exchanged his clothes for those of a peasant and came back home riding on a donkey. My grandmother didn't recognize him, and when this strange fellow came to the house she said, in effect, 'Get lost.' When he called out 'Mama!' she recognized him. He had been hit in the stomach with a rifle butt, but was otherwise in good shape.

"It was not an easy childhood. My father remarried, but my stepmother removed my mother's picture, and this deeply offended me and my grandmother. Just took the picture down. And I fought with my father, for I was caught in this messy situation with his new wife. My sister was studying in a local French school, and we had our private schemes. We collected matchboxes and filled them with ants. According to local legend, America was a sanitary, antiseptic paradise—so clean, in fact, that the anteaters of America were unemployed, totally without work. So my sister and I set about collecting ants for shipment to America. We envisioned making millions of dollars. We collected both the small ones, the Christian ones, and the big black ones, the Muslim ants. This was a venture that never got off the ground, and once we realized the enterprise was doomed we buried the ants under an almond tree. But it kept me occupied, and it removed some of the strain in the house. My grandmother had moved next door, and I was saved, in a sense, by three people in Tabriz with whom I could spend time and study—learning was becoming paramount, the main goal. One was an optometrist, another the director of a flour mill (my sister married his son), and the third a rug merchant. They were most important at the time. I profusely borrowed bicycles from them, not owning one of my own. My reading had unfortunately given me an exaggerated, literary view of a wicked stepmother, and it became fixational, something from which I felt I had to flee. In 1947—" Dr. Gregorian was interrupted by a knock on the door, and a young woman appeared. "I hate to break in," she said, "but I think it is time for you gentlemen to have some brownies. We have outrageous brownies at the New York Public Library."

We both nodded, the brownies were presented, were tasted, and were pronounced outrageously good. The young lady silently departed.

"The people who work with me reflect my moods," Dr. Gregorian said. "If I am down, they tend to be down. When I'm up, they are up. Now, in 1947 there was a province-wide examination of scholastic achievement, and I did quite well—a sixteen-point-five average out of a maximum of twenty. About this time, an important figure came into my life. Important and helpful people have always mysteriously shown up at critical times. He was a French vice-consul named Edgar Maloyan, and since there were no good hotels in Tabriz he stayed at the home of a friend of mine, and I got to know him. We talked and talked, and he taught me to play chess— I would win one game in a hundred—and he told me of the exciting capitals of the world, and of the big world outside, and he said to me, 'Vartan, you are bright and must leave here and go to Petit Paris, to Beirut.' I cannot bear to think of Beirut today, where the shellfire and the bombing and the devastation have been so severe that the ancient Roman ruins are beginning to peep up from buried layers of earth. This man told me that even if I went to Beirut with no visible means of support I could still live on a banana a day. I didn't even know that you had to peel a banana in order to eat one! Beirut seemed impossible to reach—there was so much protocol involved in getting there—but this man volunteered to write a letter to officials in Lebanon. He would help in every way. My father was dead set against the idea. He told me that he would give permission if I could obtain a passport, feeling entirely certain that a passport was impossible. I brought a petition to the governor, at his official residence. I tried every avenue. I went to hearings. I was tenacious. I know how to be tenacious. Still, my father tried to dissuade me. 'It's a strange land,' he kept saying. 'A strange land.' Finally, after more than eight months, the passport came through. My father had one last ace up his sleeve. He told me to talk with

my grandmother, the one I called Mother. He was certain she would persuade me not to leave home. She surprised them. Of course she surprised
them. She said, very calmly—I remember it so clearly—'I would like my
son to go and become a man. To become a man, he needs an education.'"

A week or so later, as we sat talking in Dr. Gregorian's quiet office, I could
not help thinking of the many other people in the building, silent yet all
around me, looking things up, pursuing facts, pursuing fancies, reading
books, perhaps fulfilling dreams, reaching back in order to reach forward.
I thought, What a curious world it is that places at the head of one of the
greatest repositories of knowledge, in the center of the island of Manhattan, this exotic man from Armenia.

"You are shaking your head in a strange way," said Dr. Gregorian.

"I am astonished," I heard myself saying, "at the meeting of different
cultures in this city and in this building. While you have been speaking of
your grandmother, quite unexpectedly I have been thinking of mine. She
was born in 1858, here in New York—then a city of nearly eight hundred
thousand—on West Twenty-second Street, in Chelsea. And educated directly across the street from where we sit, at Rutgers Female College, on
Fifth Avenue, in a series of Victorian Gothic buildings." This news excited Dr. Gregorian.

"Tell me something about her," he said.

"The paramount memory of her childhood, which she passed on to me,
was of her father taking her to City Hall in April of 1865 to see the body of
Abraham Lincoln lying in state, on its way to burial in Springfield," I said.
"Hand in hand with her father, she climbed those beautiful curving stairs,
with thousands of other mourners. When she was in school, the Croton
Distributing Reservoir was right here, where the library stands, with high
Egyptian walls of masonry and a fashionable promenade along the top."

"I imagine she walked there often," said Dr. Gregorian.

"I know that for a fact," I said. "I also remember how proud she was of
Rutgers Female College. She studied Greek, Latin, French, piano, mathematics, art, and moral philosophy."

I had now had several visits with Dr. Gregorian. I knew something
about him. He knew something about me. After all, we were in a library.

On one of many other occasions, I was back in Dr. Gregorian's office, talking with him and struggling with an egg-salad sandwich. Once again, he mercifully came to my rescue, skillfully opening the stubborn wrapping. "I left for Beirut when I was fifteen, with fifty dollars in my pocket," he said. " 'Oh, you'll be back,' said my stepmother. *That* did it. I was determined to succeed. I stayed at the Hotel Lux. There was nothing luxe about it. It consisted of several rooms on the fifth floor of a building near the port. The guests were a motley assortment, all strangers to me. There were some poets, and everybody played pinochle, bridge, and poker. After about two weeks, someone asked me about paying a bill. I sold some silver cups and silver frames I had brought with me, and one of my blankets. There were some highly competitive bridge games. Because I was poor, I actually took seriously the advice I had been given to eat a banana a day, but learned rather rapidly to peel it. I began my studies at the Collège Arménien. A turning point in my life. The college was situated in the former headquarters of the French Admiralty—a good setting. Good teachers. A vital, all-important person now entered my life—Simon Vratzian, Armenian nationalist, writer, last prime minister of the Independent Armenian Republic. He was the principal of the college, and he took me under his wing, made me his protégé. To many he was a national hero. He managed to get me a small scholarship, and room and board. I would not be here today if it were not for Simon Vratzian." Dr. Gregorian rose and walked swiftly around the yellow oak table. Then he sat down again. "I wear on the fourth finger of my left hand a gold ring with embossed black stone given to me by Simon Vratzian. It pictures a shovel for the peasantry, a dagger for the revolution, and a quill for the intellectual life. At the college, I became secretary to Vratzian. His eyesight was bad, so I read all his mail for him. I was allowed to open it. I edited his memoirs. I became indispensable to him. The going was hard. I learned French. I picked up money where I could—different jobs, everything from busboy to dormitory assistant. People were kind, discreet, subtle in helping a young man—especially, once again, three families who gave me moral, and even financial, support. Someone would ask me if I would accompany him to his dinner engagement, and this would mean that I would then get a free meal. The approach would be indirect. The same with clothes. I would be provided with secondhand suits, but in a most civilized manner. Vratzian had been a close friend of Aleksandr Kerensky, and, as I say, was a national hero. As his secretary, I achieved a certain prominence. Wherever he went, there were demonstrations—flowers, speeches, outpourings of emotion. I am speaking of the Middle East and a demonstrative people. I returned to Tabriz three times to visit my grandmother. On one occasion when Vratzian was delivering a speech there, I introduced him to my grandmother. I felt so proud when Simon Vratzian said to her, 'I thank you for Vartan Gregorian.' When I left home, she had told me to go out into the world and become somebody, and now I *was* somebody. Whenever I visited her home, we ate a great deal, and I would take her to see American movies. She insisted on walking out on the *Ziegfeld Follies*. 'I want to go this minute,' she said. 'Nobody has invited those people to take off their clothes.' When I was twenty-two, in 1956, I began to feel that it was time to move on, to leave Beirut and head for the outer world."

He was teeming with ideas, he said, but had no set focus. He knew that he wanted to be a scholar, and to pursue knowledge to the fullest extent of his abilities. He began the study of Portuguese, with the notion that he might go to São Paulo, Brazil, and become principal of an Armenian high school there. The United States appealed to him. So did England. As for the United States, he had certain fixed notions of life there: everybody wore eyeglasses (all the American missionaries in Beirut wore them); everybody read constantly (this explained the eyeglasses); and the country had a strong, masculine, outdoor dignity (he had seen a lot of American movies). Some instinct told him that America was the place for him. He was attracted to Stanford University. He had read extensively about Herbert Hoover's relief work in Europe during and after the First World War, and he knew a good deal about the Hoover Library at Stanford. He was offered scholarships at both Stanford and Berkeley. The Stanford letter arrived by airmail; the Berkeley one had been sent as surface mail. First come, first served. Gregorian decided to go to Stanford.

New York, his first stop in the United States, overwhelmed him. "I felt like a yellow ant," he told me. He had very little money. He spent several nights at a YMCA, at two dollars a night, and rose at 4:00 A.M. in order to wash in privacy. His room, he recalls, was like a cell. His shyness was acute. Cafeterias and self-service stamp machines fascinated him, and signs reading "PED XING" bewildered him. He was totally confused by a sign that said "ANIMAL HOSPITAL." The notion of a hospital for animals was beyond his comprehension. He remembers an entry in the diary he was keeping that read, "Noise and noise! I have an eerie feeling as if I have lived in New York for many years," and one that read, "On Sundays there is a special breakfast that costs thirty-five cents (great!). It has a catch—I gather a Protestant minister will be giving a sermon during the breakfast. No, thanks." The sight of people poking through garbage cans made him sad. He gave a panhandler twenty-five cents, and noted in his diary, "I know too well what it means not to have any money." The girls on the street, he thought, were exceptionally well dressed. In general, he felt that Americans ate too much—heavy breakfasts and dinners. He wandered into the New York Public Library and headed for the Slavic section, but almost immediately he turned and walked out, stunned by the size of the place. "I simply could not believe that someone could walk up those big front steps and enter that extraordinary building without any questions, without any identification, no proving this or proving that, and no one asking are you liberal, conservative, or wishy-washy," he said.

On another occasion, I talked with Dr. Gregorian at an Armenian restaurant in the East Thirties. "We will have lunch where you will not have to struggle with the packaging," he said. "I will show you Armenian food." I arrived at the restaurant, a pleasant place with spotless tablecloths, promptly at eleven forty-five and was directed to a table at the rear, where Dr. Gregorian was surrounded by a cluster of waiters, who were obviously enjoying his company. I heard him say to one of them, "I like the Serbian expression '*Mrtvo Puhalo*.' It means 'one who is dead and doesn't know it.' So many people like that are walking around."

All the waiters spread out through the restaurant except one, who said to me, "Your order?" I immediately made it clear that my knowledge of Armenian cuisine was less than rudimentary.

"You have nothing to say today, nothing whatsoever," said Dr. Gregorian. "I am doing the ordering. This is my table. I always sit here." An order was given, in Armenian, with considerable authority. The waiter smiled a smile of complete satisfaction.

"I am going to compress some of the next academic years," said Dr. Gregorian. "Undergraduate at Stanford with a bachelor's in 1958. Then a

Ph.D. in 1964. I was scheduled to study English literature, but ended up a history major. My thesis was on 'Traditionalism and Modernism in Islam.' Although I spoke seven languages, I got mixed up in English from time to time. I studied extremely hard. I even shaved my head, to avoid social engagements. Perhaps I just wanted to save on haircuts. I mixed myself up in all sorts of campus activities at the same time that I was studying. I have always been extremely active. I studied geology, but it struck me as a mystical science, and I dropped it. I studied philosophy. There was an organization of foreign students on campus, and I became head of it, and acted as master of ceremonies on different occasions. Malapropisms dropped from my lips. Once, when I was told that the top brass of Stanford was coming, I rose and announced, 'Ladies and gentlemen, I wish to introduce the brass tacks of Stanford University.' Someone told me we were in the Year of the Dog, and I rose and announced that it was a dog of a year. That sort of thing, if you can stand it."

Some dishes were brought to our table by the smiling waiter: a flaky cheese-blintz type of dish; *baba ghanouj* (eggplant salad); some grape leaves; and mussels with nuts. All very tasty. Dr. Gregorian had a Bloody Mary and ordered some white wine. "These are just the hors d'oeuvres," he said. Then for me he ordered swordfish with green peppers, onion, and rice, and for himself a highly spiced beef kebab. "Give us time with the hors d'oeuvres," he said to the waiter, "and bring some of your pickled cabbage." To me he said, "The pickled cabbage is extremely delicious. Now, back to Stanford and serious matters. For a while out there, I was dating a French ballerina. A beautiful dancer. I was slim as a reed in those days, and a good dancer. I am still very light on my feet. People are always surprised when they see this short, roly-poly figure with the jiggling beard hopping about with grace. Well, there was this fine French dancer, but each time I went to pick her up at the dormitory I was immensely attracted to a tall, blonde young woman, an undergraduate, a major in American and Ottoman history, whose papers I happened to be marking. And she played an entrancing Joplin ragtime. The ragtime gripped me, and so did the young lady playing it, Clare Russell. I fell in love with her. I remember dates well, and on May 28, 1959 all sorts of people went from Palo Alto to San Francisco to celebrate the hundredth anniversary of the publication of Edward FitzGerald's translation of the Rubáiyát of Omar Khayyám. The celebration took place at the California Palace of the Legion of Honor. Darius Milhaud composed a piece for the occasion. Stephen Spender was there. Edward Teller made a speech on the atomic theory of Omar Khayyám. Clare and I went together. Someone asked me who the tall, beautiful lady was, and I said, 'She is the lady I hope to marry.' On the way back from San Francisco to Stanford, although I was feeling quite nervous, I said to her, 'Someday I will ask you to marry me.' She said, 'If you ask me now, the answer is yes.' We have three sons—one who has graduated from the University of Pennsylvania, one who is now a senior there, and a third at Trinity School here in New York. When we called her father in Tenafly, New Jersey, to make the announcement, it was a bad connection, and he thought we said we were in jail. When I met her grandfather, he told me about their family Bible, which for three hundred years had never had a foreign entry, and I couldn't resist saying that our family Bible had sixteen hundred years of Armenian names in it. We were married in March 1960.

"I taught at San Francisco State part-time, and then full-time. I taught five courses a week. I taught European intellectual history and Middle Eastern history. I taught the history of Russia. I taught European history from 1914 to the present. I taught in the mornings, I taught in the afternoons, I taught in the evenings. I *loved* to teach. Then I taught at the University of Texas. Then, in 1972, I went to the University of Pennsylvania, and *that* is a history. I was the first dean of the Faculty of Arts and Sciences, and then I became provost. It was the most exhilarating and most painful experience of my entire life. It's on my mind a great deal. It was a searing experience. Sometimes I think I am over it, other times it still haunts me. I expected to become the president of the university." Dr. Gregorian put down his knife and fork and sighed. I could see that he was becoming agitated. He said, "When I start talking about the University of Pennsylvania, my wife says, 'Please don't talk about it again.' Sometimes she tiptoes from the room."

Dr. Gregorian said that when Martin Meyerson, then president of the university, announced his intention to retire, in 1978, it appeared that a large proportion of the faculty expected that he would be named the new president. The trustees decided otherwise. Dr. Gregorian was deeply wounded. He feels that the manner in which he was rejected assaulted and violated his most basic dignity. During the height of the decision-making process at Pennsylvania, he was under serious consideration for the chancellorship of the University of California at Berkeley, which he has always considered one of the best academic jobs in the country. Thinking that he would get the University of Pennsylvania post, Gregorian withdrew his name from consideration for the Berkeley job—only to be passed over at his home institution. There are some differences of opinion in academic circles as to precisely how far the University of California went in its pursuit of Dr. Gregorian. Most of the scholars with whom I have talked are certain that he was one of two finalists for the post. Others seem to think that he was, in fact, definitely offered the post. Some of Dr. Gregorian's opponents in the fracas at Pennsylvania claim that he was never actually offered the chancellorship. A distinguished social scientist at Harvard who was asked about such matters replied calmly, "There are no blood battles anywhere, *anywhere*, that can compare with the blood battles of academia. Horrible is the word for the massacres." In any event, on September 15, 1980—the day the University of Pennsylvania trustees announced that Sheldon Hackney, the president of Tulane, would be named the next president of the University of Pennsylvania—Dr. Gregorian announced his resignation as provost.

"I felt devastated," Gregorian told me. "And now I am going to change the subject and talk about knowledge. I sit here and I look intelligent, but we must put our minds to real concerns. What is to become of memory? Orwell didn't realize the dangers of the computer: the possibility of being *overwhelmed* by undigested information, and the possible manipulation of that information by those who process it. Furthermore, he wasn't aware of acid paper, destroying the written word. I went down to Wall Street the other day and made a talk to some businessmen, and I scared them. I told them that information is doubling every five years—talk about explosions—but that the ratio of use to available information is declining. Availability has increased, but use has diminished. Technically we have managed to perfect retrievability, but the question remains how the general public will get the information. Presumably, the scholar will be able to make his way through the new technology, but what about the individual member of the general public? How will he master the methods of retrieving information? And the cost! Nobody knows how much information will cost. Knowledge will be there, but will it be only for the rich? It costs money to use computers. Will this mean that only those with money will have access to information? I worry about this. Believe me, I worry about this. The great fear for the future is the cry 'The computer is down!'—meaning you can't get the information until the computer is working again. This puts knowledge, in a sense, in the category of airline tickets. 'Sorry, we can't confirm your reservation now, as the computer is down.' When we say that the computer is down, we give the computer itself a say in the development of knowledge. Another thing that worries me is the loss of process with the computerization of knowledge. I am contradictory about all this, for I am wholeheartedly for the new system of computers, but I do see some of the dangers. I worry about the various drafts of a story or poem or essay, the material that has gone to build up libraries. What about all the revisions of *The Waste Land* that are in our Berg Collection? Will the computerization of knowledge wipe out evidence of the process of gaining it? All the systems are dangerous, but at the same time I have great faith in them. I am an optimist at heart. Today, there are a thousand systems that one can plug into, and I foresee a system of converters all over the world, the way you plug your electric razor into a converter in a foreign hotel in order to get a shave."

A young woman at a nearby table got up and approached us. She held out her hand to Dr. Gregorian. "You don't remember me," she said, "but I studied with you at the University of Texas. The only change I can see in you is that your beard is no longer jet black."

"I noticed you," said Dr. Gregorian. "I thought I recognized you, because all the girls at Texas were beautiful."

"I see you haven't changed," the young woman said. "I would like to phone you and come and see the library." Dr. Gregorian beamed, and she returned to her table.

"Happens to me all the time," he said. "I dreadfully miss teaching. I miss the feedback, the give-and-take, but once I had decided to come to New York and the library I immersed myself in the library. I commuted every day for four months from Swarthmore, where we lived. I read everything I could get my hands on about the library. I made a thorough investigation of the place. I must have visited at least twenty of the eighty branches. I met every single trustee, in thirty or forty meetings. I talked with Daniel Boorstin, the librarian at the Library of Congress. 'You have a historical obligation to take the job,' he said. I talked to Oscar Handlin, who was then head of the Harvard University Library. I asked them not only what they had accomplished but what they couldn't do. I was twenty minutes late for my first meeting with the trustees. To begin with, the train was late. Then the cabdriver who picked me up at Penn Station didn't have the faintest notion how to get to Wall Street, where the meeting was. I found everything here so different from Philadelphia. Passion is frowned upon down there. They don't capitalize on their strengths. They allowed New York to walk off with the Bicentennial—the tall ships, for instance. Philadelphia is like an artichoke. You peel off a leaf at a time. There is Bryn Mawr. And there's Swarthmore. Philadelphians live their lives on the outskirts. Not much sense of unity. It's horizontal, not vertical. People can live off the interest down there, as in Boston, and not touch the capital. The children of the elite go to prep school there but off to college elsewhere. Incidentally, I was only the second foreign-born provost in the University of Pennsylvania's history, and proud of it."

Dr. Gregorian took a sip of wine. "No question the Pennsylvania experience left a deep scar," he continued. "I am afraid I glamorized the Anglo-Saxon tradition of fairness. I still often wear the blue-and-maroon university tie. I still know the names of some one thousand Penn faculty members. But once I made up my mind to come to New York in 1981, that was it. New Yorkers are not afraid of passion. They are not afraid of flamboyance or panache. I was struck by the deep feeling the trustees of the library who approached me had for their institution. Their excitement infected me. I was feeling pretty bankrupt, and I said to them that when the lions are hungry you feed them starving Armenians. I told them that we would face monumental problems, that we could go either up or down. Yet I knew that I could not only run an institution but build it and make it stronger. All my life, I have wanted to know the rules of the game, and I felt that the people who ran the library knew the rules. I know that some people criticize me for all the social events we put on—the big, expensive dinners, the monumental fund-raisers—but they are ways of showing the flag. I have also noticed that at a literary cocktail party one requires a distinct, exaggerated peripheral vision in order to see who is coming in the door, who is talking to whom, and so on. Once here, to get a feel of the place, I went into active duty at the information desk in Room 315, the card-catalogue room. A terrifying experience. I answered the phone. I could not believe the way the inquiries poured in. A lady called wanting certain information about Flaubert. I was so flustered I couldn't find anything about Flaubert. I couldn't even find his name in the catalogue. The lady was nervous. She said, 'It's my first day on a research project.' 'Lady,' I said, 'it's my first day, too.' Finally, a seasoned employee took pity on me. 'Dr. Gregorian,' he said, 'the lady seems to be looking for an article, not a book. You will find it in Periodicals.' I learned what these people do from day to day. I learned how long it takes to get a book onto a shelf. I began to appreciate the details of the system. I have never forgotten something I heard in an exchange between Mike Wallace and Marlene Dietrich. Wallace asked what was the most important thing she had learned, and she said it was how to overcome the routine in order to do the essential. In the library, I discovered that someone must open the front door. Not everybody can be creative. The cogs in the wheel are vital. It is essential that someone spend forty years answering economics questions.

"I am proud of many things, and especially of the money we have raised. A ten-million-dollar grant—the very largest in our history—from the Vincent Astor Foundation! Twenty-seven-point-six million dollars in a new capital fund allocated to us by the City of New York! Never before has the city given so much to the library! Exxon has donated one million dollars to our Science and Technology Research Center. The Dana Foundation has given us half a million to advance the computer catalogue system. And the National Endowment for the Humanities has awarded our Research Libraries a matching grant of two million dollars a year for three years. Under its terms, we will need to have raised eighteen million in private funds by June 1988. We have been getting matching grants from the Endowment since 1972, but this represents the largest ever to a single institution." Dr. Gregorian paused for breath. "I am often overwhelmed by the generosity and the interest. I know that each year it is another uphill struggle just to keep going. I wonder who I am, where I am. The New York *Times Book Review* once asked me what character in literature I would most like to be. I instantly replied Candide. His deep concern for humanity. His critical rationalism. His healthy skepticism. His realistic optimism. His knowledge that with a frank acceptance of man's fate life can be made endurable. Candide calls for positive action, for faith in man's eventual ability to improve the human condition. One must cultivate one's own garden."

I have been looking into the phenomenon of Vartan Gregorian. And he *is* a phenomenon. One must approach him as one would approach an extraordinary force of nature—a tornado, perhaps, or a hurricane. Of course, Gregorian is a benign force, and he leaves behind him as he whirls through New York not death and destruction but a heightened sense that, while knowledge is power, knowledge itself is the primary goal. In searching for Gregorian, I first spent many hours talking with him. I then moved around in his wide circle of friends and associates, listening to them talk about him. In a sense, the search has been like using the old card-catalogue system of the library: pull out one card and you find a reference that leads you to another, and so on, until you have at least partly satisfied your curiosity.

Brooke Astor is, among other things, the honorary chairman of the library's board of trustees. She is a lively, brilliant, attractive woman in her eighties, who gives the appearance of someone twenty years younger. She supervises every detail of the Vincent Astor Foundation from an unmarked suite of offices on Park Avenue. The suite is simply furnished, and coolly designed for efficiency. Mrs. Astor's corner office is dominated by a large oil portrait of her late husband, Vincent Astor, in the full regalia of a captain in the United States Navy. The picture faces her desk. "I've taken down most of the pictures and things on my walls—the awards and so on—because it looked too much like a doctor's office," she told me one afternoon not long ago. Not only has her foundation given millions of dollars to the library but Mrs. Astor is a close friend of Dr. Gregorian, and an adviser. She seems to have an instinctive understanding of his quixotic nature. "If I were asked to give one word for Vartan," she said, "I would say 'dynamic.' I am in awe of his fund-raising abilities. Absolute awe. He isn't feathering his own nest. Sometimes he talks too much, no question about that. His bubbling over is part of his erudition and his teaching ability. I have urged him to stick to the two-minute rule—no talking beyond two minutes—but that's hard for Vartan. He's a spinner of tales, and when he's wound up it's hard for him to stop. I am also in awe of the fact that he didn't speak any English until he was in his twenties. Imagine that!

"I am always trying to help Vartan strengthen the library's board—put people on who are valuable intellectually. I feel so strongly about New York, and especially about the use of this fund's money. The money came from New York, and it should go back here." She glanced at the portrait of Captain Astor, and at another picture on the wall, a signed photograph of Franklin D. Roosevelt. "Vincent really liked that portrait in the uniform," she said. "And Roosevelt loved to spend time on Vincent's yacht, *Nourmahal*. People still keep asking silly questions, such as was F. D. R. uneasy being on the yacht, with the New Deal and all that. Nonsense! One thing did worry me about Vartan and Clare Gregorian when they came here from Philadelphia. After all, they were part of the grove of academe down there. A quiet life. And suddenly they are thrown in with a ritzy crowd and money. I worried about Clare. It wasn't her style. The pace worried me. The different dinners every night. The fund-raising. But it's quieted down now, and they have settled in. You know, there's a fund-raising letter that went out in my name, and I keep getting phone calls about it, and all sorts of congratulations. They say they love the letter. They send in five hundred here, or a thousand there, or five thousand." She winked.

I was curious about what it would be like to work for Dr. Gregorian, and, going through my human card catalogue, I found myself, one afternoon, talking with Joan Dunlop, a stately woman who had been his executive assistant for several years after he first came to the library. She is currently the president of the International Women's Health Coalition, an organization that deals with family planning and the reproductive health of women in the Third World. Her office is in a stunning Georgian building on Park Avenue, and she herself has much of the elegance, reticence, and balance of a fine Georgian structure. "Gregorian had been at the library several months when I heard he was looking for an executive assistant," she told me. "I wrote him a letter and received no reply. Then I made some phone calls down there and they weren't returned. I knew that his office must be in some sort of disarray. I had been working for John D. Rockefeller III—for the Rockefeller Family and Associates—handling his population and abortion concerns. I had been going through a personal crisis—

cancer, from which I had most happily recovered. I had a renewed sense of life and hope. I was about to go to work for a hotel chain, but something inside told me that, with the recovery and all that, I should make some larger contribution than the hotel business. I found out later that Gregorian had received some five hundred applications for the executive-assistant post and had gone through each of them himself. Then, one day, a friend of mine called Gregorian about me—there's a women's network involved here, and news travels fast—and he tracked me down in California. I went to see him around Thanksgiving of 1981. He was in an upset state. He hadn't yet learned quite how to handle the New York press— they hadn't caught on to his special personality. There was a fuss about the library's buying him an apartment, and some tenants in the cooperative objecting on the ground that selling to an institution meant that the identity of some future tenant would be a question mark. It was messy. He was off balance. 'I am not usually upset,' he said to me, 'and a film crew is coming in later today to take some pictures.' 'Welcome to New York!' I said to him. 'They'll forget the whole thing in two weeks.'

"We hit it off. We hit it off instantly. We talked for hours. We talked of each other's strengths and weaknesses. We inquired into one another's lives. In no way was it a linear interview. I was born in England, and I told him that when I had finished preparatory school there I had not gone to college. I had done a good deal of reading and thinking. I had read White-head's *Aims of Education*. I felt that I had been defrauded by education in postwar England. England, to me, was a prison—there was no energy there, and no money. He described the duties of the job, and I said to him, 'I'll sleep on it.' This seemed to floor him, but he respected me for it. 'I would walk into the desert without water to get you in this job,' he said to me. One must understand that's the way he talks. I think he understands women better than men. He actually talks in feminist terms. That's part of the essence. Well, I went to work for him, and it was a mighty experience. He never hurts anybody's feelings. I am convinced that the University of Pennsylvania hurt his feelings, wounded him deeply, broke his private code in some way, when it didn't make him president. One must remember that when he started out at the library here he didn't get too much support from the library itself. The infrastructure there is creaky. They didn't give him too much back from the energy he expended. As for his working methods, above all he needs to trust people. This is vital in order for him to proceed. He's a master at lobbying and raising money. A turning point for him was a talk he gave to the editorial board of the New York *Times* at the end of 1981. I am told that he amazed them. He had thousands of arcane facts about the library and its history at his fingertips, and without so much as a note in his hand. He knew the history of each of the collections. He had delved into every nook and cranny of the place.

"There are dangers to his method of working, for he keeps everything in his head—*everything*. Administratively, he's a nightmare. The dialogue is a constant struggle. 'Where is the paper?' 'You have it.' 'No, you have it.' And so on. He has a passion for reading letters that contain contributions to the library—especially if they are unsolicited. These give him renewed faith in the place. There is no stopping him—he will come in and open the mail himself. Anything that's unopened he opens, and then he throws the letters all over the place. There is no such thing with Gregorian as an 'in' and 'out' basket. One day, he opened a letter and a check fell out, and he was quite excited. 'One thousand!' he shouted. 'And from someone we don't know!' He took another look. It was for a million—he had misread the zeros. Then, of course, he wanted every available fact about the person who had made the contribution.

"I think he is the strongest-willed person I have ever worked with. People find it hard to say no to him. People think his power lies somewhere in his personality and his charm, but it's something else. It's his ability to make people think differently, to alter their perspective. With Mrs. Astor, for example, you have one shrewd cookie working with another shrewd cookie. They are equals. Each gives something vital to the other. Gregorian's relationship with Mayor Koch is extraordinary and symbiotic. Mutual respect and affection. A big moment for Gregorian came in 1983, when he got four million seven hundred thousand dollars from the city for the library. Arthur Rosenblatt, his architectural liaison with the city, who knows the city, had said to him, 'Look, the *zoo* is getting eight million.' So Gregorian brought his staff in on a Saturday—he works six days a week, by the way, and fourteen hours a day. They planned their strategy, and Gregorian worked every level of the city government. He was a master at lobbying before the Board of Estimate and its various subcommittees. I had the great pleasure of watching him grow in sophistication and confi-

dence. I wish I had been one of his students; it would have been an enriching experience. I go back to that day I first met him. It was symbolic. The
city had been taking the library for granted. There it was, in that beautiful, aging building, just being taken for granted, and going downhill fast.
It had been forgotten. And along comes a man with a funny name and puts
the library back into the consciousness of the city.

"I left him in June 1984, to do the population work I am now engaged
in. I have many worries about the library. I am not certain it is being used
the way it once was, what with the great university libraries all over the
city. I know that the physical structure is being shored up, but I have some
qualms about the managerial side of things. The whole complicated system of the library is typical of the city's erosion—a little like the transit
problem. The library needs a hearty dose of personnel excellence, but it
can't compete in salaries with, for example, the Metropolitan Museum.
Although Gregorian sees a great many of the people in the library, there
are still people he never sees. It's just too big. There are wonderful and dedicated people down there who could double their salaries somewhere else
but stay because they love the place. But when they get older and retire
who will take their places? I certainly don't know the answer. I worry about
him. I worry that he is exhausting himself, running around the city for the
library. I am not sure he is consistently supported by the troops." She stood
up and took a few long strides across her office. "He hasn't defined himself
yet," she said. "This wonderful man has not completely defined himself.
His friends must help this man find himself."

Federal District Judge Louis H. Pollak, who sits in Philadelphia, is one of
Dr. Gregorian's closest friends. The two men have a deep admiration for
one another. They met when Judge Pollak, who had been dean of the Yale
Law School, went, in 1974, to the University of Pennsylvania Law School,
where he became dean the following year. Gregorian was then dean of the
Faculty of Arts and Sciences at the university. He became provost in 1978,
at the age of forty-four. They immediately became friends. I, too, felt immediate friendship for Judge Pollak when I went down to Philadelphia one
day to visit him and talk about Gregorian. Judge Pollak is a tall, personable, agile, youthful-looking man in his sixties, possessed of extreme
courtesy and friendliness. His offices, on the thirteenth floor of the United

States Court House, overlook Independence Hall and a National Parks Service structure that houses the cracked Liberty Bell and offer a sweeping view of the broad Delaware River and several bridges. The judge keeps his golden retriever, Bumpo, near him in his chambers; during my visit, the dog was not only alert but law-abiding.

"Gregorian made his presence felt on the campus," the judge said. "One must know that the University of Pennsylvania is an assemblage of baronies. The Wharton School, in a sense, stands by itself. The medical school is an enormous entity. And so on. Gregorian was the first dean of the Faculty of Arts and Sciences. He was putting together a faculty of arts and sciences in a centrifugal atmosphere. People had been conditioned to think of arts and sciences on a secondary level. Now, quite suddenly, like a whirlwind, here was a dean who was interesting, who by means of energy and enthusiasm made people feel important. This was something real, and even the most jaded liked it. I came to Penn shortly after he did, and the Gregorians gave the Pollaks a reception. Here was a professor giving a reception for a professor! It is just second nature for Gregorian to make pleasant things happen. I especially grew to admire the way Clare learned Armenian cuisine, dived into it with skill and affection. For some reason, her enthusiasm for the serving of delicious Armenian food strikes a deep emotional chord in me. And Gregorian became excited about the United States. There was a good deal of food-exchanging between the two families. We would have Monday-evening dinners together, and gorge ourselves on food and sentimentality. He is a most imaginative educator. He wanted an exchange of scholars between Arts and Sciences and the law school. He felt the need for an exchange of disciplines—putting historians and philosophers into the law school. Ideas tumbled from him, notions of interdisciplines. There were the inevitable money restraints. How do you pay a professor from one part of the university who is contributing his knowledge to another part of the university? No problem for Gregorian! He would say, 'We can work it out. If there is a sound educational reason for someone to teach in another part of the university, we can work it out.' As a result, we simply allowed trading back and forth between the two schools. I had the privilege, after I went on the bench, of presiding over his naturalization ceremony. He was extremely emotional about it. I recall that when it came time for him to speak—he spoke for all those sworn in

that day, and they came from twenty-seven different countries—he spoke
very rapidly, much faster than usual. He was truly excited. He spoke of his
deep faith in democracy. He spoke of Woodrow Wilson's notion of democracy—that one of its purposes is to reduce inhumanity and maximize
hope. He spoke of Franklin Roosevelt's Four Freedoms, and I remember
he said, 'In the words of Herman Melville, we are not a narrow tribe of
men. . . . We are not a nation so much as a world.' "

Looking up Gregorian led me rather rapidly into the world of "searching"—the widespread practice on the part of public organizations and
private enterprises of seeking talented people to become their chief executives. This cannot rationally be compared with the rigors and adventures
that confronted pioneers crossing the vast North American continent, but
discovery is the name of the game. The stakes are high, and the occupation
is serious. Foundations and universities are in the forefront of "searches."
It seems that they are constantly on the lookout for new chiefs, as the turn-
over in the higher echelons of foundations and universities bears some resemblance to the goings-on in a fun house. The more I looked into the matter, the more apparent it became that somewhere deep in corporate
philanthropic academic foundation America there is a list of "availables,"
and that this list consists of certain staple names. These staples may never
actually become the president of Yale or the head of the Ford Foundation
or the Metropolitan Museum, but nonetheless their names are always
cropping up. Once the University of Pennsylvania had turned down Gregorian for its top post, he became an accepted name in the pantheon. Is the
president of Yale about to resign? Well, then, certainly Gregorian is being
considered, and papers such as the *Times* will call Gregorian and try to
force him to admit that he is very close to the top of the list. (One afternoon
recently, Gregorian had a hard time convincing reporters that he had not
just *been* appointed the new president of Yale. "No, I have not been offered
the job." "What are your plans?" His plans were to stay at the New York
Public Library and "help secure its future.")

Richard Salomon is a public-spirited man who has been involved in his
share of searches. He is chancellor of Brown University and at one time
was the chief executive officer of Charles of the Ritz, the cosmetics firm.
He retired a few years ago, at the age of seventy, as chairman of the board

of the New York Public Library, but he remains on the board, and the library is one of his major concerns. He is extremely active in its affairs and is in almost constant touch with Gregorian. I went to see him one day in his office, an unprepossessing one, in Rockefeller Center, and he filled me in on some of the events that led to Gregorian's coming to the library. In 1981, when Richard Couper, who was then its president, announced his intention of resigning, the library first advertised for candidates, as it was legally bound to do. The institution was inundated with applications, but the list was soon reduced to three or four candidates. Gregorian turned up on everybody's list. Salomon had never met him, but a lunch was arranged, then cocktails, then dinner. As on other occasions, Gregorian made a remarkable impression. "I found him frank and forthright," Salomon told me. "One of our problems was the public's view of the library. The old regime never stuck its neck out, wasn't daring, took a negative attitude. The philosophy, I am sorry to say, was 'Nothing can be done.' Gregorian's philosophy is 'Everything can be done.' There is no such word as 'no.' But I am getting ahead of myself. When the search approached the critical period, Bill Dietel, the trustee who was head of the committee, and I took Gregorian to dinner at La Petite Marmite, a restaurant near where I live, and then we went back to my place. *Our* minds were made up at this point, but his wasn't, so we were trying to sell him on the library. We tried to sell him on the intangibles of the job. He was extremely affable. He is always affable. But beneath the affability he was being distinctly noncommittal. He told us that he had to take a phone call at nine o'clock. He felt bad about the interruption, but there was no way around it—he had to take a phone call at nine. There was something dramatic about the proceedings. Promptly at nine, the call came, and he took it in another room. The call lasted twenty minutes, and then Gregorian was back. He was rubbing his hands in a sort of slicing gesture. He was beaming. 'I'm your man,' he said. 'I'm your man.' He told us that he had been talking to the chairman of a university in an area of the country flooded with sunlight. 'I like sunlight,' he said. They had offered him a car, a chauffeur, a house, and a stipend 50 percent higher than we could meet. But he said he was our man. I wondered why. 'Well,' said Gregorian, 'if this fellow had been smart enough to tell me that he had a third-rate place and wanted me to come down and make it second-rate, elevate it to a second position, I might have considered it. But they pretended they were first-rate, and with people like that you simply cannot do business.'

"From that moment on, we held nothing back from Gregorian. We told him that we had a weak administration, that we were building bricks without straw. To give you an idea of the mood: We had been running a series of advertisements that had a negative impact on the public. They were dreadfully downbeat. In an attempt to raise money, they pictured the library in such dire straits that it had been turned into a parking lot behind the lions. We thought we were about to deal with an administrator—we had no notion we were dealing with a demon fund-raiser. He methodically went about meeting every member of the professional staff. He asked everybody at the library what his or her problems were. Every night, he takes home a bundle of work. Frankly, I don't know how he does it. His memory is encyclopedic. We are the library of last resort for the State of New York, but we had been getting only four-point-eight million from the state—not enough. Now things are looking up, and considerably more money is forthcoming. Although Gregorian has managed to get us the largest matching grant ever given anybody by the National Endowment for the Humanities, that is the only unrestricted federal help we get. His dream, and long-term plan, I think, is that one day this great national treasure will be placed on a basis comparable to the Library of Congress or the Smithsonian, as a national asset with a fixed annual amount. In the old days, the board of trustees could be counted on to throw money on the table. It would fill the bill. This is no longer true. Taxes were different then. You could accumulate money."

Andrew Heiskell is the current chairman of the library's board, and the former chairman of Time, Inc. He is an outgoing, ruddy, athletic-looking man of seventy—the archetype of what is commonly known as "the picture of health." I met him in an office he maintains on the thirty-fifth floor of the Time & Life Building. An oblong sign on his desk reads "I'D RATHER BE SAILING." On the wall I noticed a picture of him and Gregorian, with one of the library's lions in the background. Heiskell towered over Gregorian. "We don't look very much alike in that picture," Heiskell said to me, "but the bonds between us are extraordinarily strong. There is a kinship. I was born in Naples. He was born in the Middle East. We both came to the United States from foreign lands. He fascinates me, and I enjoy working with him at the library simply because it is fun. But it's nonstop. He goes all the time—morning, noon, and night. He works fourteen hours a day, and I worry about his eating habits. I had never met him until the library thing came up. I not only didn't know him—I didn't know anything about him. I marvelled at the way he went about his task. First, he had to believe in the library itself. Once he became enthusiastic, he spread the enthusiasm to others. His optimism can be quite infectious. He never says no. He always says, 'Sure, we'll do it.' It doesn't make any difference who comes in—a curator, a trustee, a politician—Gregorian rolls across the room and says, 'Sure, we'll do it.' A key is his sincerity, his conviction, and his word. People take him at his word. Sometimes his ideas fall of their own weight, but I think that being a historian has given him a broad perspective, a sense of time, that allows for accomplishments. What he did was put the library in the spotlight. He had to change the mood— of the city for the library, of the people in the city for the library, and of the people in the library for the library. In essence, he had to change the future. I think he used mirrors. You know, we had no real support in the city. People had turned their backs on the library. We weren't trusted to use money wisely. He has proved that we can handle the money."

Heiskell looked out the window for a moment, at a spectacular cityscape of Rockefeller Center and its environs. To people with an optimistic nature, such views must tend to accentuate the positive and make impossible tasks appear possible. The noises of the city, for one thing, are muted. Thousands of twinkling lights jabbing into the sky tend to make one forget the crush of bodies down on the streets, the gridlock, the mess. Mr. Heiskell is an alert and sensitive man, and I think that he guessed some of my thoughts just then. "One must never forget the troubles," he said. "There are times when I think it's hopeless. I say to myself, 'I don't see how we're going to pay for this.' It's a funny thing, but when I was in the private sector I never really thought about money, so to speak. Now I think about money all the time—in connection with the library. We are cursed by several things—one is having 'New York' in our name. The rest of the country doesn't like New York, runs it down. 'Nice place to visit'—that sort of thing. In Congress, it's some sort of hate word. Then, there's the word 'public.' That's another misnomer. It means that the public can use the

library. It doesn't mean that we get great sums of public money. Sixty percent of the research libraries' budget is privately financed. The research
budget is over thirty-six million, and we have to produce twenty-two million of that. The Library of Congress gets more than two hundred million
from the federal government. The city does give money to match the
money given to the eighty branches. And, by the way, Gregorian has re-
vitalized the branches. The mayor now gives us a lump sum for certain im-
provements in the main building, and we've been allowed to take charge
of much of the construction there, so that twice as much is done in half the
time. In the entire system, we have some eighty different construction
projects under way now, and the procedures are devilish and complex when
you are dealing with the city, and with construction unions, and with the
comptroller. We have come a long way from the days when officials at the
library wanted the books lined up on the shelves, looking neat. You have
to watch yourself in this enterprise. It is easy to look at people in terms of
money, and I try never to forget what the library is all about—the spread-
ing of knowledge."

William Dietel is a trustee of the library and the president of the Rockefeller Brothers Fund. His office, simple and functional, is in midtown, on
Sixth Avenue. He bears a certain resemblance to the current species of
foundation executive whose support is essential—the times we live in
being what they are—to the reading of a book in a public library. On the
surface, at least, these executives seem to be an entirely wholesome lot.
They smile a great deal. They keep themselves in top physical form. They
dress without a trace of display. They are educated. They make what my
grandmother used to call "good money." They speak softly. They do not
appear to ruffle easily, and they give the impression of being (always with
modesty) satisfied with themselves and the society in which they thrive. If
they lived in rural areas, one could easily imagine them as leader of the
local 4-H club. Gregorian works with them on a daily basis. They are the
linchpin of his endeavors. Dietel told me that he finds himself constantly
astounded by Gregorian—for instance, by his instinct for knowing not
only where great wealth lies but how to jar it loose and make it wend its
way to the New York Public Library. "I had never met him until the library
post came up," he said. "When I did meet him, it was love at first sight. I

must confess that we ardently courted him. We were asking him into a tough situation. We needed a charismatic character. And now we have one. New York doesn't have too many heroes, and he seems to be one at the moment. He breaks people down with that bear hug. The Calvinist mentality is dissolved by him and his approach. You know, I talked with him right here in this office. I wanted to find out something about what happened at Penn—why he wasn't made president. He wanted to know about the library. We had quite a talk. I can't tell you why they didn't make him president, and nobody at Penn gave me a satisfactory answer. As I talked with him, I realized, as Andrew Heiskell had and as Dick Salomon had, that any dream we might have of the library's future could be handled by Gregorian. He bubbles over. I mentioned casually, once, that I was going to Italy. 'You must meet my friend the Communist mayor of Florence,' he said instantly. 'He's the only bourgeois Commie I know.' Merely mentioning Greg's name opened all doors. I was treated like royalty. Incidentally, Heiskell calls him Greg the Eleventh. I remember once I felt that he looked downcast and exhausted. This worried me. I talked it over with Dick Salomon, and we decided to give him a little party in a private room at '21.' To bolster his spirits. Someone made him a needlepoint pillow with a lion on it, and we all sang a song that was titled 'Blessed Greg' and was sung to the tune of 'From the Halls of Montezuma.' " Mr. Dietel had trouble remembering the words. "I want you to hear them," he said. "I'll call my daughter." He reached his daughter on the telephone. "What were the words to that song dedicated to Greg?" he asked her. She sang something to him, and he thanked her with affection and hung up. " 'To the stacks of the New York Li-brary, from the halls of the U. of P.' " Mr. Dietel went on to say, "That song got around. It was subsequently sung at a meeting of the board of trustees. I have a wonderful family."

Barbara W. Tuchman, the historian, has a passionate interest in libraries. She has spent a large portion of her life in them, to the joy of thousands of readers. She and Gregorian have a close personal and professional relationship. I have known Mrs. Tuchman for many years, and one morning I walked over to have a chat with her, in a pied-à-terre she maintains with her husband, Dr. Lester Tuchman, on Fifth Avenue. (She spends most of her time at their home in Connecticut.) I found her, as usual, surrounded by mountains of books. She is small and alert, with features that are at once delicate and gentle and sharply angular. Dr. Tuchman, who had been busy in another room, brought me a cup of coffee. "Gregorian is wonderful with respect to the revival of the library," Mrs. Tuchman said. "He has brought it into the consciousness of the city. I have been on the board of trustees since just before he became president. I had been asked to join some years before, but I went down and looked the place over, and I got the impression that the board was somewhat stuffy—the old New York *Social Register* kind of thing. It didn't appeal to me, not at all. What was not understood until Greg came along was that public attention was needed. Not big social names but public attention. After all, the donors to the library hear the same sort of pitch day after day from the Met and the Modern and others. There is this huge fight for money in New York. It's a Sisyphean struggle. But Greg's appeal and his strength are largely that he caught on to New York so quickly and that he is a passionate librarian. Also, this city welcomes an exotic person. Lots of people feel that the social events conducted under Greg's stewardship have contributed to his success. I think it's the quality of the exhibitions—the one on censorship, for instance." Mrs. Tuchman paused and glanced out the window.

"I was speaking this morning with Dick Salomon," she said, "and he was telling me of the evening they knew Greg would come to New York. They were in Dick's apartment, and Greg said he was expecting a long-distance call." I experienced here a distinct feeling of déjà vu—a most encouraging feeling when one is going through the card catalogue. "They were so pleased when he told them he was their man. Libraries are vital to a city. You have to keep buying or the library will die. You must stay open. I myself have contributed to keeping the library open more hours. I love that library. I love the lions. Nothing sickens me more than the closed door of a library. It is unthinkable to me." It was clear that this represented to her, both as a citizen and as a historian, a true horror. "You must always remember how open New York is, how free," she said. "I can recall how the Bibliothèque Nationale in Paris was closed for hours one day when I was in the middle of some critical work—the waiting, the frustration. You need a pass for the British Library. We are open to everybody. I have worked there on Fifth Avenue, doing research, and a bag lady in the next chair at the long table was making out her Christmas cards. No question that access is a question at the N.Y.P.L. That's what I always call it—the N.Y.P.L. Unlike many great libraries, ours is in an unsafe spot. The Library of Congress is on a hill. University libraries are secluded places. Here we have the broad front steps, with everybody eating lunch. The backyard is Bryant Park—drunks, drugs. I once confided my fears about all this to Greg. 'Don't worry, Barbara,' he said to me. 'We are smarter than they are.' I admire his consciousness of intellectual and mental powers, and his conviction that these powers can prevail. I think that's why he's here. I think that's why he'll stay. It's a challenging fight. Gregorian's knowledge is pretty far-ranging. Lester and I were recently at a Lincoln Center affair— there was disco din and semi-crooning and Piaf-type songs in French. Clare Gregorian whispered to me, 'Vartan knows the words to all those songs by heart, in Persian.' "

Some weeks later, I went to the library for a strange ceremony: the temporary closing of Room 315, the card-catalogue room, the room containing some eight thousand oak drawers filled with millions of titles. This is the room that I and millions of others had been using since we could remember first going into the library. The cards were to be replaced, by eight hundred black-bound volumes—the Dictionary Catalog of the Research Libraries of the New York Public Library 1911–1971—and also by thirty-two computer terminals. The speaker at the brief ceremony in the high-vaulted room was Mrs. Tuchman. About a hundred people, including Gregorian and other library personnel, were in the room. Mrs. Tuchman stood behind a small lectern and spoke slowly. She seemed downcast. "Parting is always sad," she said. "For me, the card catalogue has been a companion all my working life. To leave it is like leaving the house one was brought up in. . . . This is a sentimental occasion, and I know I shall feel lost when the wooden drawers are gone. They are my vintage, and I shall never feel competent when it comes to giving instructions to the on-line whatever-you-call-it. . . . We are told the computer file will extend usage widely to library patrons across the country and will make their research infinitely easier and quicker . . . but the easier the process is made and the less active individual thought is employed by the researcher, the less his brain will be exercised. Use it or lose it, as they say. . . . Anyway, I would not take odds on the process being easier. Judging from the few timid pokes I have made at these machines, my hunch is that the searcher will be inundated by so many titles, and will get more than he wants to know and much that he cannot use. . . . From my own experience, many of the most interesting sources for a historical subject come from chance references in some book one has found to start with, and it requires reading the book, or at least looking through its pages, to come upon the titles one might want."

The professional librarians in the room looked at Mrs. Tuchman with troubled expressions. This was not exactly what they had expected to hear. If Dr. Gregorian was disturbed, he didn't show it. Mrs. Tuchman wound up her remarks by graciously stating, without any marked conviction in her voice, that "computerized methods are the tool of the present and the wave of the future, and the library has undertaken a great and courageous, and, I may add, expensive venture." It was late in the afternoon of a bleak winter day, and many of the wooden drawers had already been removed. The scene was austere and lonely, and the serving of wine and canapés did little to enliven the atmosphere. Gregorian circulated through the room dispensing bear hugs.

Gregorian's public life would be overwhelming for even the most hyper-active executive or politician—business breakfasts, meetings all day, lunches with donors, evening ceremonies at the library and elsewhere, the almost continuous receipt of civic and educational honors. "Personally, I don't see how he manages to keep on his feet," an executive of his acquain-tance, with bags under his eyes, said to me not long ago. "I lead a pretty hectic life myself, but I cannot even imagine maintaining the Gregorian pace."

Somehow, Gregorian does manage. For one thing, he takes Sundays off, and spends a good deal of the day sleeping. "Sometimes I tiptoe into the bedroom with our sons and let them watch their father snoozing on a Sun-day morning," Mrs. Gregorian told me recently. "It's one of the rare times they can see him in repose." Other times are those isolated evenings when nothing is scheduled—no lecture to attend at the library, no medal for good citizenship to receive—and on one such evening he invited me to dinner at his home. He lives in a sky-piercing high rise in the East Nine-ties. The lobby is flashy, with the razzle-dazzle décor that is said to inflame

Bloomingdale's customers and turn them into frenzied buyers. Mrs. Gregorian greeted me at their door; she said that her husband would be home any moment. The apartment in which the Gregorians live is two apartments turned into one. As a result, the rooms are strangely shaped, with odd angles and unexpected corners. Round pillars are to be seen here and there. The floors are covered with stunning Oriental rugs. Books are everywhere, and on the walls are many framed maps of the Mediterranean area and the Middle East. "Vartan is very fond of maps," Mrs. Gregorian said, "but I honestly don't think he knows how to read one. He just likes to look at them." I noticed a great many record albums, and a stereo system. "I happen to love Fats Waller," she said to me. "That wonderful left hand. Nobody plays with the left hand anymore."

The front door opened, with a sudden gust of air. Dr. Gregorian had arrived. He embraced his wife. He gave me a bear hug. A golden retriever, which had evidently been waiting somewhere in the depths of the apartment for the arrival of its master, bounded into the living room. "Ah, Eliza," said Gregorian, embracing the dog. Mrs. Gregorian invited me to sit down at a brass coffee table that looked Middle Eastern. Gregorian said that it came from Boston. Mrs. Gregorian is a generous hostess, and she brought out and set on the coffee table a series of succulent hot hors d'oeuvres, all with a Middle Eastern flavor. There was a plate of smoked beef. There was a plate of blanched eggplant, which was surrounded by pita bread. "I use olive oil, pomegranate seed, and scallions for the eggplant dip," said Mrs. Gregorian. She was quite obviously proud of her Armenian dishes. We moved into the dining room, a corner room with picture windows, strange angles, and a lighted evergreen tree. Dinner was spectacular—a rich beef stew with a mysterious and tantalizing sauce, and a huge salad of lettuce, red peppers, Greek olives, and feta cheese. For dessert, Mrs. Gregorian had made a pumpkin mousse with fresh, pungent ginger spread over the top. "Clare does every bit of this, and I think it's wonderful," Dr. Gregorian said. He seemed deeply content, a man happy to be home.

As he had when we first met, Gregorian spoke a bit about his church, the Armenian Apostolic. "It goes back centuries, to a real split in 451, concerning a dispute on the divinity of Christ and his human qualities. The church in which I was raised uses classical Armenian in its litany. Nobody understands more than 40 percent of it, but it's used. There are few good Armenian dictionaries extant, and only a handful of Armenian phrase books, mostly out-of-date. I was looking at one the other night and came across the entry 'Can you tell me where I can find the nearest tenement?' "

I was given a choice of American or Armenian coffee. I chose Armenian. It was delicious and so thick that I could have floated on it. We moved back into the living room. The lights of the city outside the picture windows, and the Triborough Bridge, with its green illumination, lent the room a dramatic air. Gregorian told me again how much he had enjoyed teaching, and what it had meant to him. He missed most of all, he felt, the idea of being in a position to forge young characters. "I was nervous before every lecture," he said. "I was almost sick from nerves, but once I started talking I could go on forever. I recall a lecture, one day, about Faust. I went on and on. An entire class stood patiently outside the door waiting to get in for the next lecture. I was carried away. Teachers are governed by three things. One, they must be enthusiastic. Two, they must remember that the student has never heard any of this before. And, three, they must tell the truth. Above all, the truth." Gregorian pronounced the word as though it were Holy Writ. "Just a word about origins, before you leave," he said to me. "I want you to see this ceramic tile of Adam and Eve, copied from a ninth-century Armenian manuscript. Adam and Eve are fully clothed, and the serpent still has hands. You can see the serpent handing over the apple."

The evening was at an end. Dr. Gregorian insisted on riding down with me in the elevator, accompanied by Eliza. As we stepped into the lobby, he suddenly seemed like a visitor from another world, a bustling, compact figure distinctly removed from his immediate surroundings.

"There must be many times," I said to him, "when you are overpowered by the distance you have come from your origins."

"That happens many, many times," he said, with deep feeling. "The mysteries of my life multiply. The odd coincidences, the strange turns and twists. Things happen to me that simply cannot happen. For instance, in the very neighborhood where we live, a pastry shop has opened. Nooshin Pastry and Café. Can you believe that this is the same Nooshin Café that stood on Istanbul Avenue in Tehran—one of the first places I ate when, as a teenager, I went to the capital. Transplanted here! The odds of this happening must be several billion to one, and yet it has happened to me. Just the other day, I wrote my sister of this coincidence. My life is filled with such puzzles, endlessly beckoning, endlessly mysterious, endlessly fascinating."

A few days ago, I walked over to the library. It was the middle of the day and the middle of the week, and the library was crowded. Room 315 had been reopened, after being restored to its original appearance, as designed by Carrère and Hastings. It is a dignified room with big windows. The card catalogue was gone, of course, and I missed it. Some people were pulling the huge printed catalogue volumes from the shelves; others were standing in front of the thirty-two computer terminals. I tried my luck at one of them, hitting the keyboard of the terminal with my own name, which had been in the card catalogue. Green letters instantly flashed on the terminal screen. "Type HELP," they said. I realized that I was in the grip of technology and needed patience, perseverance, and an open mind. I felt blue about this until I walked into one of the enormous reading rooms behind the catalogue room. There sat hundreds of people, quietly reading. There was a slight murmur in the room, almost a whisper, and it sounded like low music of the spheres. As long as there is this reading room, these people, this murmur, I thought, we are safe. Perhaps.

(1986)

Ladders

We had an airy, delightful Sunday lunch recently in the Oak Room of the Plaza with Max Ernst, the Surrealist master, whose current retrospective of more than three hundred paintings, sculptures, illustrated books, collages, and frottages (rubbings over textured surfaces) fills every last, curvaceous inch of the Guggenheim and is attracting huge crowds. Ernst is *almost* eighty-four years of age, small, trim, and impish, with snow-white hair, dark brown eyebrows, and a compelling smile, which appears first in the corners of his eyes and then travels rapidly to the corners of his mouth—a smile both detached and encompassing, a smile of survival. Present were Thomas M. Messer, the director of the Guggenheim, and Mrs. Messer; Ernst's wife, the American Surrealist painter Dorothea Tanning; and Ernst's trusted Boswell and observer, Werner Spies. Ernst was wearing a crisp blue suit, a crisp blue shirt, and a crisp blue necktie with a pattern of freedom-loving butterflies flying every which way. A striking Navajo bracelet circled his right wrist. We sat next to Ernst. His eyes swept over the *ancien-régime* grandeur of the Oak Room. "You know," he said, with a German accent, "we have been staying at the Pierre until today, when we moved to the house of dear friends, in the Seventies. A lovely house, with lovely *objets*. Dorothea was glad to get out of the hotel. We left a cheesecake back there at the Pierre, in an icebox. Cheesecake gets better as it gets older—much, much better—and perhaps in two hundred years, if no one pokes into the refrigerator before then, they will find this monumental cheesecake. *Ja, ja*, a cheesecake of genuine importance, an *artifact*. People will puzzle over this discovery and ascribe it to strange forces." He chuckled. When Ernst speaks, there is a mysterious buffer zone between him and others—a private, inviolate area, an area of *hush*.

A waiter came by.

"A vodka Martini," said Ernst. "That is, a Martini with vodka."

"What are you ordering?" asked Mrs. Ernst.

"A Martini with vodka," said Ernst.

"We are trying to involve ourselves with a tequila drink on this side," said Mrs. Ernst, "but we seem to have run into some insurmountable difficulties."

Ernst shrugged. "You see," he said to us, "she is interested in what I am drinking. I will take it upon myself to order the wine—a Pouilly Fuissé. One of the finest."

The waiter was back and was asking for the order.

"In New York, it is the fish life," said Ernst. "I *dream* of the fish life in New York. I want those small, delectable, delicious, perfectly exquisite little clams."

"Cherrystones?" said the waiter.

"No," said Ernst. "Try again."

"Little Necks?" said the waiter.

"*Ja, ja!*" said Ernst. "And without any side business or sauce. Just the Little Necks. And then I want oysters Rockefeller—the ones with the spinach, the ones from New Orleans."

The waiter went away.

"My imagination is slightly on strike at the moment," said Ernst. "This has nothing to do with the fact that everything is really a dream. It is impossible to tell the difference between the dream and the reality. I suddenly remember Ellis Island, when I first came to this country, in 1941. The hamburgers were especially good there. *Ja, ja*, and you had to be quick and skillful to get to the shower and then to the bed you had chosen to sleep in for the night. I had to be *fast*. I dream in three languages— French, English, and German—and when I wake up in the morning I have first to figure out what language I was dreaming in, then to sort out the dreams."

The Little Necks were placed before him, without embellishment, and he systematically and swiftly went to work on them.

"My daddy copied pictures from the Vatican," he said. "All sorts of religious paintings. My daddy was an academic painter. I could never do that. I could never copy from my dreams for my paintings. My painting comes straight from my imagination, and that is distinct from the dreams." He sampled the wine. "*Ja, ja,*" he said.

The oysters Rockefeller were placed before him. He proceeded with caution into their dark green mysteries. "It has been years since I have had them," he said. "Someone asked me the other day what I really liked, and I said, instantly, '*Good food.*'" He smiled his strange smile. "This city is so exciting," he said. "Exhilarating. I absorb what I can, I drink its spirit. But there has been the show, and parties, and friends, and receptions, and conversations, and I have had little time to explore, to move about." He was silent for a moment, and the private area was almost palpable. "I don't see this city becoming a city of silent, stark ruins, as in some of my paintings—high cities on deserted hilltops, with overgrowth of vegetation beneath. New York is too lively for that. The planet has been through so much, has suffered so much, that one must have a certain optimism in order to paint, to function. To my mind, Beckett is our truly great contemporary. *Ja, ja,* but his pessimism didn't stop him from producing his works."

One of the oysters Rockefeller appeared to distress Ernst. He circled it with his fork, then toyed with it, then abandoned it. "My mind has been running along from Ellis Island, where I was first taken, to my marriage, of short duration, to Peggy Guggenheim. Beekman Place." His eyes narrowed, and it was obvious that he had for an instant placed himself on Beekman Place. "You must watch a sense of humor with officials. I became a citizen in 1948, but in the McCarthy period I was in some sort of immigration trouble—something about not leaving the country for more than three months—and I went before a board and told them that I wanted my non-citizenship papers. They were very distressed. 'What are you laughing at?' they said. 'This is no laughing matter.' I think of this often back in France—I am a French citizen now—at our place at Seillans, near Cannes, where Dorothea fixes everything up, and I am allowed to garden. Different from officialdom. And I see now my troubles with the officials in 1942, when I went to visit my friend Matta, the painter, in his house on the high dunes overlooking the ocean, in Wellfleet. On Cape Cod. Quite isolated. Pearl Harbor had happened, and I was an enemy alien, or considered such. Never mind that I had fled before the Nazis from France. I was still German. Such strange events began to take place. One fine day, I went into some nearby woods and burned some trash. Next day, the gendarmes came around. You have been sending up smoke signals to the enemy, they said. Did you know that just a few days ago an American ship had been sunk nearby by a Nazi submarine? Ah, I thought to myself, *this* is trouble. Plainclothesmen from the Immigration Service showed up, turned on Matta's radio, and demanded to be shown through his house. Off they went. When the noise of the radio became hideous and insupportable, I quite carelessly switched it off. *I had fallen into the trap! Enemy aliens are not permitted to operate radios!* In searching the house, the authorities had come upon a telling and highly suspicious piece of evidence—a red-white-and-blue matchbox with 'Freedom House' stamped on it! My own ship was sinking rapidly. Then came the interrogation—a dreadful and comic confusion. As for Matta, they wanted to know, there were how many ladders? I understood them to mean *letters*. Five, of course, I said. M-a-t-t-a. If you keep up this mockery of us, they said, we will keep you in prison until your beautiful white hair is even more white than it is now. More talk about sending smoke signals to the enemy. How many *ladders*, they insisted— *ladders*—did Matta have, to climb on his roof and send signals to the enemy? I said he was not the type to send signals. How did I know him, they asked. He was a fellow painter, I said. What was his nationality? Chilean, I said. Ah, they said, did I not know that all Chileans were subversives? And so on, until finally we went to Boston for further questioning. Peggy Guggenheim accompanied me. The authorities were severe: I had been manipulating a radio. Peggy Guggenheim suddenly said that she was a copper heiress, someone made a phone call, and it was all over. No, no dessert, thank you."

(*1975*)

Billions of Realities

Jean Dubuffet, the French painter, is seventy-one, small, wiry, taut, bald, slightly bent because of a troublesome back, has no eyelashes, permits his mind to hop, skip, jump, and ricochet, discharges vast quantities of nonstatic electricity, and has an almost maniacal affection for New York. He has been visiting here, and we ran into him the other day at the Guggenheim, where some three hundred of his works cover every curve of the museum, hang from the ceiling (Dubuffet clouds float somewhat disturbingly in a world that is neither here nor there), and even overflow into the subterranean auditorium, where masses of giant cutout figures (his so-called Hourloupe figures) are lined up between performances of his animated-painting extravaganza *Coucou Bazar*. Dubuffet was wearing a tightly knit brown suit, a blue-and-white shirt, and an elegant brocaded gold tie, which perfectly complemented the occasional flashing of his gold teeth, of which he has quite a number. They are exhibited when he smiles, and he smiles with the regularity but suddenness of the sweeping beam of a lighthouse. We sat in the semi-dark auditorium, facing the assembled cutouts, which cannot be described as either friendly or unfriendly—just different. "When I first came to see my exhibit here, the officials were very kind to me because of my back," he said. "They permitted me the privilege of an invalid chair, a wheelchair. A wheelchair in the Guggenheim! Oh, my! A wild ride! Such slopes and instant turns. Two brakes, you understand—one for the right hand, one for the left—and all the time whirling down, down, down! An immense experience, like eating Rice Krispies, which I indulge in at all times of the day and night here, and like phoning overseas, which I do most of the night. I cannot stop expressing my enthusiasm for New York. You cannot imagine how much I enjoy it. Every day here is a week in Paris. I feel the creativity, the tempo, the thinking, the deciding. I think I have a better view than New Yorkers. You must understand that a man who has not seen a frog very much has a pretty good idea of what a frog is like. But if you slowly become a frog yourself, how can you tell what a frog is like?" [Flashing beam from lighthouse.]

M. Dubuffet has long, sinewy fingers. He rapidly lighted a cigarette. "When I was here for six months back in 1951–52, I saw very little of the city," he said. "My wife and I had a flat on Charles Street. I would take a bus across Eighth Street to an immense store—Wana . . . , Wana . . . , *Wanamaker's*—and then take another bus to Bond Street, just off the Bowery, where I had a loft. I worked all day long. Nothing mattered but my work. At noon, my wife would come with a basket of food, we would lunch, and then I would work until evening. Here now it is a holiday. But not that first visit. Friends kept saying, 'You must see New York, you must see the Empire State Building, you must see this and that.' I didn't need to see it. I *felt* it. I enjoyed the remnant dealers down there, but suddenly it was time to leave, and when I went to the boat I had seen nothing. But I *felt* it. This time, I have been very busy; I have seen a great deal. I have a chauffeur, Ben, and he and I are pals; we are very comrade, and we go about the city. New York is at an extraordinary point in history, and in *its* history. Perhaps at some time back in ancient China there may have been a similar high point of creativity, of inventiveness, of intelligence. It is fantastic! [Beam of golden light.] In fact, there is something on this continent to stimulate people to insanity. The climate has always been exciting for the mind. I understand that the Indians were stimulated to a collective insanity—perhaps ten to fifteen thousand massacres a day! [Lighthouse.] It stands to reason that the settlers were stimulated by the insanity of the Indians. They were infected. They were driven to their own madness. I see it today in the walk, the tempo; I hear it in the talk. Before I made my *Four Trees* sculpture, which stands down in Chase Manhattan Plaza, I would go there in the mornings, quietly, just to watch. I was impressed by the intensity of the people who cross that plaza. Serious, tense, earnest faces. I was stimulated. Those trees down there are forever expanding into space. They are restless. They have something to do with insanity."

He leaned forward and stared for a few moments at the silent Hourloupe figures—some red, white, and blue and some silver, some of stratified resin and others of painted sheet metal. "For me, insanity is supersanity," he said. "The normal is psychotic—a collective psychosis. Normal means lack of imagination, lack of creativity." He moved his right arm up and down in a chopping motion. "Creativity! *There* is a flowering, a bursting forth. What is called reality by everyone is something very conventional, an accepted interpretation of the world. I have wanted to make my own translations, my own interpretations. Why not re-create the ordinary translation—what one ordinarily knows as reality—and produce a reality no less legitimate than someone else's? [Pause for cigarette, and sudden flash from lighthouse.] Some people say, 'Dubuffet, when you attempt a new reality, you are expressing the ultimate nihilism, the ultimate desperate nihilism.' That's not my view of it. Instead of one reality, we can have billions of realities. Each person can legitimate his own reality. Is this not enriching for the human mind, is this not the negation of a surface approach to life, is this not *very* positive? [Two rapid flashes.] People who are conditioned to any one reality are prisoners. We all seek to share a reality. I have sought it several times in my life. It's the desire to feel fraternity, not to feel alone." He had become more intent than before, as though stripped for a race. "This business of reality and nonreality," he said. "A dangerous business. My strange Hourloupe figures here in front of us—are they distinct personalities? During the *Coucou Bazar* they will move about and be moved, and in five cases actors will climb into Hourloupe costumes and also move. I see them all as little, mysterious figures coming from our world, in still another transcription or translation. They have their own reality, and I want them to have the power to convince. If they have the power to convince, they will make our reality seem like nothing. In essence, I see them as contesting the *being* itself. They will challenge it. As they move about, the audience will not be able to determine what is real, what is nonbeing, what is permanent. A dangerous matter. One paints a guitar on a canvas, or a bed on a canvas. Translate the painting of that bed into three dimensions, and, oh, you are in trouble! Is it a bed to lie down on, or is it still a fantasy? We have reached the ambiguity between the figurative and the literal bed. Very frightening. [Series of rapid golden flashes, signalling intense danger.] But it is all mental anyway. One must lose one's conviction of reality, dispense with the main food of one's life. One must conclude that all is accident, question what is real, what is false, reach a state where there is no north, no south, no compass. I truly enjoy cutting the links with reality. But I am not proud of my success; I am not happy with it. Bring into being something really new, and nobody will understand it. I feel the need to change my work when I have success or someone imitates me."

Dubuffet lighted another cigarette and sent forth a comforting series of beams. "I feel that fun is the high point of the mind," he said. "There is a close and tender link between comedy and the very highest productions of the mind. New York has such a strong sense of jokes—even frightening ones. Often they are very serious. I hear them with my bacon and eggs in the morning at the counter across from my hotel. The whole place is joking, very seriously joking. The jokes are magic. They are like the highest point of a religious service." He was speaking slowly now, and not smiling. He blew out a long puff of smoke and watched it drift toward the figures. "Yes," he said. "The joke is magic. It brings the sanity of life into question. It questions the reality."

(1973)

Liberace

Our man Stanley somehow managed to snag a ticket to the Liberace concert at Madison Square Garden last Wednesday evening, and he dropped by the office several days later, still shaken, to leave the following notes:

"It's love, and love alone, that makes the world go round. Arrived outside Garden fifty minutes before concert, scheduled to begin at 8:30. Huge crowds pouring into place, police prowl cars standing by on Eighth Avenue, in case of emergency. Shuffled through, clutching passport to accommodations: Side Arena, Section 120, Row D, Seat 13, $5. First concert I ever attended with accommodations in side arena. Countless men in inner lobby wearing white cards attached to white hats, reading, 'NOVELTIES $1 NOVELTIES.' Men peddling Liberace souvenir programs. Cries of 'Program! Official program! Here's your program! There is no other program!' Thought maybe I was at hockey game. Bought official Liberace program. One dollar. Directed to seat toward west end of Garden, overlooking platform on floor of arena occupied by giant grand piano—top up—and musicians' stands. Garden filling fast, mostly with women of forty-one plus, wearing glasses. Men present, too, but subdued-looking. Buzz of romantic expectancy in air. Settled down in seat, read souvenir program. Read 'LIBERACE (pronounced Liber-AH-chee) was only four years old when he seated himself for the first time at the family piano in Milwaukee and then proceeded to unveil the soul of a supersensitive child as he played simple melodies seemingly with some strange and invisible guidance.' Rapidly turned pages to pictorial section. Saw picture of Liberace at home, sitting at edge of piano-shaped swimming pool. Saw picture of Liberace having Sunday buffet with Mother Liberace. Saw picture of Liberace giving autographs to fans. Also saw pictures of Liberace's brother, George Liberace. Read 'George has developed a flair for comedy.' Getting on toward 8:30. Excitement mounting. Musicians entered, took seats. Many women in Garden carrying binoculars. Program hawkers now shouting their wares inside Garden. Garden draped with American flags and red, white, and blue bunting; huge turquoise hanging at west end with piano symbol. All seats filled now, with exception of several in uppermost reaches of east end, at approximately eighteen thousand feet.

"Lights dimmed at 8:48. Magnificent stir throughout huge assemblage. George Liberace appeared, to applause, raised baton, conducted orchestra in something by Bizet. George looked tired. Multicolored spotlights focused on southwest corner of Garden, where elephants emerge during circus. Tense moment. No sound in entire Garden, other than heavy breathing. The entrance! Liberace! Himself! A poem in white tie, white tails, white shoes, and pancake makeup! Auditorium beside itself. Scenes of pandemonium. Ladies waved handkerchiefs, chirped greetings, shouted welcome. Cries of joy! Great happiness! Liberace smiling like well-fed baby. His dark curls gleamed under spotlights. 'It's a dream come true,' he said. 'Playing here tonight! Did you count them, George?' George smiled wanly. 'I wonder if we could turn on all the lights,' said Liberace. All lights immediately turned on. Liberace able to grasp size of audience for first time. Obviously delighted. Sat down at piano, burst into 'Cornish Rhapsody.' Fast and loud. Strong fingers, this fellow. Loves to run them up keys, back down, then up again. Series of runs and flourishes. Pedal work difficult to analyze. Keeps pumping feet up and down and sidewise, as though he were on electric horse. Keyboard technique interesting. Bang, bang, bang; up, down, back up. Ended number with huge gesture—hands in air, high over head, and head thrown back. Triumphant. Women beside themselves. Shrieks and cries. Liberace still smiling. George looked tired.

"Liberace introduced entire orchestra, one by one. Said they were all great. Played Parisian number, played Mexican number (George shook gourds, slowly), played number of his own creation, sang song to himself, sang 'Cement Mixer (Put-ti, Put-ti).' All numbers pretty much the same—up keyboard, down keyboard, up again, bang, bang, bang. Talked about some of his television sponsors—a tuna firm, a railroad, a tissue company, a detergent outfit, and a beer crowd. Mopped his brow with handkerchief, said it was 'the beer coming through.' House beside itself with laughter. Talked about inspiration he had received from Paderewski. Said Paderewski last pianist to give solo concert in Garden. Said he wanted to dedicate next number to Paderewski and to Chopin. Said he and Paderewski had same ideas about music, played for happiness of masses. Masses applauded. Played some Chopin. At conclusion, Liberace introduced his mother. Fine-looking woman, under spotlight, in side-arena box. Liberace wept. Crowd wept.

"Liberace announced intermission but promised to return and 'go real crazy.' Mother Liberace held court during intermission, leaning over box to shake hands with well-wishers. Photographers ever-present. Great scenes of affection and appreciation for Mother Liberace. Liberace returned after intermission in gabardine dress suit. More banging. Liberace disappeared for a moment, reappeared to do hayseed act, with tattersall vest and farmer hat. Did a soft-shoe shuffle around stage. Reminded me of Paderewski, and old days at Garden. Auditorium hysterical. Liberace disappeared again for a moment, returned through elephant door wearing brocaded dinner jacket. 'I'm not the least bit tired, if you're not,' he said. More banging. Up keyboard, down keyboard, up again. Liberace called for request numbers. Ladies began to shriek titles. Liberace played medley. Recognized 'Tea for Two.' Sounded like 'Tea for Three Hundred.' Grand finale—head thrown back, hands over head. Thanked throng. Thanked mother. Promised to return and play in Yankee Stadium."

(1954)

Notes on Freedom

For our money, the most impressive moment in the I Am an American Day ceremonies in Central Park a couple of Sundays ago was a brief speech by Learned Hand, senior judge of the United States Circuit Court of Appeals for the Second Circuit (New York, Connecticut, and Vermont). Next day not a newspaper in town quoted his remarks, so we went down to the United States Courthouse on Foley Square to get a copy from the Judge himself. He is a rugged, stocky man of seventy-two, with bushy eyebrows. During our call he evidenced a tendency to prowl around his chambers, which are approximately half the size of the Grand Central waiting room. "Three or four people have called me about the speech," he said. "I'm glad they liked it." He handed us a typescript and we will quote some excerpts, with the wish that we had space for more: "Liberty lies in the hearts of men and women; when it dies there, no constitution, no law, no court can save it; no constitution, no law, no court can even do much to help it. . . . The spirit of liberty is the spirit which is not too sure that it is right; the spirit of liberty is the spirit which seeks to understand the minds of other men and women; the spirit of liberty is the spirit which weighs their interests alongside its own without bias; the spirit of liberty remembers that not even a sparrow falls to earth unheeded; the spirit of liberty is the spirit of Him who, near two thousand years ago, taught mankind that lesson it has never learned but has never quite forgotten: that there may be a kingdom where the least shall be heard and considered side by side with the greatest."

Judge Hand told us that all his decisions and speeches are written in longhand, frequently after hours of intense struggle. "For me, writing *anything* is like having a baby," he said. "I take long walks through the park and think and think before putting down a word. I don't deliver a speech to the trees, like Roscoe Conkling, or anything like that. Never dictate. Can't get the hang of it. But I've written countless thousands of words, and the Definitive Hand," he said, pointing to the bookshelves, which lined the room from floor to ceiling, "is along those walls. Mighty dull stuff."

Judge Hand feels that latter-day oratory has taken a turn for the worse. "Too many people have other people write their speeches," he said. "Why, just the other night I was sitting on the dais with the waxworks at some banquet and a fellow rose and made some intelligent introductory remarks. Then he reached into his pocket, pulled out a paper, and said, 'I paid fifty dollars for this speech, so I better deliver it.' *I* ducked out." Judge Hand said that when he was a boy up in Albany, orators were the most envied personages in town. "There wasn't much theatre or music in those days, so the orator satisfied everybody's yearning for drama," he went on. "The orators talked a good deal of fustian—lots of Webster is fustian, for example—but they were creative and did their own writing and nobody much cared what they said." He had little traffic with Fourth of July speeches when he was young, concentrating instead on firecrackers, but his cousin, Judge Augustus Hand, who is also a colleague on the bench, took a more serious attitude toward Independence Day. He used to go out in the fields with his sisters and together they would read aloud the Declaration of Independence.

The maiden name of the Judge's mother was Learned; hence his first name. Few people can resist calling attention to its relevancy in his case. For instance, when President Conant of Harvard presented him with an honorary degree some years ago, the citation read, "A judge worthy of his name, judicial in his temper, profound in his knowledge, a philosopher whose decisions affect a nation." Judge Hand has been on the Circuit Court of Appeals since 1924; for fifteen years before that he was a judge in the

Federal District Court, Southern District of New York. Lawyers don't seem to mind much when cases of theirs are lost by reversals on appeal, if the reversal is made by Judge Hand, and jurists rank his decisions with those of Holmes and Brandeis. His remarks in Central Park were a simplification of many earlier speeches and a lifetime of thought. "Democracy can be split upon the rock of partisan advantage," he told us. "Believe me, if majorities in legislatures pass bills merely to press their advantage and say, 'Let the courts decide,' liberty will not be preserved in the courts, it will be lost there." Judge Hand moved to the window and looked down on Foley Square. "I believe Holmes felt that way," he said.

(1944)

Mr. Secretary

Dean Gooderham Acheson, the forty-ninth Secretary of State of the United States of America, has been engaged most of his life in a running battle with his appearance. He is an impressive example of the maxim that there is more to a man than meets the eye. What meets the eye that looks at Acheson is an austere, tall, slim, long-legged, and outrageously mustached fashion plate, a parody of the diplomatic virtues, with matching tie and handkerchief, brown leather dispatch case, and black homburg. The discrepancy between the outer Acheson and the inner Acheson is huge. The inner Acheson is gregarious and warmhearted, possessed of a quick wit and a skeptical mind, impatient of procedural form, self-analytical to an advanced degree, and a taskmaster who will accept from himself nothing less than what he considers perfection. Often, shifting from foot to foot at an official function, Acheson is painfully conscious of the impression his appearance is making on strangers. Some perverse devil deep inside him compels him to play—for a time, at least—the role expected of him. Not long ago, at a particularly humid gathering of people who concern themselves with foreign affairs, the outer Acheson pulled noncommittally at his mustache, raised and lowered his thick eyebrows in a manner that could signify everything or nothing, engaged in talk so small as to be almost invisible, and bowed from the waist with punctilio. Not until a stranger in striped trousers approached him and said fatuously, "Mr. Acheson, you must be proud indeed of your achievements in life" did the outer Acheson send forth a hurry call for the inner Acheson. "Sir," replied the secretary, dipping into his gag file, "all that I know I learned at my mother's knee, and other low joints."

The secretary's remark was characteristic but inaccurate. His formal education was extensive and included attendance at such high joints as Groton, Yale, and the Harvard Law School. At Groton, he learned that people are expected to have a fervent juvenile loyalty to something about which they basically don't give a hoot, such as a freshman class or a baseball team. "At Groton, I didn't happen to feel like conforming," Acheson said recently, "and to my surprise and astonishment I discovered not only that an independent judgment might be the right one but that a man was actually alive and breathing once he had made it." At Yale, he learned that life can be fun. At Harvard, he learned that the human mind, though complicated, is probably the most effective instrument available for solving the problems of the human race. "This was a tremendous discovery—the discovery of the power of thought," Acheson says. "Not only did I become aware of this wonderful mechanism, the brain, but I became aware of an unlimited mass of material that was lying about the world waiting to be stuffed into the brain. It was just one step further to the philosophic approach to matters—to learning that you need not make up your mind in advance, that there is no set solution to a problem, and that decisions are the result of analyzing the facts, of tussling and grappling with them."

Acheson's informal education has been even more extensive, and certain aspects of it have been equally fruitful. When he graduated, fifth in his class, from the Harvard Law School, Felix Frankfurter, who was then teaching at Harvard, recommended him for the post of law clerk to the late Louis D. Brandeis, an associate justice of the Supreme Court. Acheson received the appointment and remained with Brandeis two years. They were years of hard, almost uninterrupted work. Justice Brandeis believed that the quality of a man's work was more important than the quantity, that there was something attainable beyond "best," and that anything less was not enough. A man of fiercely moral makeup and with an acute feeling for the larger problems of society, he sharpened these same things in Acheson. The association with Brandeis was not confined to the justice's chambers, and a strong bond developed between the two men. "Throughout these years we brought him all our problems and all our troubles, and he had time for all of us," Acheson said when, two decades later, in 1941, he spoke at Brandeis's funeral. "In talk with him, the problems answered themselves. A question, a comment, and the difficulties began to disappear; the dross and shoddy began to appear for what it was. . . . I have heard him speak of some achievement of one of us with all the pride, and of some sorrow or disappointment of another with all the tenderness, of a father speaking of his sons. We are the generation which has lived during and between two wars. We have lived in the desert years of the human spirit. Years when the cry was 'What is truth?' . . . In a time of moral and intellectual anarchy and frustration, he handed on the great tradition in the mind and spirit of man."

Acheson's association with Brandeis led to friendships with other members of the Court, notably the late Oliver Wendell Holmes, who appears to have been a magnet to anyone who came anywhere near him. The influence of Holmes was of quite a different character. Whereas Brandeis exhibited certain of the forbidding qualities of an Old Testament prophet, Holmes was a caustic, aged, all-wise Grand Lama. In his wisdom there was a magical, twinkly leaven. Brandeis saw through to the heart of a matter after a painstaking sifting of the evidence, then reached his conclusion and stood four-square behind it. Holmes followed the same process, but having reached a clear conclusion he could, with equal sureness, demolish his own argument. Throughout his early years in Washington, Acheson paid monthly calls on Justice Holmes at his house. The Justice did most of the talking. "I felt that he had all knowledge in his head," Acheson says. "Of course, the old man relished his nuggets. He would hit on a rich, ripe phrase and repeat it over and over. He used to say and say again that man was created to form general principles and none of them was worth a damn."

Acheson's intellectual style is his own, but observers of his career feel that it happily shows the influence of both Brandeis and Holmes. As a practicing attorney in Washington on and off for twenty-eight years, he was further schooled in the value of objectivity in the face of facts. "Dean never let facts throw him," a former legal associate has said. "He always maintained a cool detachment. Some lawyers get so steamed up they think their client is the Lord God Almighty fifteen minutes after he has stepped into the office. Acheson always saw the client as representing a soluble

problem, and little more." Some years ago, a prominent New York indus-
trialist asked Acheson's firm—Covington, Burling, Rublee, Acheson and
Shorb—to handle the appeal of a case that had been badly bungled in the
lower courts. Acheson agreed to plead the case in a higher court, came to
New York to talk over matters with the client, and that same day wrote a
brief that was a model of conciseness, clarity, and persuasiveness. The
client ordered several hundred copies printed on deckle-edge rag paper
and planned to distribute them among his plant managers, executives,
and salesmen. A couple of evenings later, he spied Acheson at a table in the
Oak Room of the Hotel Plaza, nursing a nightcap and pulling abstract-
edly on his mustache. "Mr. Acheson," said the client, wringing his hand,
"your brief is a work of art, a masterpiece of legal thinking." Acheson gave
the man the long, gentle, tolerant look he reserves for persons whose enthusiasm gets the better of them. "Not a bad brief," he said slowly. "It
almost convinced *me*."

Acheson's convictions are numerous and deep, but for the most part he
naturally confines his official remarks as secretary of state to clear exposi-
tions of established public policy. His speeches are an anomaly in Washington, since he writes most of them himself and they are in English that
can be parsed. They are seldom indicative of anything beyond the outer
Acheson, the lawyer-diplomat stating his case in formal terms. Of the
North Atlantic Treaty, for example, he has said, "The treaty is the practi-
cal expression of the determination that an aggressor cannot divide these
nations and pick them off one by one." Of the United Nations, "The future of America is closely related to the extension of democratic principles
and practices in other areas; we believe the United Nations is the proper
agency for promoting that extension by peaceful and proper means." Of
the anticipated meeting in Paris of the Council of Foreign Ministers, in
the spring of 1949, "I cannot . . . honestly state whether or not this new
attempt will end in success. No one can tell. The answer will have to await
the meeting." Once, however, in the summer of 1946, when he was under-
secretary of state, Acheson revealed to a public gathering some of his more
private thoughts. Invited to address the Associated Harvard Clubs in Boston, he accepted, with the intention of discussing in generalities some major problems facing the State Department. A few of the younger men in

his office felt that there was no point in his making that kind of speech. "Dean," one of them said, "why not put down on paper what's really on your mind? To hell with the old-fashioned speech!" The under-secretary decided to take the suggestion. On two successive evenings, he sat at his desk in his study writing in longhand. He kept a Scotch highball at his elbow and sipped from it occasionally, the more readily to summon the inner Acheson. The result was a speech entitled "Random Harvest," which holds a high place among Achesoniana. As Brandeis and Holmes were in their day, Acheson is the center of an admiring and devoted group of young men, mostly lawyers with a Harvard background, and in this circle "Random Harvest" is favored reading. In it, his friends feel, the two Achesons merged and found a common expression. "If one is to spin from his own visceral wisdom," Acheson declared at one point, "he must say, first, 'I shall not be a fake,' and, second, 'What do I know, or think I know, from my own experience, and not by literary osmosis?' An honest answer would be, 'Not much; and I am not too sure of most of it.' . . . One thing, however, seems pretty sure—that the tasks which grow out of the relations of our country with other countries are hard ones. . . . For a long time we have gone along with some well-tested principles of conduct: That it was better to tell the truth than falsehoods; that a half-truth was no truth at all; that duties were older than and as fundamental as rights; that, as Justice Holmes put it, the mode by which the inevitable came to pass was effort; that to perpetrate a harm was always wrong, no matter how many joined in it, but to perpetrate it on a weaker person or people was particularly detestable. . . . Our institutions are founded on the assumption that most people follow these principles most of the time because they want to, and the institutions work pretty well when this assumption is true. . . . It seems to me the path of hope is toward the concrete, toward the manageable. . . . But it is a long and tough job and one for which we as a people are not particularly suited. We believe that any problem can be solved with a little ingenuity and without inconvenience to the folks at large. . . . And our name for problems is significant. We call them headaches. You take a powder and they are gone. These pains about which we have been talking are not like that. They are like the pain of earning a living. They will stay with us until death. We have got to understand that all our lives the danger, the uncertainty, the need for alertness, for effort, for discipline will be upon us. This is new to us. It will be hard for us. But we are in for it, and the only real question is whether we shall know it soon enough."

The secretary of state leaves his ivy-covered, white-doored red brick house, on a quiet street in Georgetown, at approximately ten minutes to nine in the morning. In one hand, he carries his brown dispatch case. On his head there is a black or a gray homburg. These cool mornings, he wears a trim, gray topcoat. His sartorial equipment stops just short of undue elegance. He is partial to gray or blue suits with white stripes, ties with commanding, colorful diagonals, highly polished shoes, and blue-and-white candy-striped shirts with stiff white collars. In the morning light, his big reddish-gray mustache is an object of remarkable distinction. It has a personality of its own, and people who have happened by and seen Acheson emerge in the morning have often experienced the disquieting illusion that two entities are on their way to work, the secretary and the secretary's mustache. "Honestly," a neighbor who goes to work at about the same time said recently, "some mornings the mustache appears to be a step or two ahead of the secretary; other mornings it appears to be a step or two behind." There is a solid basis for this illusion. Acheson is enormously fond of his mustache. It is for him not only a major link with his past but a guide to his present and his future. As a public figure, Acheson without his mustache would be like Roosevelt without his smile or Churchill without his cigar, but the mustache is more than a convenient cartoonist's symbol. Acheson's father, the late Edward Campion Acheson, Episcopal Bishop of Connecticut, wore a mustache, too—a Guardsman's mustache, thick and imperious, with a disdainful droop. While still in college, young Dean cultivated a similar growth, partly in defiance of and partly out of respect for his father. Throughout his early years at the bar and his first years in government service, his mustache was large, unruly, and reasonably aggressive. It was a pushy mustache, but its very pushiness betrayed it owner's uncertainty. Not until Acheson had become undersecretary of state, in 1945, was the mustache somewhat reduced in size and tilt. Though it once seemed about to climb his cheeks, like a vine seeking the sunlight, it now is comparatively self-controlled and at peace with itself, quietly aware of its responsibilities. While still bushy, it is no longer impenetrable, and while still giving off gay hints of the unpredictable, it is the adornment of a man who has conquered not only himself but his mustache. Acheson uses no wax or artificial flattener on it. He engages a great deal in the art of thinking, and with some violence, and while doing so he unconsciously pulls on the mustache and this gives it a bristly, well-tailored appearance. Most mornings, when Acheson leaves his house, taking a sharp look up and down the street from his front door, moving briskly along his short brick walk, and almost leaping down a flight of stone steps to the street, he and his mustache are in perfect harmony. On mornings when the secretary is disturbed by a problem, the mustache asserts its independence, once again giving the impression of being a separate entity.

The secretary walks to work. On every morning that it isn't raining, he covers the distance—a matter of a mile and a half—in the company of Justice Frankfurter, who is now one of his closest friends. Some mornings, Frankfurter, a short, bouncy man, picks Acheson up in front of the secretary's house (they live three and a half blocks apart); on other mornings they meet at an agreed-upon spot. Conversation, on a variety of topics, is the mainstay of their walks. Frankfurter is one of the celebrated conversationalists of our day, and, whether he is standing or sitting, his talk covers a staggering range of subjects. Acheson himself is no slouch at conversation, but it's possible that he is at a slight disadvantage when on foot. Both men jealously guard the contents of their talks. "I'll tell you one thing," Justice Frankfurter said a while back to an inquiring acquaintance. "We never talk about the government or foreign policy. We just talk." Heading down a tree-lined street of Georgetown, they would be an artist's delight—the small, compact justice taking two or three steps for every seven-league one of the tall, rangy secretary, and both engrossed in conversation. On overcast mornings, the justice's car creeps along behind. If it starts to rain, the two men hop in and the driver proceeds to the Department of State. The department, which used to be in the antique, fricasseed structure across the street from the White House, on Pennsylvania Avenue, is now housed in a seven-story building that was constructed just before the last war for the War Department, which later moved to the Pentagon Building. It is in a section of Washington locally called Foggy Bottom, a term that refers not to the State Department or its policies but to the fact that it is a low area near the Potomac and often foggy.

About nine-fifteen on a good morning, the secretary and the justice, still talking, round a corner of the State Department Building. They walk together as far as the front steps. Acheson says good-bye to Frankfurter and starts up the steps. On four out of five mornings, Frankfurter has one final morsel of conversation, and he calls after Acheson, who pauses to listen and then goes into the building. Frankfurter's car then picks him up and takes him to the Supreme Court Building. Acheson enters his official world through a dark lobby, with square marble pillars, reminiscent of Egypt and of Hollywood, and takes a private elevator to his office, on the fifth floor. He steps from the elevator into a panelled waiting room containing some chairs and sofas upholstered in blue leather and several small mahogany tables. When he became secretary of state, the walls of the antechamber were hung with colored reproductions of modern American paintings, including a Fiene, a Hurd, a Zorach, a Levi, and a Marsh. Mrs. Acheson, herself a painter, felt that the room should have something different, and she borrowed several lively primitive prints from the National Gallery as replacements. These include one of Old Rough-and-Ready Taylor on his horse. She also borrowed some scenes of the Mexican War, but out of diplomatic discretion the secretary saw to it that they weren't hung. Acheson enters his office from the antechamber through a dark wood door. He is still staggered by the size of his office. Not long ago, he said of it, "I always have the feeling that I am walking into the cabin-class dining saloon on one of those old North German Lloyd liners." It is of Mussolini-type proportions, with a huge refectory table at one end, beneath a large oil of former Secretary of State Henry L. Stimson. The secretary's desk, a massive mahogany object installed in Secretary Marshall's day, is midway along the windowed side of the room. His chair is high-backed and upholstered in red leather. At one side of his desk is an unabridged dictionary, at the other a globe of the world illuminated from within. This is also a holdover from the tenure of Secretary Marshall. Against the wall opposite is a tremendous grandfather's clock. High above the clock, almost at the ceiling, are two dark paintings, which Mrs. Acheson borrowed from the Smithsonian Institution, one of the signing of the

Treaty of Ghent and the other, painted by Mrs. Acheson's grandfather, John Mix Stanley, of the signing of a treaty with the Cherokee Indians. In a corner of the room is a group of comfortable red leather chairs, a sofa, and a coffee table. On the table are generally a dozen books of paper matches bearing the seal of the Department of State.

Acheson has a personal office force of two assistants—Lucius Battle, a young lawyer, and Miss Barbara Evans, who has been shuttling with Acheson between his law office and the Department of State for years—and three stenographers. Once Acheson has deposited his homburg and top-coat in a closet and has sat down at his desk, either Battle or Miss Evans brings him the Logbook, a black leather-bound loose-leaf volume with "Top Secret" in silver across its cover. In the Logbook have been placed copies of the most important cables (to and from State Department offices in all parts of the world) of the last twelve hours. These have been carefully winnowed out by the Communications Room, the twenty-four-hour-a-day nerve center of the department. Within a few minutes, the secretary can bring himself up to date on the latest developments in the more critical problems facing the department. Under each cable is a note or two of pertinent information. Acheson studies them until nine-thirty, and sometimes, following a practice that goes back to his early days in law, jots down salient points in longhand on sheets of yellow foolscap. Then, unless, of course, hell has broken loose somewhere in the world during the night, he holds a conference with Under-Secretary of State James Webb, Battle, and Carlisle Humelsine, the Director of the Executive Secretariat. Humelsine is the traffic policeman in charge of all the messages flowing in and out of the offices of the secretary and the under-secretary. His office is halfway down a lengthy corridor that begins at Acheson's office and ends at Webb's, a chamber as vast as the secretary's. These meetings generally last half an hour. During them, Acheson discusses the new cables and plans his day's work. From ten o'clock on, his day is more or less flexible. He may start out by meeting with a group of departmental experts to discuss important business. In conference, he follows a well-established pattern. Leaning far back in his red leather chair, taking notes in pencil, he listens to each man's exposition of his conception of the problem and his suggested remedy. Occasionally, Acheson asks a question, but he rarely expresses an opinion until everyone else in the room has had his say. He then summarizes what he has heard, points out the conflicts between the several points of view, attempts to reconcile them, and finally offers a solution based on the other men's opinions and his own. "His summations are much on the order of those of a fine judge charging a jury," a State Department official recently said. "He weighs, balances, thinks, and then gives his orders." Acheson may hold four or five such meetings during a morning, and meet briefly with foreign diplomats or other visiting dignitaries as well. In his encounters with foreign representatives, he is almost invariably good-humored, sympathetic, brief, and cryptic. Lord Halifax, the British ambassador to the United States during the war, saw a lot of Acheson at that time. Halifax, a master of diplomatic nuance himself, once remarked to a friend that he envied Acheson's skill in that field. "I would be halfway back to the embassy, still chuckling over some remark of his, before I realized that he hadn't told me a single, blessed thing," Halifax said.

Acheson is aware that a large number of visiting foreigners are eager to have a conversation with him, however short, to enhance their prestige back home. He obliges as far as he can, making the interviews as short as possible. Not long ago, a politician who had held high office in a Western European country and was attempting a comeback asked for an appointment to see the secretary. "I really didn't have the time," Acheson told an acquaintance, "but I knew that this fellow would be crushed if he couldn't cable back home that he had stepped across the threshold of the secretary of state's office. He had nothing to say, I had nothing to say, but he badly needed the cachet of having been in the office of the secretary of state. He was very friendly to us during the war, so I had him in. He entered ceremoniously, bowed ceremoniously, shook hands ceremoniously, and said, 'Mr. Secretary, what of the future?' 'What of it?' I said, and the man shook hands and left. He had achieved what he wanted, and I had lost, at the most, forty-five seconds."

On Wednesdays, at eleven, the secretary holds his weekly press conferences in the State Department auditorium, three floors below his office. Usually a hundred or more newspapermen turn up. Acheson's conferences rank high in attendance and popularity, as Washington press conferences go. Their popularity is indicative of the importance of foreign affairs in America today, but Acheson is more than a little responsible himself, because he brings his wit into fairly steady play during the sessions. Wit is in short supply among high government officials. There is a good deal of unconscious humor and an overabundance of horseplay of the hotfoot and dribble-glass variety, but little wit. From time to time, however, the shock of hearing a secretary of state operate with the light touch is more than some of the old press hands can take, and Acheson guards himself against being too funny. Lately there have been complaints that he is also guarding himself against saying yes or no and has been falling into the Washington habit of talking around a question.

Acheson prepares himself assiduously for his press conferences. Every Tuesday night, he takes home a portfolio of reports and memoranda on topics that he and his aides think may be asked about by the journalists in the morning. For several hours before he goes to bed, he studies these and sketches out his answers. The consequence is that he is rarely presented with a question he is not prepared to answer. In a single conference, he may be called upon to discuss Ruhr policy, the ex-Italian colonies, the Egyptian ruling house, Indonesia, China, Tito, the extension of the lease on the United States Air Force base at Dhahran, an obscure section of the United Nations Charter, the atomic bomb, the financial condition of the United Kingdom, and several score other topics, the consideration of any one of which would have been considered a half week's work by a secretary of state a quarter of a century ago. Acheson is ruefully amused by the eagerness of the press. "One of the happy things about this conference," he said one Wednesday, "is that I learned what it was about over the radio before leaving the house. That seemed to me to be a triumph of modern journalism." On another occasion, he told the assembled group, "There is a certain dilemma between the great need for as full and as quick public information as possible and the equally great need for a certain amount of privacy and calm in reaching a formulation of the matter which you are going to discuss publicly." He is adroit at ducking a question he doesn't want to answer. Asked for detailed information on the postwar allocation of steel to Germany, he replied, "You have now gone over the narrow edge of my knowledge." Occasionally, to avoid answering, he will fall back on reminiscence. "I'll tell you a story," he said one morning in response to a query about something still secret. "My old law partner Judge Covington once went to an oyster roast down on the Eastern Shore of Maryland and had a fine time eating those wonderful oysters, until he was handed a red-hot one. Why, that oyster must have been two hundred and seventy degrees Fahrenheit. Old Judge Covington took one look at the oyster and said, 'A man would have to be a damn fool to swallow *that* one.' " "Thank you, Mr. Secretary," said a voice from the rear of the room, and the conference was over.

Fridays, at ten, the secretary attends Cabinet meetings at the White House; every other Thursday afternoon, he attends a session of the National Security Council, a group consisting of the president, the vice-president, the secretary of state, the secretary of defense, the three service secretaries, and the head of the National Resources Planning Board. Mondays and Thursdays, at twelve-thirty, he goes over to the White House to talk with the president. He may see the president two or three times more every week, and he talks with him frequently on the phone. Like the other Cabinet officers, Acheson has a white telephone on his desk that is connected by direct wire to the White House. The relations between Acheson and Truman are among the happiest in Truman's official family. Cynical observers have said that Truman admires Acheson because he looks the way the president thinks a secretary of state *should* look. "If Harry were a painter, and had never laid eyes on Acheson, and sat down to paint a picture of a foreign minister, he would come up with a life-size oil of Dean," a Republican congressman once remarked. Seated in the president's oval office threshing out questions that would stagger the gods, the president and his secretary of state hit it off in a curiously old-fashioned comfortable, confident manner. Superficially different, the two men have startlingly similar aspects. Both come from small towns—Truman from Independence, Missouri, Acheson from Middletown, Connecticut—and both have roots in a relatively carefree and easygoing America. Politically and economically, both are to the left of what is customarily known as center but are lodged there in a conservative way. Both have a highly developed sense of loyalty. When Acheson appeared before the Senate Committee on Foreign Relations during the hearings on his nomination for secretary of state, he spoke of his concept of the job. "The policies which President Truman has followed since he took office have been evolved with the help of two secretaries of state," he said. "I served under both of them as their under-secretary. I think I know something of the circumstances and the problems which the president's actions were designed to meet. I think I know something of the need in American foreign policy for steadiness and continuity. During these years and the four years preceding . . . I think . . . I learned something about the function of an adviser to his chief— that that function was to be frank and forthright and vigorous in counsel, that it was to be energetic and loyal in accepting decisions and carrying them out."

"I would imagine," said Senator Tydings, "that there is also the inference that when any situation came up that you felt you could no longer adhere to, you would no longer be a member of the president's family."

"I anticipate nothing as unhappy as that, sir," replied Acheson, "but should it arise, of course your answer would be the only answer that an honorable man could give."

For his part, President Truman undoubtedly remembers that when he returned to Washington from Independence in November 1946, after the Democratic Party had taken a severe beating in the congressional elections, Acheson was the only high government official on hand to meet him at Union Station.

Acheson carries to his meetings with the president what he calls his Briefing Book, a loose-leaf volume of summaries of problems he wishes to discuss. He is never didactic or dramatic with the president, and asks him to question any ambiguous passages in his presentation. "Acheson never pushes a policy with Truman," a State Department official said a few weeks ago. "Rather, the two of them appear to evolve a policy working as a team. Of course, Acheson skillfully plants a seed here and a seed there, but he never marks them as his own and he wants no credit for them." From all reports, President Truman is delighted with the working methods of his secretary of state. Secretary Byrnes is said to have proceeded somewhat arbitrarily, rather than by the patient, detailed, step-by-step method toward which Acheson is disposed. The president was so awed by Secretary Marshall that the relationship was never an entirely natural, relaxed one. Truman has perhaps more respect for Marshall than for any other living man—a feeling shared by Acheson—and this very fact made it impossible for the president to establish a give-and-take relationship with him. The president is unstinting in his praise of Acheson. "He's doing a whale of a job," he told a recent visitor at his office. "One of the finest men in government, and the results are already showing. I never wanted him to leave government service in the first place, but as I've said many times, you need an elephant hide and a barrel of money to stay." "A great chief," Acheson frequently murmurs to his aides in the State Department after a call at the White House.

On Mondays, the secretary has lunch with the rest of the Cabinet at the White House. Other days, he lunches across the corridor from his office, in a small, upper-echelon dining room containing a half dozen or so tables and pallid etchings of several of our embassies. Ordinarily, he goes into the dining room by himself and sits down with two or three other top officials wherever he finds an empty chair. The conversation is mostly confined to State Department business. Acheson generally eats a light lunch and returns to his office for sessions with a steady stream of department officers. He holds many telephone conversations with senators and representatives, sometimes about vital business, sometimes about nothing more pressing than a request for a letter of introduction to the ambassador of some country a friend of a congressman intends to visit. The secretary is on chummy terms with a host of congressmen, partly because he was once assistant secretary of state in charge of liaison with Congress. Much to the surprise of many of his friends, he got along famously with the senators and representatives; he not only had a great affection for various members of Congress but had as many rambling jokes stored away in his head as Vice-President Barkley. He took a liking to meeting with Leslie Biffle, the secretary of the Senate, and Biffle's cronies in Biffle's office in the Capitol, where bourbon and branch water are consumed in moderate, *gemütlich* quantities and state business is discussed in an atmosphere of anecdote and knee-slapping.

Of necessity, Acheson devotes considerable time to congressional relations. When the State Department is advocating a piece of legislation, he may spend as much time on Capitol Hill as in his office, appearing in executive session before a congressional committee or at an open hearing in one of the large, marble-pillared rooms in the Senate or House Office Building. Open hearings have the atmosphere of a bullfight, with the secretary as the bull. The bull usually emerges from the fight unscathed. The sessions ordinarily begin with the secretary's reading a prepared statement in a dull, bored, nasal voice. Acheson is not at ease with prepared statements; they cramp his style. He comes into his own during the question-

and-answer period. He has often sat for two or three hours under steady questioning, for several days running, without losing his poise or his air of deep concern with every question. He will repeat phrases like "You are entirely correct, sir," or "I cannot see how the position could be better expressed," or "I am glad you brought that matter up, Senator," with such conviction that sometimes, before the question period is over, the members of Congress are pleading the proposition Acheson has set out to prove.

Acheson tries to finish each working day by being alone in his office. "It's humanly impossible to handle all the problems that come across this desk in a day," he told a caller a few weeks ago. "I try to delegate as much authority as possible and leave myself toward evening with just a little time to think. There are usually half a dozen crises on hand before supper, you know." The secretary's late-afternoon thinking is frequently interrupted by the flow of paperwork. All day, Mr. Humelsine, down the corridor, has been gathering papers for the secretary's signature. He has devised a method whereby Acheson does not lose much time in scanning them. Every paper to be signed reaches the secretary's desk clipped to a batch of other papers pertinent to the matter involved. He can simply read the first page of the attached batch, which summarizes the facts and presents the recommendation of the department, or, if he has doubts about the problem, refer to the attached file. A small green oblong blotter bearing the word "SIGN" in black letters is clipped to the paper to be signed over the point where Acheson's signature is to be placed. At six-thirty sharp, in a garage in the basement, Rudolph, the official chauffeur of the secretary of state, tunes up the secretary's official black Cadillac. Upstairs, sometime between six-thirty and six forty-five, having walked approximately a quarter of a mile up and down his office in deep thought, and having stopped at his desk to sign twenty or thirty papers, Acheson crams a challenging bunch of documents into his dispatch case, puts on his homburg and coat, descends in his private elevator to the basement, gets into his car, and goes home for supper.

Few things delight Dean Gooderham Acheson quite so much as reminiscing about his childhood. The more complicated his official life becomes, the more pleasure he derives from taking a rare few moments off to recall, wistfully and sometimes perhaps romantically, certain aspects of his early days. Once he gets going on the life of a small boy in Middletown, Connecticut, at the beginning of the century (i.e., himself), only pressing problems of state can divert him. Early last spring, during a brief lull in the delicate negotiations for the lifting of the Berlin blockade, the secretary sat down in his office with a reporter to talk over the old times. As Acheson spoke, the pressures of his high post seemed to lessen. Features that are normally forbidding—his bristly reddish-gray mustache, his penetrating, almost popping eyes—became youthfully and gently mischievous. Crossing and uncrossing his legs, the secretary painted an idyll of boyhood in which every lad on every block was a Tom Sawyer, every day was filled with explosively carefree adventure, and there was chicken every Sunday. Suddenly, the door swung open, and an aide looked in. The secretary waved him back and said, "Just a couple of minutes more, please." He continued for a couple of minutes to spin his tales of pony rides and Wild West shows, of sandlot ball games and hitches on ice wagons, until, once again, the aide interrupted. "I must see you for a few minutes, sir," he pleaded. His arms were filled with papers. Acheson got up and turned to his visitor with a shrug and a sigh. As the reporter left, he noticed that the secretary's mustache, a moment before as impish as a false mustache attached by a piece of wax to the face of a small boy, was stiff and commanding.

Dean Acheson was born with at least a silver-plated spoon in his mouth. His father, an Englishman of Scotch-Irish descent, emigrated in 1881 from England to Canada, studied for the Anglican ministry at the University of Toronto, received his theological degree, and came to New York as assistant rector of St. George's Church. Soon thereafter he married Eleanor Gertrude Gooderham, a member of a wealthy Canadian distilling family, and moved to Middletown, a town of twenty thousand, thirty miles north of New Haven, on the Connecticut River, where he became rector of Holy Trinity Church. The Achesons settled down in a large, roomy brick house on an elm-lined street, where two sons and a daughter were born to them. Acheson's father, who became Episcopal bishop of Connecticut in 1915, was tall and imposing, had decided views on a variety of topics, from child-raising to the need for improving conditions in factories, and in the house often wore a blue jacket with bright silver buttons. Shortly after Dean was born, on April 11, 1893, a neighborhood couple brought two of their sons, in their teens, to call one evening. "Fine boys you have there," said the rector. "Where do they go to school?" He was told that they attended a new academy called Groton, and that they were receiving what appeared to be a sound, classical, and disciplined education. "I have a new son upstairs," said the rector. "We'll enter him in Groton." "And that's how I went to Groton some fourteen years later," Acheson recalled not long ago. "Father's method was direct—a simple question asked and a decision reached."

For the first few years, his elementary education was put in the hands of a governess, but he persistently managed to elude her with admirable ingenuity and light out in his pony cart. In those days, the secretary says, a child didn't have many serious problems. "Today, heaven help them, children face nothing but problems," he says. "They can't do this, they can't do that. They dare not go into the street, for fear of being run over; they must not stay in the house, for fear of becoming sheltered. Our pleasures in Middletown were of the simplest, most beautiful kind. The high spots of each day came after supper, at twilight. There were two major events. One followed immediately after the other. First, all the boys and girls raced down to the firehouse, where every evening the shining wagon and the well-brushed horses were brought onto the street. Firemen slid down poles. The horses and wagon were put back in the firehouse. That was all, but, oh, what pleasure! With perhaps sixty seconds to cover the distance, everybody then raced to the wharf to watch the arrival of the Hartford boat. She stayed only a couple of minutes, picking up passengers, and started downriver toward the Sound, on her way to New York. To me, it seemed that the ladies and gentlemen promenading the deck of that ship were the most fortunate people on earth, and watching them, night after night, I imagined myself ploughing across the open sea, some nights to Europe, some nights to China, some nights to darkest Africa. But the moment the boat disappeared, I was happy to be still in Middletown—there were so many things to do."

The comings and goings of the Hartford boat were young Acheson's only contact with the world beyond Middletown, except for occasional excursions to New Haven with his father. "From the time of my first trip to

New Haven, Yale was the college I wanted to attend," Acheson says. "This was, in a sense, strange, since Wesleyan is in Middletown, and one of the juicy thrills of my boyhood was to make for the Wesleyan ball field and hang around the outfield for an hour or so during batting practice. Sometimes, if you hung around long enough, a fly ball might come your way and you were allowed to catch it and toss it back to some big boy with a *W* on his sweater, who would sometimes actually say, 'Thanks, kid.' A rather impressive moment." Problems of foreign policy rarely intruded upon the Middletown cosmos. "The only foreign-policy problems I remember," Acheson says, "were created by Father, who would always hang out the British flag on Queen Victoria's birthday, enraging the Irish, and the Irish flag on St. Patrick's Day, scandalizing the so-called proper elements. When the Boer War came along, Father chose to side with the British, and this made the Irish quite sore. They were never sure where he stood—nor was anybody else, for that matter. But really, as far as problems beyond our shores went, why should anyone have been bothered by them? The pattern of one's life in Middletown had an ordered regularity. Life flowed easily and pretty democratically. Take Mr. Bostick. Poor Mr. Bostick! Everybody was upset about *that*. It shows how much people cared in those days. Mr. Bostick was a conductor for the New Haven Railroad, on the Saybrook-Hartford run. He was also in overnight charge of the train and was supposed to see it safely parked on a siding in Middletown. But by the time Mr. Bostick got to Middletown each evening, he would be famished. He'd leave the train out on the main track and go home for supper, and a brakeman would come along later and roll it onto a siding. One night the train went off the track, or rolled off the track, or something, and Bostick was docked thirty days for not having attended to his duties. Most of Middletown was incensed and felt it was a dreadful punishment and quite unjust."

Acheson's easygoing life came to an end when he went to Groton. He had been sent to Hamlet Lodge, a less lofty boarding school at Pomfret, when he was nine, but for only a short period. "The first thing I noticed at Groton was the seriousness with which teams were chosen and the sudden and arbitrary loyalties one was expected to entertain," he says. "Back in Middletown, if you wanted a ball game, you went out to a lot and found some other fellows and chose up sides. The games went merrily along until someone got into a fight or was called for dinner. At Groton, it was a more intense procedure." In 1911, outfitted with a splendid wardrobe and a fairly large allowance, Acheson went to Yale. He was only a passable scholar there, but he was a rousing success at the art of living. His classmates remember him chiefly for his dazzling wardrobe and his quick tongue. "Dean moved in a fast circle and seemed to have a great deal more money than he actually had," a former classmate recalled recently. "He was never what you could honestly call gay—just as he isn't today—but he was refreshingly bright, and intent upon enjoying himself. He shunned the abstractions, for example, and kept far from the literary life on the campus, or anything that might have smacked of culture with a capital *C*." Acheson rowed on the freshman crew but was too light to make the varsity. He joined a number of clubs, including the Turtles, the Hogans, the Mohicans, and the Grill Room Grizzlies. Mostly, the members met to talk, sing songs, and tell rather poor jokes. More important, Acheson was tapped for one of the Yale secret societies, Scroll and Key, a big tap in the Yale world.

After graduating from Yale in 1915, Acheson went on to Harvard Law School, where he roomed for a year with Cole Porter. Acheson was immensely stimulated by Harvard. He discovered that he possessed a mind and that, applied to legal problems, it functioned with ease and swiftness. In 1917, while still at Harvard, he married Miss Alice Stanley, the daughter of a Detroit railroad lawyer; she had been a roommate of his sister's at Wellesley. Soon after that, the United States having entered the First World War, Acheson signed up with the navy as an ensign in an overseas-transportation unit. He was stationed in the Brooklyn Navy Yard and never got overseas. After the war, he went back to Harvard, received his degree and served the two fruitful years under Brandeis. He then was invited to join the new Covington, Burling and Rublee firm. Today, the firm is among the most successful in the country.

One of the original partners, Edward Burling, a tall, thin, agile, sardonic-looking septuagenarian who bears a resemblance to the fictional Mr. Tutt, is still active in the firm. According to his associates, Burling has a mind that can clearly see eight sides of every question. He has always surrounded himself professionally with young men who not only know law but give him intellectual pleasure. Impressed by young Acheson, he put him to work, as a starter, on an important case, a matter involving a number of neutral Norwegian ships that had been seized by the United States government during the war. Covington, Burling and Rublee represented the Norwegian government. The controversy was over the amount of reparations the United States owed Norway. The United States felt it owed no more than three million dollars; Norway felt she should get eighteen. Acheson spent a year digging into the law, went to Oslo in 1922, with Burling, and soon afterward pleaded his first case in any courtroom before the old Permanent Court of Arbitration, at The Hague. He was toweringly arrogant. On the opening day of the trial, mounting the staircase to the small box where pleading lawyers stood, he told the court that the attorney for the United States government had, a few moments before, insulted his client, the Royal Norwegian government. He demanded an apology.

"Do you mean to say that you are demanding an apology from your own government?" asked one of the five presiding judges.

"I am, sir," said Acheson. Burling, who was sitting in the courtroom, experienced a sensation of dizziness. He hurriedly scribbled a note, and handed it to an attendant.

"From your own government?" repeated the judge.

"Indeed, sir," said Acheson. At that moment, the note reached him. He opened it ceremoniously, read "For God's sake, come down fast," and went down the staircase, with aplomb. Mr. Burling mildly suggested a bit more caution, and Acheson remounted the stairs. He achieved a highly satisfactory settlement of twelve million dollars for Norway.

Back in Washington, Acheson settled into the traditional routine of a successful lawyer in a successful firm. He bought the house he still lives in, near the corner of Twenty-eighth and P Streets, in Georgetown, and enlarged it. The Achesons now have three grown children, as well as two grandchildren. Jane, their oldest child, is married to Dudley Brown, who is vice-president of the Milwaukee Gas and Light Co. David, a lawyer, works with the Atomic Energy Commission. Mary, the youngest, is married to William Bundy, who is associated with Acheson's old law firm. In the late twenties, the Achesons bought a piece of land near Sandy Springs,

Maryland, on which there was a run-down farmhouse built in 1795 as a tobacco barn, and set about remodelling it. Acheson is an incorrigible amateur architect and has often told friends that he feels he missed his vocation. The Achesons turned the house into a weekend place, a cozy maze of book-filled rooms and hooked rugs. During the twenties and thirties, Acheson kept horses and cattle. He rode strenuously and taught his children to ride. "The riding lessons were supposed to be taken quite seriously," his younger daughter said not long ago. "Father insisted that we have the proper form on a horse, and no excuses."

Given complete freedom of professional choice, Acheson would unquestionably have patterned his legal career after that of the English barrister, who pleads cases before the courts but has no direct contact with the people whose cases he is pleading. Clients often bored and distressed Acheson. He did not feel any obligation to comfort or sympathize with them. Some of them, desiring a combination legal adviser and family doctor, felt that he was too disinterested. In 1926, when he was thirty-three, he was made a partner in the firm. For years, although he was not even slightly charmed by the work, he handled a great many tax problems. Acheson's reputation, however, was made as an appellate lawyer for complicated cases. "Once you have acquired a reputation as a noted appellate lawyer, you get cases with a hopelessly sour posture," a prominent attorney has remarked. "Once one of our kind gets into the mists and convolutions of appellate work, he is doing splendidly, we like to think, if he emerges victorious in ten percent of his cases." Acheson won around twenty percent of his cases before the United States Supreme Court. A lost case often brought him as much kudos as a victory, lawyers being as sensitive to the skill of a jouster as to the decisions he wins. In 1931, in a case that gave him considerable renown, Acheson represented the State of Arizona in a suit against the States of California, Nevada, Utah, New Mexico, Colorado, and Wyoming. Arizona wanted to retain what she thought was her just share of the water of the Colorado River for irrigation. That share, she claimed, was threatened by the building of Boulder Dam, a project to which the other states, under an act of Congress, were parties. At one point in his argument, Acheson offered to prove that the Colorado River was not navigable and hence the federal government had no jurisdiction over it. The Colorado River, he said, was a wild, turbulent stream. It had deep gorges, rapids, falls, treacherous curves, and other deathtraps. It was beautiful—one of nature's incomparable pearls—but not navigable. The Supreme Court thought otherwise. Justice Brandeis, who was like a father to Acheson, delivered the blow. Records had revealed to the Court that ten or twelve voyagers had navigated enough of the river to render it legally navigable. Among them was one unsung hobo on a raft.

In 1933, when Franklin D. Roosevelt became president, one of Acheson's close friends, Lewis Douglas, of Arizona (it was Douglas who had wanted Acheson to take on the Arizona case), urged the president to appoint Acheson solicitor general. The president had someone else in mind for that post, but he made Acheson under-secretary of the treasury. Acheson was forty. The secretary of the treasury, William H. Woodin, was ill most of the time he held office, and a large portion of his work was turned over to Acheson. Acheson was spiritually inclined toward the New Deal, but temperamentally he was never entirely at home in the theatrical hurly-burly of its early days. Plans to improve man's lot on earth appealed to him enormously, but, being a lawyer, he occasionally felt the need for a few hours to think matters over. He was a vast admirer of the president and was stunned by the scope of Roosevelt's interests and the ease with which he could shift his attention from one large project to another. Early in the New Deal era, Acheson went to the White House with a group of other government people to see the president. The door to his study was open. Seated at his desk was Roosevelt, surrounded by a milling group of advisers. In his mouth was his long cigarette holder, cocked at the customary angle. Someone thrust a paper at him. He read it rapidly and signed it, listened briefly to two or three of his advisers, smiled, jotted down some notes, answered the telephone, signed some more papers, whispered to a man at his elbow, and, glancing toward the door, spied the waiting group outside. "Come on in!" cried the president. "We're doing a land-office business!"

Acheson parted company with the administration less than six months after he had become under-secretary. The president, in his desire to hoist prices from their disastrous Depression level, got the notion that he should fiddle with the price of gold. Acheson demurred. The government, he claimed, lacked the right. The president is said to have replied, impatiently, that he was interested in finding a method of accomplishing what he had in mind, not in being told that the scheme was impossible. Stanley Reed, now an associate justice of the Supreme Court and then counsel for the Reconstruction Finance Corporation, upheld a plan by which the government would raise the price of gold, and thus devaluate the dollar by buying gold with discounted Reconstruction Finance Corporation short-term obligations. Once again, Acheson demurred. "Those were trying days for Dean," one of his old friends, a distinguished legal scholar, recently said. "He had run head-on into the great moral dilemma of our age: At what point can undesirable means be justified by a socially desirable goal? In other words, when do you, in all conscience and pondering the imponderables, break the egg to make the omelet?" Quite a few of Acheson's well-to-do friends considered the scheme simply a scatterbrained fantasy, likely to destroy their hearths and homes. Although displeased with their point of view, Acheson found himself, for an entirely different set of reasons, on their side. He took the problem to his friend Brandeis, who fortified his former law clerk's resistance to the proposal. Acheson sent the president a memorandum expressing his objections to the Reed plan. "Quite clearly," he wrote, "it would not be a discount justifiable for revenue purposes . . . to consider it as a discount at all within the meaning of that term as used by legislators would be to open wide the door for any and every kind of manipulation for ulterior purposes." Would Mr. Acheson be willing to accept an opinion from the attorney general, the president asked the Treasury Department. Of course, replied Acheson. He added that he was also willing to resign. Before any opinion was presented, the president announced Acheson's resignation to a group of newspapermen, some of whom, in turn, mentioned it to Acheson, who had not been informed but was not entirely surprised. His code does not permit him to show distress, shock, or disappointment, and when his successor, Henry Morgenthau, Jr., took the oath of office, he was on hand, cool, genial, and in complete control of his mustache. The president, a man with an acute appreciation of gallantry, watched Acheson throughout the ceremony. When it was over, he said, "Dean, you're a sport!"

Feeling none too sporty, Acheson returned to his law firm. He had more clients than he could handle, and he prospered, but he was not a contented man. "Something came over Dean," a former partner said a while ago. "At some point along the road, he lost a measure of his self-confidence. He began to ask himself questions—where he was going, by what route, for what reason—and this was a new and strange experience." One thing that bothered Acheson was his attitude toward the practice of law. What had originally appealed to him was the excitement of the pursuit, through a labyrinth of circumstances, of a logical solution to a problem, but now this pursuit was only mildly exciting. "Dean took pleasure in finding the answers to riddles," the former partner said. "The nature of the riddles did not concern him. He was not a man to wander into the penumbra of thought." Acheson practiced law through the rest of the thirties, but he also kept up an interest in public affairs. He had enjoyed government service.

Acheson supported Roosevelt in 1936 and again in 1940. He was deeply concerned about the rise of Hitlerism, and he became an influential member of the Committee to Defend America by Aiding the Allies. "We must focus the full power of America," he told the fortieth-anniversary convention of the International Ladies' Garment Workers' Union, in 1940, "first, to produce the materials with which the free peoples of Europe may fight; second, to prepare ourselves to fight; and, finally, to harden and discipline our wills so that if and when the moment comes we shall not be defeated by irresolution or doubt." Acheson felt that the survival of one free nation was bound up with the survival of all free nations. It was inconceivable to him that the United States should watch Great Britain go down without making every effort to save her. In August of that year, along with Charles C. Burlingham, Thomas D. Thacher, and George Rublee, Acheson signed a lengthy and now historic letter to the New York *Times*, setting forth, in involved legal language, the proposition that old United States destroyers could legally be exchanged for British bases without congressional sanction. The letter, which was composed by Acheson, created a furor in Washington. "Dean, when he made up his mind about the destroyer deal, once again faced the great moral dilemma," the legal scholar who commented upon his attitude toward the gold problem said in the same conversation. "The free world had to be saved. Those old destroyers would help to save it. Dean is a resilient man, and here was a case in which the eggs, in all conscience, could be broken—indeed, *had* to be broken."

In February 1941, Acheson was appointed assistant secretary of state by Roosevelt. He held office in the State Department for six and a half years—through the days just before this country got into the war, through the war itself, and through the disillusioning period that immediately followed it. He served as assistant secretary under Hull and Stettinius and as undersecretary under Byrnes and Marshall. In those years, he mastered the workings of the Department of State and mastered himself as well. When he entered the department, his mustache was a good quarter inch longer at each end than it was when he resigned, in the summer of 1947. Its diminution was almost imperceptible—a slow, gradual change, signifying his increasing self-confidence. He was then known in Washington as the "Number One Number Two Man," a term he did not relish. His assignments were of the kind that could be called big and hot potatoes. Under Hull, he was, among other things, in charge of coordinating economic matters in the Department of State. Many people in the department had the impression that their duties were identical with his; practically every fourth person considered himself an economic coordinator, or at least an economist. Acheson soon came face-to-face with large, amorphous, intense, prerogative-minded groups in charge of such matters as trade agreements, the gathering of vital commodities, the collation, analysis, and hashing over of economic data, and the preparation of speeches based upon the collation, analysis, and hashing over of the data that had been collated, analyzed, and hashed over. He also came face-to-face with stray, isolated groups, some of which had gone without solid food for months. While Acheson was economic coordinator in a State Department of seven thousand employees, and while handling the subsequent hot potatoes, he had an opportunity to learn more about the intricate inner workings of the State Department than any other high departmental officer within memory. Now that he is secretary of a State Department with twenty-two thousand employees, this knowledge is of inestimable value. "Acheson is one of the few foreign secretaries, in any country, who are not, in a sense, trapped by their departmental experts," a student of foreign policy has observed. During his early years as assistant secretary, Acheson many times felt like resigning. He was restrained by his sense of duty and by the notion that he would be doing himself a great disservice if he withdrew a second time from the government.

Except for one trip to Montreal, Acheson remained in this country all during the war. He attended neither of the Roosevelt-Churchill-Stalin conferences, but by the end of the war he had rung up a record for attendance at international conferences in the United States. He had a great deal to do with the formation of the International Bank for Reconstruction and Development (at the Bretton Woods conference), the United Nations Relief and Rehabilitation Administration (at a conference in Atlantic City), and the Food and Agriculture Organization (at a conference in Hot Springs, Arkansas). His most difficult task came each time after the conference was over, when he had to go before congressional committees and plead for the passage of implementing legislation. His approach to a conference was all business. When there is official work to be done, he has a compulsive desire to get it done. To his amusement and occasional dismay, he discovered that a great many international conferences had a way of turning into *Kaffeeklatsche*, at which old League of Nations hands would renew acquaintance and talk over the bittersweet days on the shores of Lake Geneva. He displayed a cultivated impatience less toward the time-consuming social side of the conferences than toward their tendency to postpone action by wandering down procedural bypaths. Perhaps in part because of this attitude, some of Acheson's critics accuse him of being unsympathetic toward the United Nations. Many other observers see no possible basis for this accusation. In the spring of 1949, he informally told the members of the United States delegation to the General Assembly that he was heartily in favor of the foreign ministers' attending the opening session as "an outward and visible sign of our inward and spiritual grace."

Acheson occasionally became conference-happy, notably at the gathering that resulted in the formulation of U.N.R.R.A. At Atlantic City, he worked eighteen hours a day, rising at seven-fifteen, having breakfast with assistants to plan the day's program, meeting all day in conference sessions, having a cocktail around five or six with delegates, eating dinner with his assistants, and then returning to his hotel room for four or five more hours of studying tables, charts, and reports. One night, reading a speech over the radio, he deviated from his prepared text and announced that U.N.R.R.A. aid of two billion dollars was contemplated. The text said two billion five hundred million. A newspaperman later asked him what had become of the missing half billion. "A split-second decision after a martini," Acheson said. Although noticeably weary by that time, he insisted upon exactitude in the wording of U.N.R.R.A. agreements, suggesting, for example, that a phrase in a paragraph that dealt with eligible beneficiaries be changed from "expectant mothers" to "pregnant women." "A maiden aunt of fifty-one told me once that she was an expectant mother," he told a group of foreign delegates. "What you mean here is 'pregnant women.' " The delegates, aware that they were dealing with a man with a Continental mind, willingly made the change.

Patience, a prime requisite for a successful career in diplomacy, came slowly to Acheson, by nature an impatient man. His wartime dealings with Russian representatives taught him the necessity for patience. "In the old days before the war, Dean would argue quite eloquently with many of his young associates," one of his friends has said. "The Soviet system was a tyranny, he would say, and make no mistake about it. But once the coalition had been struck—and he believed it was the only course to victory—he determined to do everything he could to see it through. The Russians would haggle over some point, get it settled—or appear to get it settled—and then be back in his office two or three days later for more haggling. Dean gritted his teeth, kept his temper, explained and explained and explained that we were friends, that we wanted to be friends, then and after the war." Patience became a pressing personal necessity in Acheson's life in 1944, when his daughter Mary was stricken with a lung ailment and went to Saranac to recuperate. Mary, who had been doing code-breaking in the War Department, had been in the habit of spending a half hour over a bedtime glass of milk with her father in the kitchen. She would tell her father what was on her mind, and he would tell her some of the things that were on his. These sessions had become a ritual, and when Mary went to Saranac, a large gap was left in both their lives. Acheson knew that only a slow cure would restore his daughter's health. What his temperament demanded was a quick one. He resolved that he would never betray his impatience or his anxiety. Every evening while Mary was in Saranac—she was there for more than a year—he sat down at the hour he used to talk with her in the kitchen and wrote her a long, chatty letter. To cheer her, he began each letter with a family joke. Acheson took up gardening to occupy his mind. He began to raise dahlias and gladioli and became expert in the growing of bulbs. "Mary's illness marked a tremendous crisis in Dean's life," an old friend said recently. "It was perhaps more important to him as a statesman than meeting with hundreds of diplomats or tackling hundreds of ticklish world problems. He became reconciled to slow, hard answers to difficult questions."

As assistant secretary of state, Acheson's salary was nine thousand dollars a year, a small figure compared with his income at the bar. In the summer of 1945, he told Secretary Byrnes that he could no longer afford to continue in office. Both Byrnes and President Truman urged him to remain, but he said that his decision was final. He went to Saranac to visit his daughter. Byrnes telephoned him there and said that President Truman refused to accept his resignation, insisted that he accept the post of undersecretary, and had already dispatched his private plane to bring him back to Washington. Although the new job paid only a thousand dollars more a year than the old one, Acheson found it impossible to resist; it would place him near the highest level of government service. He accepted the appointment and flew back.

Byrnes was out of the country two hundred and forty-five of the five hundred and sixty-two days he held office, leaving Acheson behind as acting secretary. One of the most important questions he faced was the problem of international control of atomic energy. He knew that the creation of the atomic bomb upset the whole relationship of nation to nation. World peace, he felt, depended to a large extent upon a swift, intelligent attack on the problem. If an atomic-arms race could be avoided by the setting up of an international agency devoted to the gradual, safeguarded sharing of atomic knowledge by peacefully inclined nations, the world, he was sure, had a reasonable chance of preserving itself. Byrnes appointed Acheson chairman of the secretary of state's Committee on Atomic Energy, which included Vannevar Bush, James B. Conant, Major General Leslie R. Groves, and John J. McCloy. This committee appointed a Board of Consultants, consisting of David E. Lilienthal, as chairman, Chester I. Barnard, Dr. J. Robert Oppenheimer, Dr. Charles A. Thomas, and Harry A. Winne, to prepare a report "anticipating favorable action by the United Nations Organization on the proposal for the establishment of a commission to consider the problems arising as to the control of atomic energy" and "to study the subject of controls and safeguards necessary to protect this government."

While the Board of Consultants was preparing its report, Acheson learned as much as he could about atoms. He asked Dr. Oppenheimer to stop by his house from time to time in the evening and give him an informal lecture on the subject. Oppenheimer would turn up with blackboard and chalk. Each of the sessions lasted for several hours. Oppenheimer has since remarked that Acheson grasped the essentials with astonishing speed. When the Board of Consultants brought in its report, Acheson ironed out some major differences of opinion between his committee and the Board of Consultants. Several members of the secretary of state's committee felt that the report was excellent as far as it went but that it should give a more detailed exposition of methods of setting up and operating international control. "You have a fine ship here," Dr. Conant is said to have remarked, "but how are you going to get it in the water?" Overcoming some opposition, Acheson convinced everybody that a chapter, to be composed by Dr. Oppenheimer, should be added to the report to cover this ground. "Acheson was a remarkable chairman, especially in the way he helped us reach workable compromises," a member of the Board of Consultants said not long ago. "He helped, too, by stressing in his introduction to the report that it was not a final paper but, as he put it, 'a place to begin, a foundation on which to build.' " The report, known as the Acheson-Lilienthal Report, was the basis of the proposals made by the United States to the United Nations in the Baruch Plan, accepted by the U.N. Atomic Energy Commission, and approved by the General Assembly, for control of atomic energy. The Russian government, however, has not approved, and for the moment, at least, the atomic situation is deadlocked.

When Marshall succeeded Byrnes as secretary of state, in 1947, Acheson agreed to remain in the State Department for only six more months. This time, he said, he would not change his mind; his financial situation demanded a return to the law. Like Byrnes, Marshall was away from the State Department much of the time, and again Acheson was acting secretary. Marshall, Acheson, and Will Clayton, who was roving about Europe for the department on economic missions, all independently reached the conclusion that Europe's economy could be restored only by large-scale aid from the United States. Marshall realized this from the moment he began to deal with the Russians; their policy, he felt, was to stall European recovery. Clayton, travelling from country to country, came to understand Europe's need for dollars to strengthen shattered currencies and replace destroyed factories. Acheson, at home, scanning reports and surveying the problem from the vantage point of distance, is credited in Washington with having evolved many of the details of the Marshall Plan. The first inkling that it had been formulated was contained in a speech Acheson made before the Delta Council, a gathering of farmers and planters, at Cleveland, Mississippi, in May 1947. President Truman was to have addressed the group, but he was unable to attend, and asked Acheson to speak in his place. Instead of preparing a routine speech, Acheson, at Marshall's suggestion, jotted down some of Marshall's, Truman's, and his own thoughts on United States aid to Europe. Armed with a rough draft of a speech, he climbed into the president's plane and flew to Mississippi, putting the finishing touches on his speech while aloft. The plane landed in a large field outside Cleveland, where a welcoming committee greeted Acheson and took him to the schoolhouse for a fried-chicken lunch and then to the school gymnasium, where several hundred farmers, in galluses, were awaiting his talk. Acheson removed his coat, discarded his prepared text, and spoke to the group earnestly and at length. The gist of his remarks added up to the Marshall Plan. Acheson went back to the field in a station wagon and, while the plane was being warmed up, drank a mint julep prepared by his hosts. A month later, Marshall, feeling that the time was ripe for a pronouncement by the secretary of state himself, delivered an address at the Harvard Commencement exercises, dropping a large hint that if European nations were interested, the United States was willing to give them aid.

Acheson resigned from the state department in July of 1947 and returned to his law firm. He especially regretted severing relations with Marshall, with whom he had worked in a harmonious atmosphere occasionally lacking during the regimes of other secretaries of state. For the next year and a half, although pleased to be with his old partners again, he had a gnawing desire to get back into public life. "Once a man has tasted public power, he probably never forgets the taste," a former law associate of Acheson's said recently. Acheson pleaded several civil-rights cases and, as vice-chairman, under Herbert Hoover, devoted a great deal of time to the work of the Commission on Organization of the Executive Branch of the Government, paying special attention to increasing the efficiency of the State Department. When Truman was elected, in November 1948, he almost immediately asked Acheson if he would become his secretary of state in January. Acheson, surprised, but knowing that Marshall intended to resign, accepted with solemn enthusiasm. "It has taken years and years," he told a close friend, "but now I am on my own."

The after-dark activities of Rudolph, who has been for over twenty-five years the official chauffeur of the secretary of state, indicate the extent of a secretary of state's social life. Under Hull, Rudolph was certain of going home every evening, and staying home, once he had driven the secretary to the Wardman Park Hotel, where he lived in Washington. When Stettinius succeeded Hull, Rudolph remarked to a State Department colleague, "The honeymoon's over." Stettinius was a gregarious man and spent many evenings visiting friends. Byrnes kept Rudolph on call nearly every evening. Since becoming secretary, Acheson has spent an average of only one night a week visiting friends or attending social functions. Unless there is a conclave of high-ranking foreign diplomats, and the concomitant schedule of full-dress events, Acheson usually stays home at night. These days, high government officials rarely give formal dinners at home; that custom died with the war. If Acheson is obliged to entertain visiting dignitaries formally, he does so at a hotel. He has had his name removed from the telephone directory, and only the most important phone calls are relayed home to him by the Department of State. Most evenings, he and Mrs. Acheson have a quiet supper together and talk a while. One or more of the Acheson children may drop by, and then the secretary will talk with them or maybe read aloud to them for a half hour. Felix Frankfurter may telephone to read Acheson a passage of a book he is reading. Acheson, in turn, may read Frankfurter a passage from a book *he* is reading. Occasionally, a friend stops in for a chat. Sometime before ten o'clock, Acheson usually goes into his study to put in several more hours of work. The Achesons spend almost every weekend at their house in the country. "I try to see that the secretary has a proper weekend—without interruptions," Mrs. Acheson says. They drive there on Saturday afternoon and remain until Sunday night, the secretary pottering about the farm in slacks and sport shirt. Lately, he has become interested in old furniture and has installed a small carpenter shop, where he hopes eventually to turn out replicas of antique chairs and tables. During the last few months, he has found himself taking so much State Department work along with him that his achievements up to now have not gone beyond a few wall brackets and other small knickknacks.

When friends make an early after-dinner call on Acheson in Georgetown, they usually find him sitting erect in a large upholstered easy chair by the fireplace in the living room. The room is an elegantly comfortable picture-book room, with large windows overlooking a brick-walled garden, soft draperies and lights, oil paintings, vases filled with flowers, and an English-country-house dignity. Acheson rarely discusses the broader aspects of his job with his friends. He is more inclined to relate a humorous incident of the day or to discuss the work of his visitors. Once in a while, though, he will speak for a moment or two about some of the problems that concern him most deeply. This happened one evening recently, when he and a friend were having a quiet talk about family life. "When you come right down to it, the purpose of foreign policy is to preserve the freedom of our homes," he said, "and also the freedom to do one's work, or move on and do one's work somewhere else. There are millions throughout the world with the same aspirations—to be allowed to live out their lives in their own way." The secretary of state thoughtfully pulled at his mustache. The secretary and his mustache looked equally calm and resolute. "War would end all this," he said. "War would mean regimentation— every man assigned to a hard task, dispersed industries, human beings living underground in caves like beasts, a nightmare. It would mean the very end of all freedom. Peace is freedom, and freedom is our life."

(1949)

Good of You to Do This

for Us, Mr. Truman

A friend of mine who works for Doubleday and Co., which has just published the first volume of former President Harry S Truman's *Memoirs: Year of Decisions*, called me up a couple of weeks ago and said that Mr. Truman was going to autograph copies of the book on Wednesday, November 2, in the grand ballroom of the Muehlebach Hotel, in Kansas City, Missouri. "I think you'd have a lot of fun out there," he said. "It's the first time, as far as we know, that a president or an ex-president has agreed to sit down and sign copies of his book. Mr. Truman says that he'll start at ten in the morning, stop at noon, resume at two-thirty, and stop for good at five-thirty. May I read you a letter he wrote me just the other day?" I urged him to fire away, and he said, "Mr. Truman wrote, 'I will set aside one day near the book's publication date, and I will autograph as many as I can. I am not an expert with a machine, and I would rather do it by hand. As you know, I am accustomed to signing my name a great many times a day. I cannot possibly enter into a program which would look as if I were selling autographs instead of a book. I want the book sold on its merits. If it cannot be sold that way, then it's not worth having. I have a very strong feeling about any man who has had the honor of being an occupant of the White House in the greatest job in the history of the world and who would exploit that position in any way, shape, or form.' "

I decided that I'd like to go out to Kansas City.

The train ride to Kansas City is a beauty. Overnight to St. Louis, change of trains for K.C. I boarded a Pennsylvania train called the Penn Texas at seven-forty on Sunday evening, and when I woke up the next morning, we were rolling across the flat, broad, golden Ohio countryside, somewhere between Columbus and Dayton. Soon we were in Indiana, and not much later we were speeding across Illinois. At East St. Louis, we crossed the Mississippi, and pulled into St. Louis's Union Station at around three. I got out (I had an hour between trains) and inspected the bold and impish fountain of Carl Milles, called *The Meeting of the Waters*, that stands in front of the station. The waters that were meeting were the waters of the Mississippi and the Missouri, and you could tell in an instant that Mr. Milles derived a great deal of personal satisfaction from their union. When I went back into the terminal and tried to open the locker I had put my luggage in, I had some trouble with the lock. An elderly gentleman who was walking by stopped and came over to me. "I can see you're having difficulty," he said, "and I should like to be of some service." He was, too, since he knew how to open the lock and I didn't. I thanked him, and he said that I was to think nothing of it, and that if I would just hang around St. Louis, instead of rushing away, I could see a great many fine things. He struck me as one of the most relaxed gentlemen I had ever met, and he was the advance guard of a whole population of relaxed gentlemen I was soon to meet in the Middle West. I thanked him again, and boarded a Missouri Pacific train for Kansas City.

This train was called the Colorado Eagle, and the dinner menu in the dining car was a far cry from the ham-sandwich, Ry-Krisp, and tomato-juice card that is so often presented on Eastern trains. I had my choice of fried oysters, roast loin of pork, club steak, rainbow mountain trout, or chicken flakes. A great many trimmings went with the dinner, such as herring tidbits and Waldorf salad. I ordered the rainbow mountain trout, along with Brussels sprouts and sauerkraut, and I hardly had time to notice that a lot of the men in the dining car looked like Harry Truman before the trout arrived. The sauerkraut was absolutely marvellous, and I told the waiter how much I admired it. A moment later, the chef was by my side.

He was a tall, dark man, and his face was a moon of happiness. "I understand that you like the sauerkraut," he said. I admitted that I did, and his smile grew even wider. "I *am* glad," he said. "It's got apples in it, and it's got bacon in it, and it's got mashed potatoes in it, and it's all strained." Then he added, "I got something for you," and ducked back into the galley, returning with some pickled cantaloupe rind. "Try that," he said. "We put that up ourselves." I tried it, and it was delicious. This fellow's attitude reminded me of my grandmother; she used to put up cantaloupe rind and would never let you leave her house unless you took along a jar of it, or of something else she had put up.

When I got back to my seat, the porter told me that I was foolish to sit up there in the Pullman with the rich folks—that I should head back into one of the Planetarium-Dome coaches, take a seat, and look out at the beautiful Missouri. He felt strongly about the Missouri, and I did as he suggested. The Missouri was indeed beautiful; we were running right alongside its bank. From those coaches you can see everything to the sides and ahead and above, including the gleaming red and green signals along the tracks. The moon was full, dusk was setting in, and I sat there until, before I knew it, we were in Kansas City, Missouri.

I hopped into a cab at Union Station and asked the driver to take me to the Muehlebach Hotel, where I had reserved a room. It was Monday night, and the autographing party wasn't scheduled until Wednesday, but I wasn't worried about how to kill the time out there, because I had written to Mr. Truman and he had told me to drop by his office on Tuesday and have a chat. I told the cabdriver that I had come out to Kansas City to watch the former president sign his books. "Saw Harry Truman just the other day," he said. "He was going into Frank Spina's place on Tenth Street for a haircut. See him all the time on the streets. I see him come downtown in the mornings along Truman Road—that used to be East Fifteenth Street— and then he goes into his office in the Federal Reserve Bank Building. That's at Tenth and Grand. Truman Road runs right out from Kansas City to Independence. It also runs from Independence to Kansas City." And then he added, "You know something? Harry Truman is going to fool them with this book, too." I asked whom he meant by "them." "Well," he said, "whenever Harry Truman starts anything, there's a crowd of them that think he's going to fall on his face. 'Them' are the people who don't know what's going on. Harry fools them every time. He always lands on his feet. I bought a copy of his book the other day at Frank Glenn's bookstore. Frank has sold thousands of copies of Harry's book, and he'll sell thousands more before he's through. For one thing, Frank's right there in the Muehlebach, and it stands to reason that if you got a bookstore right in the Muehlebach and Harry Truman is coming to the Muehlebach to autograph the book, why, you're bound to sell 'em. And this Frank Glenn is working every minute. He sells books in his sleep." This was the first cabdriver I had ever met who talked about books. "Here we are, Twelfth and Baltimore," he said. "You're at the Muehlebach Hotel, and I've enjoyed every minute of the ride."

The Muehlebach has a friendly lobby, done in wood of a rich mahogany color. The clerks are courteous—or at least the clerk who signed me in was courteous. "We're glad you're here," he said, and he sounded as though he meant it. The bellhop who took me to my room was an energetic fellow. I asked him if he ran into Mr. Truman often. "Mr. Truman and the Muehlebach have a lot in common," he said as he switched on the lights in my room, opened the window, and hung my coat in the closet. "You know, the night he was elected in 1948, he slept over at the Elms Hotel, in Excelsior Springs, and woke up at four o'clock in the morning and learned he had been elected president of the United States. He hustled right over here to the Muehlebach, and got here at five o'clock in the morning. He went straight up to the penthouse, which had been reserved for him. The president of the Dominican Republic is up there now, buying cattle. I have to go on another call now. The penthouse costs fifty-five dollars a day."

I went down into the lobby for a couple of minutes. Frank Glenn's bookshop, I noticed, has a Twelfth Street entrance and a lobby entrance. One of his lobby windows was filled with copies of *Year of Decisions* and a reproduction of an oil portrait of Mr. Truman. A sign pasted on the window read, "THE BOOK OF THE AGES BY THE MAN OF THE AGES." I wanted a drink, so I went into the Terrace Grill, where I came upon a lanky comedian piano player called Norm Dygon, who has solved, once and for all, the problem of working with a wooden dummy. He has the dummy somehow mechanically attached to a pedal on his piano (the dummy sits at an adjoining instrument), and by pressing his foot on the pedal Mr. Dygon can make the dummy stick his tongue out, raise his eyebrows, and play his piano. Mr. Dygon doesn't even have to be a ventriloquist; the dummy's voice is a tape recording. "Hail, hail, the gang's all here! Where the hell's the restaurant?" cried Mr. Dygon, while the dummy stuck out his tongue. At the end of his act, he inquired, "If you can't get a good steak, what's the use of living?" It was too late for a steak, and I went upstairs to bed.

The next morning, I called Mr. Truman's office, and one of his aides, Gene Bailey, told me to come right over. "It's only about six blocks from where you are, and it won't take you but a couple of minutes," he said. I went right over. The Federal Reserve Bank Building looks like some of the older buildings on Wall Street, or the big business buildings in cities like Cleveland and San Francisco. I got off the elevator at the eleventh floor and walked down a broad corridor. At one end of the corridor, a sign on a door read, "HARRY S TRUMAN, ROOM 1107," and an arrow pointed to the right. I went in the door to the right. A blonde lady at a desk said that Mr. Truman would see me in a couple of minutes and asked me to sit down. I took a seat beside a gray-haired man who had a copy of the *Memoirs* in his lap. Mr. Truman suddenly walked into the room. He came over and shook hands with me and asked if I would mind waiting a minute or two in a reception room next door. "I'll be right with you," he said. As I left the room, he was shaking hands with the gentleman who had been sitting next to me. The reception room was lined with green-backed volumes, all marked "POLITICAL SPEECHES—ORIGINAL." A calendar hanging on one wall had a picture of the Capitol and the legend "HOUSE OF REPRESEN-TATIVES." A self-possessed young man wearing tortoiseshell glasses came into the room and introduced himself as Mr. Bailey. "I'm glad to see you," he said. "The president will be with you in a minute." I asked him how he happened to be working for Mr. Truman. "It's interesting," he said. "I met him on a train. I was working for the Southern Pacific. After Mr. Truman left the presidency, you may remember, he and Mrs. Truman and Margaret took a holiday in Hawaii, and Averell Harriman lent him his private car as far as Ogden, Utah, which is as far as the Union Pacific runs, and at Ogden, I was delegated to pick him up and escort him to San Francisco on a Southern Pacific train. We had a great deal of time on that train to talk, and we talked. I had a fascinating trip. Some weeks later, when Mr. Truman got back from Hawaii, he wrote me and asked if I would like to be his secretary. And here I am. And I'm having a wonderful time."

"Well," said Mr. Truman, appearing in the doorway. "I'm sorry to have kept you waiting. Come into the office." He led me down an interior hall that was crammed with photographs and into a large, comfortable, warmly furnished room. Books filled one wall. Along the other walls were pictures of Andrew Jackson, Franklin Roosevelt, Miguel Hidalgo y Costilla, San Martín, and Bolívar. Also on the wall, I noticed, was a framed letter from Lewis and Clark to the War Department; it had something to do with an expense account for a hundred and sixty-one dollars. A couch was piled with copies of the New York *Times*. In one corner of the room was a bust of Chaim Weizmann. Several flags, all furled, stood behind Mr. Truman's desk. Mr. Truman sat down at his desk, and I sat down across from him. He looked fine. His complexion was pink, his face was firm, and his eyes gleamed behind thin-rimmed bifocals. He was wearing a brown suit, a brown-figured tie, and light brown shoes. "That was the Greek ambassador out there ahead of you," he said. "He wants me to come to Greece." He sounded as pleased as could be. I told him that I liked his book very much. "I hope you won't be disappointed with the second volume," he said. He sounded like any writer. He told me that he had dictated at least 60 percent of the book. "Right here in this room, too," he said. "It was a tremendous job, with all those documents and files to go through. I'd spend several hours each morning dictating. I called in a great many of my friends, such as Dean Acheson and John Snyder, to go over the manuscript, and we would sit and discuss disputable points. All in all, I must have dictated a million words or more, and we threw out a half million when it came time to publish the book. I'm not getting any tax break on this book—I'm paying 62½ percent. But that's not the point." Mr. Truman leaned across his desk. "I wanted to get the facts straight," he said, moving his hands up and down, parallel to one another and about twelve inches apart, in his familiar gesture of emphasis. "I have been misrepresented—outrageously misrepresented—and I wanted to put the truth down. I wanted to get the facts on record. Of course, the columnists who misrepresented me at the time will continue to do the same thing, and they won't like the book." He swung around in his chair toward a globe standing beside his desk. "There's the trouble spot now," he said, indicating the Middle East. "I'd do something about that. The trouble there goes back two thousand years. The Jews and the Arabs—they're like cousins, and, like cousins, they hate each other. Come along," he added, and he rose abruptly and led me back into the reception room.

Mr. Bailey was still there. "Gene," said Mr. Truman, "let's open that cabinet." Mr. Bailey opened a file cabinet standing against a wall. Mr. Truman reached in and brought out a thick packet of letters, in envelopes of different sizes, bound together with a couple of rubber bands. "These are the letters to my mother and sister," he said. "The ones I put in the book as the 'Dear Mama and Mary' letters. And across this room," he said, with a sweeping gesture, "is the bulk of the files that went into the book. Now I want to show you something else." He led me down the hall toward his office. "I've got something here I'm very proud of," he said, pointing to a photograph on the wall of the corridor. It was of him and Prime Minister Churchill. They were standing in front of a painting of a naval engagement, and an inscription, in Churchill's hand, read, "To President Truman, whose decisive stroke against aggression in Korea turned the fortunes of the Free World to the sure hope of peace." "That was taken aboard the presidential yacht, the *Williamsburg*," Mr. Truman said, "and I maneuvered Mr. Churchill in front of the painting." The painting depicted the sinking of the British vessel *Guerrière* by the *Constitution*, the forty-four-gun frigate known as *Old Ironsides*, on August 19, 1812. "Just as we were having our photograph taken," said Mr. Truman, "the old man turned to me and said, 'You put one over on us that time.'" Mr. Truman chuckled.

In his office, I asked him if he was worried about the autographing party, and he said no—he was used to signing his name, and he had often signed six hundred documents a day in the White House. "Once, in 1930," he went on, "when I was presiding judge of the Jackson County Court, I signed three thousand county bonds in two and a half hours. Of course, that's different from books, because the bonds are all lined up for you and you just run down the list." I asked him about the flags behind his desk. "That blue one is the presidential flag," he said. "That belongs to the presidency. I will always keep it furled, because it goes with the high office."

"Mr. Truman," I said, "in your book you mention the time that you were sworn in on the night President Roosevelt died. You say it was 7:09 P.M. I was wondering how you could possibly have remembered the time on that dreadful day."

"It *was* a dreadful day," he said. "Dreadful, dreadful." He led me out into the corridor again and showed me still another picture on the wall. It was a photograph of his swearing-in at the White House. There were Mrs. Truman and Margaret and Chief Justice Harlan Stone and members of the Cabinet, and there was Mr. Truman, his left hand on the Bible and his right hand in the air. "See that picture?" Mr. Truman said. "The very moment. And you will notice that the clock above the mantel, right below President Wilson, says seven-nine." He glanced at me and then broke into a grin. "But I looked at the clock at the time," he said. "I looked, all right." We went into the reception room again, and Mr. Bailey joined us there. I said that I wanted to go out to Independence and poke around. Mr. Bailey instantly volunteered to lend me his car. "It's fully covered," he said. I thanked him and said I'd take a cab.

"Whichever way you go," said Mr. Truman, "take Route 24 to Truman Road."

Mr. Bailey saw me out and asked me if he could pick me up later at the Muehlebach for dinner. I said I would be delighted.

I walked back to the Muehlebach, and after lunch, by one of those inscrutable coincidences, my cabdriver of the evening before was right in front of the hotel. I asked him if he would take me out to Independence. He said sure, and I got in. "We'll head first to the northeast," he said. "That's where the gang wars used to be. And then we'll head over to Independence Avenue—that's Route 24. We got a new thruway running through here—cloverleafs and all. Everything is cleaned up now. Kansas City, Missouri, is so cleaned up you can sneeze and cause a riot." After a few minutes, he said, "This is the Inter-City we're going through now. Not part of either Kansas City, Missouri, or Independence. There are two towns here, Fairmount and Sugar Creek, and they have their own mayors. Independence is a town of thirty-six thousand people; it's about eleven miles, or twenty-five minutes, from Kansas City, Missouri, and it's practically a suburb." At Van Horn High School we turned left onto Truman Road, which seemed to be nothing but a double line of auto-supply shops and auto sales agencies, including one called the Jack Garner Auto Company. A few minutes later, we were in Independence, and another left turn, onto North Delaware Street, brought us in front of Number 219, the Truman house—a twelve-room white house, Victorian Gothic, with a slate roof and a lawn amply covered with handsome maple leaves. There was colored glass in some of the front windows. An ancient flagpole stood in the yard, and a black metal fence surrounded the property. A motorcycle was parked across the street. There wasn't much traffic. The place had an air of self-assurance, dignity, and quiet. Mr. Truman has a large two-car garage with a green roof, which looks like a barn. We drove around the house, and then down to the center of town. It has the air of a frontier town that has gone to finishing school. There's a smell of the Far West about it, and yet it has a gentility and propriety that are unmistakable. I walked into the Herald Bookshop—the windows were filled with copies of Mr. Truman's book—and I noticed that most of the stock, aside from the general run of best-sellers and some children's books, consisted of religious works. There was a red-haired lady in charge. "We are looking forward to tomorrow," she said. "We'll be there for sure." I walked on down the street. A wooden Indian stood in front of Jay's Tavern. Walker's Café had a sign in the window reading, "BREAKFAST AT ALL HOURS," and another sign reading, "HAMBURGERS 15¢, 7 FOR A DOLLAR." Next to Earl's De Luxe Barber Shop was a store selling something called "Lucky Me Ointment." I walked into the Jackson County Courthouse. It housed the offices of the County Clerk, the Director of Buildings, the Sheriff, the Constable, as well as the Magistrate Courts. A plaque in a hallway read, "TO THE MEMORY OF JAMES HENRY SHEPARD, ONE OF THE EARLIEST SETTLERS UPON THE SITE OF INDEPENDENCE, MISSOURI, WHOSE NEGROES SAM AND BEN HEWED THE LOGS FOR THE FIRST JACKSON COUNTY COURTHOUSE IN 1827." I left the courthouse and walked across the street to S. S. Kresge, which had a parakeet department. The parakeets were a dollar and seventy-seven cents apiece, and a number of them were flying freely around the store.

On the way back to Kansas City, I asked my driver where I could find some good hot jazz. "There isn't much left out here," he said, "but if you go down to 5505 Troost Street, to Johnny Baker's Number Two Club, you'll hear something that will make you sit up and take notice."

When I got back to the Muehlebach, I went and said hello to Mr. Glenn, the bookseller, and he told me that he had already sold more than thirty-five hundred copies of the Truman *Memoirs*. Around six o'clock, Mr. Bailey met me and took me to dinner down near the stockyards, at a place called the Golden Ox. On the way, we passed a huge, lighted tower, on top of which stood a huge, lighted Hereford. I think that the three-dollar-and-ninety-cent Kansas City sirloin at the Golden Ox ("Where the Steak is Born") is the finest piece of meat I have ever tasted. After dinner, Mr. Bailey dropped me off at the Muehlebach, but I went on to Johnny Baker's Number Two Club. The jazz was sweet. When I got back to the hotel, I ran into some of the Doubleday people. They were as nervous as birds, afraid that nobody would turn out in the morning for the autographing. I told them not to worry—that Harry Truman would fool them every time.

The next morning, the phone in my room jangled violently. "Good morning!" said the operator. "It's eight o'clock, the temperature is thirty-nine degrees, and it's Harry Truman Day." I got dressed in a hurry, went downstairs to the coffee shop, had some breakfast, and then went up to the grand ballroom, which is about as big as the grand ballroom of the Waldorf-Astoria. It was nine-fifteen. There were some six hundred people in the room, every one of them with at least one copy of Harry Truman's book under his arm. Fourteen bookstalls had been erected around the edges of the ballroom, for the booksellers of Kansas City, Missouri, and Independence. The stalls were occupied by Cokesbury, Kline's, Macy's, American Baptist, Fred Harvey, Herald, Emery Bird Thayer, the Baptist Book Store, Bennett Schneider, Caruso, Frank Glenn, Ace Reed, Katz Drug, and the Jones Store Company. Each stall had a length of royal blue velvet draped over its counter, on which were copies of *Year of Decisions*. Ace Reed had a striking portrait of Mr. Truman's mother at the rear of its stall, and Mr. Glenn had removed the portrait of Mr. Truman from his window and put it in his stall. I spied Mr. Glenn, and we shook hands. "It's going to be a knockout," he said. A man called Sam Pasternak, a celebrated Kansas City confectioner, marched in with an immense cake in the shape of Mr. Truman's book. This was placed on an easel that stood on a platform at one end of the room. On the platform, too, was a table covered with royal blue velvet. A bottle of Parker Super Chrome ink stood on the table, and near it were three fountain pens, along with a vase of red, white, and blue carnations. This was the table at which Mr. Truman was to sit. Behind it were six unfurled American flags. To one side, a battery of television cameras had been set up. Although the people in the room were quiet, I had the feeling that there might be some trouble, for there were several lines of applicants in front of the dais, making it inevitable that a great many people would be crowding around Mr. Truman at once. At ten o'clock, a trio consisting of an accordion, a violin, and a guitar came onto the floor and struck up the "Missouri Waltz." They followed this with selections from *Oklahoma!* A few minutes after ten, there was a flourish from the trio, and the people in the room applauded. Mr. Truman walked in, looking as though he were having the time of his life. His bearing was military, and he marched with quick steps to the platform, where he sat down. Mr. Bailey took a seat at his right, and a stocky gentleman with dark glasses took a seat at his left. It was evident that Mr. Truman was attacking this task with great seriousness; he had obviously figured out his approach in advance. There were some eight hundred people in the room now, and the autographing was about to begin. The lines looked like the lines you see on Election Day—neighborhood people whom you know, but who keep their distance, because they have come to the polling place on a special, private mission.

Five hundred roses had been provided by the Floral Industries of Kansas City, Missouri, and these were distributed to the first five hundred women in the crowd. Mr. Randall Jessee, a jolly gentleman who works for Station WDAF-TV, in Kansas City, took hold of a microphone and said, "Ladies and gentlemen, welcome to Harry Truman Day." He then led his five-year-old daughter to the platform. She was carrying a copy of the book, and Mr. Truman signed it. It was evident that he was eager to get along with the signing. People stepped up, Mr. Bailey took their books, opened them to the page before the title page, handed them to Mr. Truman, who signed them and passed them on to the gentleman at his left. He signed "Harry S Truman" and nothing else, doing this with astonishing swiftness and mechanical precision. Whenever he looked up, he flashed a smile.

Whenever anyone spoke to him, he answered. A good many of the people were shy when they reached the platform, and said nothing. Others spoke up. A lady came by and said, "Will you last?"

"I've lasted many harder days, and I have worked overtime, too," Mr. Truman said.

The trio broke into "Tea for Two." The ballroom now had at least a thousand people in it. I walked around and noticed that there was a large number of small boys in the lines, some of them carrying as many as ten copies of Mr. Truman's book. At ten-twenty, the B'nai B'rith arrived, in a group, and presented Mr. Truman with an award.

"The B'nai B'rith Women's Division of Greater Kansas City proudly presents this distinguished-service citation in honor of his outstanding services in the cause of human relations," a lady in the group said, reading aloud from a printed document. Mr. Truman rose and accepted the award. "I may not deserve all the fine things you are saying about me now," he said, "but I hope to be worthy of them before I die." He still had a fixed smile on his face as he sat down and went back to the grind of writing "Harry S Truman," "Harry S Truman," "Harry S Truman." The long lines moved forward. "Good of you to do this for us, Mr. Truman," said a lady with a book.

"You're more than welcome," said Mr. Truman.

"I had eight boys in the service, Mr. Truman," said a lady with a book.

Mr. Truman looked at her and said nothing, and went back to autographing.

Shortly after ten-thirty, an assemblage of gentlemen wearing flowing cloaks of green and yellow and large turbans of green, yellow, and red arrived, and took up positions behind the president. There was a moment of genial and general handshaking. The Oriental-looking gentlemen were members of the Ararat Shrine of Kansas City, and they had just dropped in to pay their respects. They stood around behind Mr. Truman for quite a while. His pace seemed to be picking up. "I'm doing nine a minute now," he whispered to Mr. Bailey. "It was eight a minute a while back."

"The crowd goes all the way down the stairs to the lobby," a man from Doubleday said to me, "and out into the street, and it's *snowing*! They're standing out in the street in the *snow*." It was evident that he thought he had another *Ben-Hur* on his hands. A second group of Shriners arrived, and they, too, took up positions behind Mr. Truman. These gentlemen wore fezzes, rather than turbans, and together the two groups made quite a backdrop for the machinelike autographing that was going on at the table.

"I've come five hundred miles," said a gentleman to Mr. Truman, "and I would have walked every inch of the way."

"My thanks to you," said Mr. Truman. "I hit ten a minute there," he whispered to Mr. Bailey.

"Hello, Harry," said a gentleman.

"Hello, John," said Mr. Truman, signing John's book.

The lines moved on. They were endless. There was a sudden burst of noise as some thirty men marched into the room to the tune of "The Caissons Go Rolling Along." It was Battery D, 129th Field Artillery—Mr. Truman's battery from the First World War. Mr. Truman looked up and smiled, but he kept on signing. He was in the rhythm now and he wasn't going to stop. The turbans and the fezzes departed, Battery D took up its place behind him, and the signing went rolling along.

"My feet are killing me," said a lady to Mr. Truman.

"I'm sorry that you have to stand up," he replied.

A rather elegant lady in a purple dress and a fur piece stood in front of the table. "This is a great privilege, sir," she said, "and it is the only autograph in my sixty-three years of living that I have ever sought."

"Thank you," said Mr. Truman.

I thought that the lady's remark was extremely graceful, and I followed her to the ballroom exit. She was a Kansas City, Missouri, lady, and she knew a good deal about the Trumans. "People from the East don't know that the Trumans are aristocrats," she said. "And people from the East don't understand that the aristocrats of Independence are more aristocratic than the aristocrats of Kansas City. Independence was the gateway to the West—to the Santa Fe Trail and all the rest—and was where the covered-wagon trains started. They went to California from Independence. The mules and the oxen got rested up in Independence, and got put in shape. My daughter, who lives in Alabama, wrote to me when Mr. Truman was elected president in 1948 and told me how tickled she was, and I sent the letter along to Mr. Truman. He wrote back that the letter was a dandy. He also said that he had known he would be elected, because he could see it in the faces of the people. Take a look at him now. He's watching the faces, and the faces are watching him, and he isn't missing a stroke of his pen. He's always been that way. I've got to get home now."

There was a hubbub of excitement at the platform end of the grand ballroom. The lines had broken and people were crowding around Mr. Truman. An official of the hotel went to the platform and announced in a soapy voice, "You folks just going to have to stand around with love in your hearts and wait your turn." That did the trick.

Mr. Truman was scheduled to stop the morning session at noon. At noon, however, the ballroom, the staircase, and the lobby were still filled with people carrying books to be signed. Someone had the sense to close the ballroom doors, but that still left several hundred people inside. A man from Doubleday went over to Mr. Truman and told him that it was twelve o'clock. "To hell with it," said Mr. Truman. "I'm going to sign for everybody in the room. Lunch can get cold."

The man from the hotel again took the podium. "Don't let another soul in, Officer!" he cried to a Kansas City policeman at the door.

Mr. Truman made a brief speech. "I agreed to sign only one book a person," he said. "Lots of people are bringing in more than one book. I'll sign for everybody in this room, but just one copy. I'm hungry." There was applause. I caught sight of Mrs. Truman at one side of the room. She was talking with Thomas Hart Benton. Shortly before one o'clock, Mr. Truman had signed books for all the people left in the ballroom.

Mr. Truman went out to lunch at a restaurant around the corner called Bretton's with Douglas Black, the president of Doubleday, Mrs. Black, Mrs. Truman, and a small group from Doubleday. At two thirty-three, he again strode into the grand ballroom of the Muehlebach Hotel. The trio broke into a few bars of "Hail to the Chief" and then shifted to the "Missouri Waltz." Mr. Truman marched to the platform at his military gait, sat down, and started to sign his name again. The stairs were still crowded, the lobby was still filled, and people were still standing out in the street. It had stopped snowing. During lunch, some of the Doubleday people, having observed that the morning arrangements had been conducive to chaos, suggested that the afternoon crowd move through the ballroom in a serpentine line. Thus, only one person at a time would approach Mr. Truman. This worked well. Mr. Truman was in form. He was signing nine a minute. During a pause, I asked the gentleman on his left if he had known Mr.

Truman long, and he nodded, and handed me his card. He was Paul (Mike) Westwood, a member of the Independence, Missouri, Police Department. On the back of his card was the printed legend "I have been bawled out, balled up, held down, hung up, bulldozed, cheated, squeezed, and mooched on. I have been stuck for war tax, dog tax, and syntax. I have worked like hell and been worked like hell. I have been cussed, discussed, talked about and talked to, lied to and lied about—and the only reason I am sticking it out now is to see if I can't help make Independence a safer place in which to live."

Mrs. Truman had come back from the lunch and was sitting in a chair at one side of the room. I went over and introduced myself. "We did nothing all last summer but work on the book," she said. "We didn't do another blessed thing. I'm glad it's over—it's been a tremendous job. I don't know how he does all that signing. I signed ten notes yesterday at home, and my hand began to hurt. He has a trick of signing. People have been coming to me for my autograph, and I can honestly say no to them, since I have arthritis in my right hand. It's the first and only time that arthritis has been a blessing." The musical ensemble again struck up the "Missouri Waltz," and Mrs. Truman said, "I wish I had a nickel for every time I've heard the 'Missouri Waltz.' That's all I'd need." I said that she must be tired of sitting around and watching the signing of the books. "Out here in Kansas City we have plenty of time," she said. A Mr. Weatherford, the mayor of Independence, came over and introduced himself to me. "Come out to Independence and spend the night," he said. I told him I had to take a train back home. The line was still moving, and Mr. Truman was signing and signing. "There are other trains," said Mayor Weatherford. "They go every night."

The retired Episcopal bishop of West Missouri came up to Mr. Truman and handed him a book to sign. A man from Bombay presented him with a picture of Mahatma Gandhi. A lady presented him with a tie clip that bore the flag of the Confederacy. "Thank you for your strong right arm and your good heart for a day like this," said another lady. Still another lady, armed with four books, said, "My grandchildren can never say that I didn't love you, Mr. Truman." Mr. Truman kept smiling, and he kept signing.

I noticed a tall, eager-looking gentleman who was keeping people in line, and I introduced myself to him. "I'm Tom Evans," he said. "I'm one of Mr. Truman's oldest and dearest friends. Why don't you stay over a couple of days?" I told him I had to catch a train. "Oh, hell," he said, "the trains leave every day." I asked him what he did for Mr. Truman, and he said, "Twenty-five years ago, Harry Truman put me in charge of his wearing department."

"His what?" I asked, and he said, "For the past twenty-five years, I've been in charge of Harry Truman's wearing department."

I didn't have the nerve to ask him what he meant, and after a few minutes he turned back to the line. A reporter from the Kansas City *Star* was standing beside me, and I asked him if he had overheard the conversation. "I did," he said. "I did indeed, and he wasn't shooting you any bull. He's been in charge of Harry Truman's wearing department for at least twenty-five years." I asked if he would mind spelling the word. "Wearing," he said. "W-o-r-r-y-i-n-g."

The line was still endless, and the trio played on—mostly the "Missouri Waltz." At four-twelve, Mr. Evans closed the doors. There were hundreds of people in the ballroom. I spotted Norm Dygon, the man from the Terrace Grill, standing in line with a book. "The least I can do for Mr. Truman, who is willing to sit here and autograph the book, is to stand here and have him autograph one for me," he said. A gentleman said to Mr. Truman, "We saw Margaret on television last night and she was fine."

"I'm prejudiced in that department," said Mr. Truman. He nodded toward his wife. "Stop by and see the boss, who's sitting over there. She'll be tickled to death."

At five-thirteen, when, according to a Doubleday man's estimate, Mr. Truman had signed very close to four thousand books, the last person in line appeared in front of the desk. His name was David Nasaw, and he was twelve years old. He lived at 7520 Eaton Street, Kansas City, Missouri. Mr. Truman signed his name in the book, and he did something else, too. He wrote, "With best wishes to David Nasaw." The boy's father, Irving Nasaw, who was standing nearby, was almost overcome. "That's what we hoped you would do, Mr. President," he said.

Mr. Truman looked up. "If he hadn't been the last one in line, I wouldn't have done it," he said. "I haven't done it for the others." He put down his pen and threw his arms in the air. "Finish," he said.

(1955)

Hooray!

As an art form, the spontaneous demonstration has reached new heights under Marshal Tito of Yugoslavia, as I discovered not long ago when I spent a few weeks in and around Belgrade. Spontaneous demonstrations kept popping up at all hours of the night and day. They are a matter of high policy, an integral feature of Marshal Tito's government, which solemnly refers to them as "spontaneous," especially when describing them to visitors to the country. The lack of spontaneity in a spontaneous demonstration does not, in the government's eyes, detract from its restorative and invigorating qualities. Marshal Tito and his colleagues evidently feel that a good, long, well-planned spontaneous demonstration is just what the doctor ordered for Yugoslavia, and that four or five doses a day will make the patient really sit up and take notice. For the most part the demonstrations involve civilian adults, but thoughtful provision has also been made for the kiddies and the army, which consists largely of ex-Partisans, to demonstrate spontaneously as well. That takes care of everybody, and on a fine, clear day in Belgrade, men, women, and children, both in and out of uniform, are to be seen spontaneously demonstrating all over town.

The ordinary, or civilian, demonstration is generally in the nature of a parade—not a parade as we know it, with plenty of brass bands and drum majors, but a sad, slow, solemn procession, or shuffle. At the head of the column walks a fellow carrying a large Soviet flag, flanked by two men struggling to hold aloft huge cardboard portraits of Marshal Tito and

Marshal Stalin. Then comes a group of about fifty men and women in ragged ranks, then a man supporting a large Yugoslav flag, then several hundred more men and women, many carrying banners reading, "Long Live Tito," "Long Live Stalin," "We Want Trieste," "Hooray for the Glorious Soviet Union," "Death to the Enemies of the People," and so on. At approximately four-minute intervals, everyone shouts, "*Živio Ti-to, Živio Ti-to, Živio Ti-to!*" This means "Hooray Tito!" or "Long live Tito!" and it is uttered mechanically, with the accent on both the "ti" and the "to." When several hundred people take to chanting in this manner, "Ti-to" becomes a meaningless and yet somehow frightening sound. Hearing it again and again and again, I lost all sense of its connection with any living man; it might just as well have been "Bi-bo, Bi-bo, Bi-bo!" or "Wi-wo, Wi-wo, Wi-wo!" or *"Sieg heil, Sieg heil, Sieg heil!"* Except when the marchers are shouting *"Živio Ti-to!"* they make little noise. They pad along, reading newspapers as they walk or talking quietly with one another. These parades are forever wheeling suddenly around corners and tangling with unsuspecting strollers and with the horse-drawn carts that fill the streets. Now and then two parades turn into a street from opposite directions, and there is considerable delay while the outriders decide which has the right of way. Meanwhile, the marchers mark time by turning the pages of their newspapers and sounding off at intervals with salvos of *"živios."*

Some of the army's marching can probably be classified as spontaneous, by government standards; the rest of it is more openly in line of duty, for armed soldiers stand guard at all public buildings and utilities. They are constantly coming and going between their posts and their mess halls and barracks, and occasionally units of them march to eastern Serbia to round up bands of from thirty to forty still belligerent Chetniks who, under Mikhailovitch, collaborated with the Axis. Whatever the reasons for the troops' marching, it gives them ample opportunity to express fealty to the boss, and the military demonstrators, like the civilian ones, shout their *"Živio Ti-to"*'s once every four minutes. The soldiers march briskly, in close formation, swinging their arms and thrusting their legs forward in a stride that is almost but not quite a goose step. During the war singing played a large part in any Partisan march, and sing the army does today—lusty, violent songs, with the music of traditional folk tunes and words born of the recent fighting. One can be translated, roughly, thus:

> Through forest, villages, and cities
> Partisan battalions are marching
> Against the German bloodsuckers and dirty dogs.
> The working millions are rising up.
> We are the young army of Tito.
> With us is coming the whole of our people.
> Our country will be free; only Ti-to, Ti-to, Ti-to,
> Let him be alive and healthy!

And the refrain of another goes:

> We don't want wealth, we don't want money.
> We want freedom, work, and justice!

My room in the Hotel Moscow overlooked Belgrade's main street, where, at night, the clip-clop of soldiers' heels on the pavement often awakened me. From my window, I would watch units of the vague, shadowy, automatic figures marching past in numbers that seemed excessively large to dispose of a handful of Chetniks. I heard two theories concerning the purpose of these nocturnal exercises. In the opinion of many persons in the city, they are a hangover from the days of guerrilla fighting, when all Partisan mass movements had to be undertaken at night. Another school of thought holds that people march at night only when they don't want other people to know where they are going.

The children demonstrate spontaneously in a variety of ways. For one thing, not too surprisingly, they march through the streets singing. The songs the children sing are hardly less martial than those of their older brothers in the army. This is natural enough, for most of the children between the ages of five and fifteen have been mustered into a juvenile army called the Pioneers.

Among the songs the youngsters sing is this one:

> When the National Army passes,
> The country will be called happy.
> Happy time, happy. Come with us to war.
> And you, the old, where are yours, your sons?

And this:

> Comrade Tito, when are you going to Russia?
> Please convey our gratitude to the Red Army
> And tell them all the youth is for them.

The words of a haunting melody sung by soldiers on the Salonika front after the First World War began:

> Far over there, by a seaside,
> There is my dear village, my sister, my love.

To the same tune, the Pioneers now sing:

> Far over there, by a seaside,
> There is the leader of the workers,
> The great comrade, Stalin.

Although there is a severe shortage of clothing in Yugoslavia and many of the citizens go barefoot, the Pioneers have complete uniforms. Every unit of the organization has its own chief of staff, an assistant chief of staff, and a youthful commissioner in charge of each ten members. Children who do not join the Pioneers are not allowed to participate in mass sports, receive lower and lower marks in their classes, and are deprived of the delicious privilege of spying on their parents, required homework for Pioneers. Nonmembers are also not allowed to attend such spontaneous mass demonstrations as the one in a Belgrade park last April that I was told about. On this occasion, the Pioneers gathered to swear allegiance to Tito. "We will fight to the end for Ti-to, Ti-to, and never spare our lives," they shouted in unison. Nor could nonmembers join in a program of war games that was held in the park a week later and that involved hiding behind trees, crouching behind rocks, leaping forth to surprise enemies, and, in general, having the devil's own good time.

The streets of Belgrade, through which these interminable processions pass, are littered with the wreckage of four years of war. The German bombing of April 7, 1941—a memorable day, on which the Yugoslav people, while Tito was still holding hands with the Axis, arose on their own in a heroic, if hopeless, revolt against the Nazis—ruined a substantial part of the heart of the city. Belgrade is situated at the confluence of the Danube and the Sava Rivers. Its one bridge across the Danube is down, and the only bridge across the Sava is a temporary one that will support pedestrians and motor traffic but not trains. This leads to the fertile and relatively unravaged agricultural area known as the Voivodina, to the north. For some reason, the American Air Forces bombed Belgrade on a number of occasions, notably on Easter Sunday of 1944, when several thousand persons who had run out into the streets to wave at what they thought were friendly planes were killed. Belgrade suffered further, and willingly, during its liberation by the Red Army from the Nazis, who, intent on destroying whatever they could not dominate, fought violently for every foot of ground. Russian and Partisan soldiers were buried where they fell, and their graves, surmounted by small red stars, now dot the city.

Belgrade's citizens show the effects of what they have been through. Everywhere you go you see one-legged men and women, often with the stumps of their limbs merely wrapped in soiled rags. The children have the drawn, gray, tight little faces of the very old. With a terrible frequency, former Partisans suffer seizures on the streets, falling down in a frenzy, waving their arms and screaming. When this happens, a number of passersby instantly and almost casually sit on the stricken man, pin down his arms and legs, and hold open his mouth to prevent him from biting off his tongue. After several minutes of writhing, the veteran, apparently recovered, gets up and walks off. He remembers nothing of the seizure. Some doctors, in spite of the similarity of this ailment to epilepsy, call it "war sickness," a reaction to the awful tension of guerrilla fighting; others call it "postwar sickness" and consider it a reaction to the disparity between the ideals for which the Partisans fought and the realities of Yugoslav life today.

I thought it odd that a government would permit its citizens to spend their energy marching through a shattered city rather than clearing away the rubble, but I found the parades interesting at first and, during the early days of my stay there, I stopped to watch a considerable number of them. I soon noticed that few people, except for myself and those waiting to cross the street, paid any attention to them. I was fortunate in having a sketchy familiarity with the language, which enabled me to understand some of the remarks I overheard in my wanderings around town, remarks that, though casual, led me to wonder further about certain aspects of the Yugoslav government. One afternoon, for example, a large, handsome, elderly man sat down beside me in a park and, looking straight ahead, said in a tone of utter resignation, "May they take away everything I have, and I have nothing, but merely because I am tall, please do not always force me to carry one of those damn banners!"

After my first week or so in Belgrade, I began to get the impression that

I was being followed by small, dark men in dirty raincoats. Now, this is a dangerous frame of mind to fall into anywhere, especially in the Balkans, and I resisted the thought, but the more I tried to shake it off, the more the small, dark men in dirty raincoats seemed to be following me. Eventually it became quite evident that I *was* being followed, and also that Yugoslavs follow not only foreigners but many of their own countrymen as well. The men who did the following were of a curious uniformity; all were around five feet four, with ferret faces and hungry expressions. They followed at a respectful distance, usually about thirty feet. They worked in shifts, one man stalking his prey for five blocks, then giving way to another man, and so on. The switch points were generally unoccupied storefronts, where four or five other men with ferret faces and hungry expressions lounged, smoking and talking. After the person being followed had walked past, one of the loungers would leave his companions and start down the street, while the man whose place he had taken would sidle up to the store, lean against its window, and casually light a cigarette. The process was painfully naïve, its variations pathetically limited. Cross a street and your follower would cross it; recross and he would recross. Stop short and let him glide past, and you would observe the swift, panicky twists of his head and his frantic efforts to maneuver into position again. Then off once more—the hunted and the hunter!

Since coming home from Yugoslavia, I have often wondered about the dossier of my activities that is unquestionably on file in the offices of Ozna, the Yugoslav secret police. Ozna is short for Odelenje Zastite Naroda, or Committee for the Protection of the People. My feeling is that the people would willingly settle for a little less protection, since Ozna has succeeded in creating the widespread impression that it spies into every phase of Yugoslav life and that its agents are wicked and all-powerful. The success of secret police as a political weapon depends less on what the police actually do, I have concluded, than on what people *think* they do; a Yugoslav who merely suspects that Ozna agents are watching him can hardly be more terrified if he suddenly discovers that they actually are on his trail. Since all of Ozna's activities are secret, the organization has become the subject of many rumors, the most widely circulated of which is that its agents are trained by N.K.V.D., the Russian secret police. This suspicion is part of a current tendency to blame all evils of the Tito regime on the Russians. I ran across one man in Belgrade, though, who believes the issue is not quite as simple as that. He told me that he thinks Yugoslavia is a case of the tail trying to please the dog by wagging on its own, often wagging so violently that it causes the dog some embarrassment, if no real displeasure. Physically, the Russians are not much in evidence. Red Army officers help with the training of the army, but there are no longer any Russian troops in Yugoslavia.

However that may be, if the Ozna men who traipsed behind me turned in accurate reports, they must have wasted the taxpayers' money in some such way as this: "American C-3 left Hotel Moscow in rain at 4:30 A.M. and went to marketplace to watch long lines of citizens waiting to buy food. Stood first by a vegetable line, then by a fruit line. Talked with citizens and was told that acute food shortage in Belgrade is partly attributable to unenlightened attitude of peasants, that with few exceptions peasants have refused to bring produce into town because government cut produce prices 30 percent, and that peasants have demanded similar cuts in prices of consumer goods. Housewives said they stand in line until 8:30 or 9:00 A.M. and sometimes go home with apples and potatoes, or a few grapes, and sometimes not. Best scheme, they said, is to bring several members of family along, thus covering all lines at once. Most people manage to survive because friends and relatives in countryside give them extra food.

"American had breakfast at shop near hotel—bread, ersatz jam, and coffee. Asked proprietor what coffee was made of and was told dried acorns, for one thing. Did not take second cup. Went to Ministry of Information and asked again to be allowed trip to devastated area in Bosnia to see government work of reconstruction; also asked for interview with Marshal Tito and answers to questions submitted to Ministry three weeks ago on wages and prices. Man in Ministry said he had misplaced questions but would have answers in due time. He reiterated that trip to Bosnia is absolutely guaranteed sometime soon but suggested this was awkward moment to leave Belgrade. Told American mass press conference is being arranged by Ministry to prove conclusively that anybody opposing Marshal Tito is reactionary Fascist collaborator. Also said that interview with Marshal is most difficult to arrange, that Tito has upset stomach. American asked how come sixteen Polish journalists had interview with Tito day after their arrival in Belgrade. Ministry representative suggested visit to exhibit of Partisan activities from 1941 to 1945, now open at Prince Paul Museum.

"American said exhibit sounded fine but he preferred to stay at Ministry and ask a few questions. He and Ministry man talked about Yugoslavia for two hours, and American learned things quite possibly he should not have learned. Man in Ministry is not too bright. He talks too much, gets excited too easily. To him, as to so many other sincere and hardworking Yugoslav officials, everything done under Tito is so fine and so wonderful that he admits to activities that may be questionable to many outsiders. Man admits that people are forced to participate in spontaneous demonstrations of loyalty to Marshal and new Yugoslav government; that orders are issued by government to all shops and offices, naming hours and starting places of processions; that those who fail to turn up are subject to severe questioning by Ozna; that failure to participate often results in loss of civil rights, including disfranchisement for not only culprit but his family, as well as loss of job, confiscation of property, and inability to procure medicines, shoes, clothing, etc.; that same penalties apply for failure to attend weekly block meetings addressed by political commissars, or for expression of unsound views at weekly discussion groups held in all shops and offices; that Yugoslavs who talk to Englishmen or Americans are liable to questioning by Ozna; that superintendents of Belgrade apartment houses are instructed to report fully on goings and comings of tenants and friends; that keys to front doors of apartment houses have been taken away from tenants, so anyone entering or leaving must have door opened for him by superintendent; that, although country has been devastated by war and disease, new national budget allots only ten million dinar to Ministry of Health and ninety-three million to Ministry of Construction but provides four billion for Ministry of War and National Liberation Army; that right now Tito is almost exclusively concerned with consolidation of his political power, rewriting of history to give himself credit for revolt against Axis in 1941, and denouncing all opposition, liberal or otherwise, as Fascist. American left Ministry and returned to hotel. Looked slightly ill."

Guided tours for foreign correspondents in Yugoslavia may well be compared to guided tours through large factories in the United States. In the factory, the reporter is accompanied by a nuisance from the company's public-relations department. In Yugoslavia, the reporter is attached, like one fish to the underbelly of another fish, to a man from the Ministry of Information. In either case, the reporter sees only what the authorities wish to show him. One Saturday morning, a young English-speaking army captain assigned to the Ministry of Information bundled me and three other American journalists into a Ford and drove us seventy-five miles north to the industrial city of Novi Sad. We rode along a road that runs straight to the Hungarian border through the rich, flat wheat and corn country of the Voivodina. Many of the villages looked prosperous, with large, gaily painted terra-cotta houses and people coming and going along the streets. Other villages were silent and deserted; their occupants, *Volksdeutsche* who had welcomed the German invaders, either fled with the retreating Germans or have since simply disappeared.

As we approached a bridge over the Danube near Novi Sad, a young military guard stopped the car. For twenty minutes our captain guide from the Ministry of Information showed him one pass after another, none of which seemed to impress him. The guard would take a pass, hold it up to the sun, turn it upside down, squint at it, and then hand it back to the captain with a shake of his head. At last the captain asked him whether he could read and he said no, he couldn't. The captain went off to an army post across the bridge in search of higher authority. While we waited, the guard told us that he had been liberated from a German prison camp by the American First Army and had accompanied it for several months. "I love Americans," he said. "We always had fun and lots to eat. They are my friends." The captain returned with a large and impressive new pass, which the guard stared at for several minutes. "Hooray for the Americans!" he shouted at last, waving us on. We drove across the bridge, past several hundred German prisoners who were repairing it. Novi Sad turned out to be a bustling, modern city. As we stopped in front of the municipal building, a striking black-and-white marble structure, a group of ragged soldiers marched past. No "*živios.*" Our guide told us that they were captured Poles who had fought with the Germans. "They are marching home to Poland," he said.

We were ushered into a long, panelled chamber and introduced to the president of the Provisional Assembly of Voivodina, a tall, strapping, bushy-browed man named Alexander Sevitch, who said, "I understand you are interested in land reform." For the next half hour, he told us, with our guide acting as translator, about the Yugoslav government's plans for dividing large estates into small farms. From now on, he said, the maximum amount of farmland any individual will be permitted to own will be thirty-five hectares, which is about eighty-five acres. People who work in towns and want a small country place for weekends or the summer will be entitled to from three to five hectares. The land to be redistributed belonged to large landowners, or to *Volksdeutsche* who were disloyal to Yugoslavia; a hundred and fifty thousand hectares will be taken from the former, four hundred thousand from the latter. People of the area who have no property of their own have first call on this land; second choice goes to former residents of such ravaged areas as Bosnia and Montenegro; third come the families of Partisans who were killed during the war. The land will not be given away free. The price has not yet been determined, but colonists will be allowed twenty years to pay for it. During that time, they may neither sell, rent, nor mortgage the land. At the end of twenty years, the land will be theirs, subject to the law of primogeniture. Whatever tools are found in the farmhouses will become the property of the new owners, but all tractors will be pooled in central tractor stations for common use. Each year the farmers will be required to plant a certain percentage of their land with sugar beets, wheat, maize, or whatever crops the government designates. They may use the rest of their land as they wish.

Sevitch said that the process of resettling persons from devastated areas was already under way. Until a new owner arrives to take over his parcel, the land is worked by the local farmers, assisted by troops and members of youth organizations. Civilian workers are paid partly in cash and partly in produce for their efforts, soldiers receive their regular army pay, and the young people serve as volunteers. Sevitch was proud of what had been accomplished; during the past year, he said, more than 95 percent of the land had been farmed, despite the fact that his aides had been able to rustle up only a thousand tractors and very little gas and oil and that Italian invaders had stolen a hundred and twenty-five thousand of the region's three hundred thousand horses. Sevitch's figures were impressive, and all of us asked to be shown some of the land and some of the colonists, but our guide said that it was time for lunch. The meal was served in a restaurant in the center of town and, for present-day Yugoslavia, was sumptuous: first, the national drink, *rakija* (a plum brandy), then soup, meat, salad, and coffee.

Lunch over, we were bundled into the car again. I assumed that our desti-
nation was a colony of new settlers, but after being driven eighty miles
farther north, we stopped and got out at a state horse farm. "I thought you
might be interested," said our guide, as the head of the farm, a robust vet-
erinarian named Masuric, led two magnificent stallions from his stable.
The Hungarians, Masuric said, had driven away fifteen hundred horses
and he had been able to get, as replacements, only six hundred and fifty of
an inferior breed. His stallions were available to farmers in the province at
a stud fee amounting to forty cents. "We must be off," said our guide, as
Masuric led the stallions back to the stable. We climbed into the car and
drove another eighty miles along dusty roads to the village of Buljkes.
"This village," said our guide, "was formerly occupied by *Volksdeutsche*. It
is now occupied by forty-three hundred Greeks who escaped from the terror in Greece." I noticed that S.S. death's-heads were still painted across
some of the house fronts and that one of the streets bore the name of Truman. We were led into a gray stucco house, where we were introduced to
Vanie Nicholas, the president of the local Greek colony, who summoned
several men and women to tell us of their sufferings at the hands of the
Greek government. "Show them your bruises," Nicholas said, and the ladies lifted their peasant skirts and exhibited welts on their legs and thighs.
Suddenly I heard the sound of marching men and cries of "Truman, Stalin,
Attlee!" and, glancing out a window, I saw several hundred men with
pitchforks over their shoulders marching past the house. "A spontaneous
demonstration," Nicholas said. For the next two hours, while we listened
to the stories of Greek refugees, the paraders stood massed in front of the
windows, shouting, in rhythm, "Up Elas! Hooray Truman, Stalin, Attlee!"

When we moved to an adjoining room for another sumptuous meal, the
crowd outside moved, too, and stood right outside the dining-room window. Throughout our meal, they shouted, "Truman, Stalin, Attlee!" It
was quite dark when we started back to the car, and the crowd seemed to
be all around us. "Truman, Stalin, Attlee!" the demonstrators cried. "Truman, Truman, Truman, Stalin, Stalin, Stalin, Attlee, Attlee, Attlee!"
they shrieked. Suddenly they seemed to lose themselves in the swirling
sound of their chanting and they broke ranks and pressed in on us. Several
of them hysterically grasped my necktie and shook me up and down. "I
was born in New York!" a boy shouted in English, as he took hold of my

coat. "Tell the people our troubles!" We reached the car at last and climbed in, but the crowd surged around and began to rock it from side to side. "Truman, Stalin, Attlee!" they went on yelling, and an aged woman climbed onto the radiator and brandished a pitchfork at the windshield. Our guide looked somewhat shaken by the spontaneity of this demonstration and urged the people to disperse, but apparently they were all Greeks who understood no Yugoslav; at any rate, they continued to rock the car. Our driver finally put his foot on the accelerator, raced the motor furiously a moment, and we ploughed our way through. We got back to Belgrade after midnight. That was the only guided tour offered me by the Ministry of Information.

The Ministry hemmed and hawed about my request to go to Bosnia, and I had ample time to explore Belgrade while I waited. One could always go to the movies and see newsreels of Molotov with other leaders of the Big Three, or visit the National Theatre, a comfortable playhouse with soft, red-plush seats and a seventy-five-cent top. At the National, excellent ballet alternated with performances of *Mr. Perkins Goes to the Land of the Bolsheviks*, a Russian comedy that had been a wartime success in Moscow and was now enjoying a prosperous run in Belgrade. The play deals with the visit to Russia of a prominent American businessman, accompanied by a disgruntled and hypercritical newspaperman. Wearing a silk blouse and high Russian boots, Mr. Perkins, the businessman, calls on a typical Russian family and discovers that they feel a sincere friendship for the people of the United States, visits the front to observe at first hand the heroism of the Red Army, and finally turns on his companion (who has spent the whole time sulking in corners and mumbling, "Propaganda, propaganda"), denouncing him for his attitude and delivering a rousing speech in which he urges strong and friendly American-Soviet relations. "The weak spot in the Soviet people," says Mr. Perkins, "is that they themselves are not conscious of all that they have done, and that they have not done all that they are able to do. Ah," he adds sadly, as the curtain falls, "that was the case with us, too."

One could always take a trolley to the outskirts of town, walk along the muddy roads, and stop in a wayside tavern for a glass of *rakija* and some Serbian music on a one-stringed violin. Or one could visit the exhibit devoted to Partisan activities during the war. It provided convincing testimony to the military tactics of Tito and to the indescribable brutality of the Germans, the Ustachi, and the Chetniks. The exhibit included photographs of the fighting, copies of Tito publications issued during the war, desperately primitive medical instruments, and crude pitchforks, axes, and other handmade implements used as weapons. A jarring note was introduced during one of my visits to the exhibit by the presence of several hundred young people who were being ushered through it under what seemed very much like compulsion. I was somewhat depressed, too, by the brash attempt of the government to take credit, by means of photographs and captions, for the revolt of March 1941, in which they actually took no official part.

And there was always the zoo—the pathetic, windswept zoo, where the only things to look at now were two tired, hungry lions, whose roars were like the bleats of lambs, several undernourished pheasants, and many cages filled with rabbits and pigs, which, I was told, were there solely to provide for the keepers' dinners. I last visited the zoo on my final day in town. I couldn't think of any other place to go. The Ministry of Information had ceased to offer any hope whatever—the word was definitely no on the trip to Bosnia. A young girl in a Partisan uniform slipped up beside me as I was staring into a rabbit cage. "What you have seen in this country is our shame," she said. "We wanted peace and justice; we have war and bitterness." I could not help remembering what she had said when, an hour later, I paid a good-bye visit to the Ministry of Information. "I hope you have enjoyed your stay here," said the guide who had taken me to Novi Sad. I told him that I had wished to see a little more of his country. "If you are referring to the difficulties of our trip that day," he said, "rest assured that the unruly guard at the bridge has been severely punished."

(1946)

Winds off the Pampas

The terrible notion that Hitler, Eva Braun, Martin Bormann, and other choice Nazis are alive and breathing somewhere in Argentina has been gnawing at the Argentine imagination since the end of the war in Europe. Like practically every other notion in Argentina today, it is nourished by accumulated rumors, national anxieties, and scraps of circumstantial evidence. The chances are that few of the many people who tell over and over again the same anecdotes about Hitler's presence in Argentina believe that the flesh-and-blood Hitler is literally on the premises. He is, rather, an obsessive symbol of their deepest fears and frustrations. Stories about him turn up wherever one goes, and he is unexpectedly injected into the most unlikely conversations. Not long ago, travelling in Argentina, I heard the Hitler stories. When I began to hear them again and again, from different groups in different places, their meaning became somewhat clear to me. For one thing, they serve to bring closer together segments of the population that formerly had little in common and communicated with each other hardly at all. The law student, the elevator operator, and the owner of an *estancia* (or ranch) are united by a body of Hitler lore. Through him, they all share the same fear, mainly that if he were indeed in Argentina, nothing official would be done about it. Moreover, many high-minded Argentines are uneasily aware that the wartime conduct of their country made it the sort of place Hitler might well have chosen for his postwar residence. And although the Argentina of Perón today cannot reasonably be compared with the Germany of Hitler, the very fact that the stories are told carries the painful implication that the Führer would not totally disapprove of the current course of Argentine events.

The origin of the Hitler stories is obscure. They appear to be based upon the mysterious and unheralded, and possibly legendary, arrival of two U-boats at the popular seaside resort of Mar del Plata, two hundred and forty miles south of Buenos Aires, in the latter half of 1945. Some people say that the submarines surfaced at sea before docking, while others say that they came alongside the big quay there before rising. As some tell it, the landing was made in daylight; others claim that it happened after dark. In the daytime version, knots of the curious flocked to the oceanfront as word went around that U-boats had been spotted. Police prevented anyone from getting any nearer to the scene than the top of a high bluff overlooking the quay. Onlookers are said to have watched several people pop out from the submarines' hatches, scramble onto the quay, and enter waiting automobiles. All the men were wearing the type of greatcoat worn by German field marshals. One, who walked with a limp and had one arm that dangled loosely at his side, was approximately the size and shape of Hitler, while the one woman looked like Eva Braun. The group was driven away at high speed, the crowd was dispersed without getting answers to any of its questions, and no mention of the incident appeared in the newspapers. The nocturnal version has even more sinister overtones. The submarines arrived by moonlight, disgorged the same group—including the lady and the man with the limp—which entered cars and was driven away at a normal speed. A young policeman, patrolling the waterfront, observed all this, unknown to the participants. As one of the cars drove past, he saw, seated inside, a man who looked like Hitler, and beside him a lady who looked like Eva Braun. He reported the episode to his superiors, who passed it along to *their* superiors. Within a few hours, he was summoned to headquarters, discharged from the force for being intoxicated on duty, and sent, under guard, to his home. The next morning, he was removed to an institution for the incurably insane, and its doors closed permanently behind him.

In both versions, the scene now shifts to Patagonia, the Far South of Argentina. Mostly, it is barren, windswept, and rainy, a dreary, remote stretch of rock, thorn, and sand, of black lava and volcanic ash. Only its western part is irrigated and under cultivation. Scattered about are lonely sheep ranches, many of them owned by settlers of German descent. To an ex-Führer of *Ein Reich* and *Ein Volk*, Patagonia would presumably be an attractive refuge. The way the Patagonian part of the stories goes, shortly after the arrival of the U-boats, with their mysterious human cargo, travellers throughout this vast region began to hear tales of a huge *estancia*, remote almost beyond imagination and surrounded by an electrified fence. Behind the fence, fierce dogs bark continuously. Once a month, the gates of the *estancia* swing open and a large black truck races down the driveway, careens onto the main road, and heads for the nearest hamlet, many miles distant, where a dozen stalwart blond men hop down and wander through the streets for ten or fifteen minutes, purchasing a bite to eat here and a trinket there, answering no questions. Then they hop into the truck and race back to the *estancia*. Nothing but the barking of the dogs is heard for a month; then the performance is repeated. In matters of this sort, one alleged fact leads to another, and over the years the blond men have become a guard of honor pledged in blood to defend their Führer to the death. The Führer, naturally, is behind the fence. He never leaves the estate. He is unable to do so. Drugs, defeat, and the shattering of his nervous system have left him monumentally wrecked and insane. He looks like a man of over seventy. Eva Braun stays with him, for there is no other place for her to go. Martin Bormann, the man who succeeded Göring as heir apparent, is there, too. He is in better shape than Hitler, but he is certainly not having a good time. He maintains the ghostly charade by addressing Hitler as *"Mein Führer"* and adding an occasional *"Heil!"* Bormann turns up half-heartedly for the weekly reviews, when Hitler summons his honor guard, watches it goose-step past him, and then delivers a lengthy and unintelligible harangue against Roosevelt, Churchill, and the Jews.

The Hitler stories have filtered through layer after layer of Argentine society. Who is to vouch for their truth, and who is to deny it? In any country, the people can weave and twist and enlarge upon a rumor. In Argentina, which is such a curious combination of the real and the fantastic, the odder an idea is, the quicker it takes hold. After travelling about that strange country, so different from the rest of the world, so far removed and other-planetary, I was quite willing to believe not only that Hitler was there but that I, along with several million others, had actually seen him.

Hitler intruded himself into a visit I paid to Mar del Plata. I had settled down in a large, modern, impersonal hotel in the center of Buenos Aires when, one morning, a lady of my acquaintance invited me to spend several days at her villa in Mar del Plata. (For fairly obvious reasons, the identities of all the characters in this article have been disguised.) She is wealthy, the proud bearer of an old and honored name, and related to almost everyone of importance in pre-Perón Argentina. Her roots are deep in the rich, black soil of the pampas from which her money is derived. Cattle and wheat are her heritage. Her father, a Spaniard, came to Mar del Plata more than half a century ago, drawn by the soil and by the fertile warmth of the days and the bracing chill of the nights. Mar del Plata is on a point of the coast exposed to winds from the antarctic. On a map, it is parallel with the southernmost tip of land in Australia, halfway across the world. The lady's father, like other enterprising Argentines of his generation, set about conquering and molding his environment, to make it fit his needs and fulfill his desires. Inland from Mar del Plata are the pampas, and in her father's time their section of the pampas was treeless, except for a few ombús, majestic shade trees of tremendous girth, whose wood is too soft even for firewood. Their leaves, which are poisonous, were often prescribed for the very sick by herb doctors in ancient times. Wherever he settles, man requires trees, it would seem, not only for shade and shelter but to provide some sense of permanence. Her father planted non-native trees by the thousands, and his friends and their friends planted others, and millions of them now grow in and around Mar del Plata and on the great ranches that lie on the long, lonely, sometimes flat, sometimes undulating sea of plains and grazing lands that stretches inland. The sons and daughters of the tree planters and *their* sons and daughters are considerably different. Many of them have been educated abroad, in French, Italian, or English schools. The wealth from the land has brought the opportunity to pursue one's leisure and turn it into one's profession. Thus, my friend became a painter and, although possessed of a passionate fondness for the land, grew away from it and from those who work on it. She is typical of those Argentines who visit the United States—rich, cultured, sophisticated, avant-garde in a curiously laborious and defensive way, and with an extreme sensitivity that betrays itself in an intense, nervous, easily aroused pride.

Over the phone, my friend had said that two friends of two cousins of two cousins of second cousins of hers would come for me at my hotel at five forty-five the following morning, Sunday, and drive me to Mar del Plata, six or seven hours away. They themselves were headed for a vacation spot farther south, and would drop me off. They arrived on time, in a new Buick. I had been astonished by the hundreds of new American cars I had seen on the streets of Buenos Aires. It had also been impressed on me that Buenos Aires has more than one city's share of wild and hysterical drivers. With a population of millions, it does not have a single traffic light. A trial set of lights was diffidently installed several years ago at one of the main downtown intersections, but the idea of mechanically regulating traffic so offended not only drivers but pedestrians that, in a burst of indignation, they ripped out the lights. The only regulating of traffic now is done by an occasional policeman, standing on a wooden platform, who waves the traffic on with excessive dignity, and even this happens only during rush hours. The rest of the time, it is Liberty Hall. Cars slide out from side streets, shriek to a halt, lock bumpers with each other, back up, tug, pull, and push; drivers get out and scream; pedestrians have to climb over the bumpers; and so on. Wise men in Buenos Aires wear holy medals to ward off danger and walk slowly and cautiously, looking both ways three times before crossing a street.

It was with understandable reluctance that I climbed into the backseat of the Buick. The capital was still asleep, and it seemed to me that the couple in the car were asleep too. They were husband and wife. He was middle-aged, of slight build, and had a combination of names common in Argentina; his surname was Irish, his Christian name Spanish. I shall call him Ricardo Kelly. Señora Kelly was an expressionless woman. Señor Kelly pushed the accelerator as far as it would go, and we were off. We raced over a bridge at the edge of town, dashed across a railroad track a bare second ahead of a hooting freight train, and shot down a flat stretch of road at eighty miles an hour, on the wrong side of the road. I asked Señor Kelly about this. By now, he seemed fully awake. He turned completely around to talk to me, without slackening speed. He told me that until three years before, Argentina had followed the British custom of driving on the left-hand side of the road. Then the government had ordered a shift to the North American way of driving. "I am still adjusting to the new method," he said. Looking me in the eye solicitously, he continued, "You are a stranger in the city, and I think it only fair to warn you against travelling in the *collectivos*. They are most dangerous." A car heading our way obligingly veered into what should have been our lane. Señor Kelly was still facing me, and this incident escaped him.

"What are *collectivos*?" I asked.

"Those small buses one sees on the streets of Buenos Aires," he said. "Overcrowded. Reckless drivers. No sense of timing or direction."

"Pardon me, Ricardo," said Señora Kelly. Señor Kelly turned to face front and tore off onto the grass alongside the road; he screeched back to the pavement after a hundred feet or so.

"Stupid!" said Señor Kelly, shaking his fist at a car we had barely missed.

"Ricardo," said his wife, "at this very point you lost your teeth three years ago."

"I recall it well," said Señor Kelly.

"Could we stop for some coffee?" I asked.

"At your pleasure," said Señor Kelly. He seemed to gather that I was hinting at something, for he switched into the proper traffic lane. "Last week," he said, "two *collectivos* overturned on Avenida Roque Sáenz Peña, and the same day one *collectivo* crashed into a storefront on Calle Bernardo de Irigoyen, pinning four children against the counters. Dramatically, it was a toy store." He turned around again and smiled. "So you see," he said. "Avoid *collectivos*."

We stopped at a crossroads for coffee. Our car slapped into the rear of another, whose front bumper was locked with the rear bumper of the car ahead. Seven or eight men were jumping up and down on it. They were too busy to bother about us, and since we had done no damage, we went into the restaurant, a white plaster building that was the only structure as far as the eye could see in any direction. The interior was divided into small booths containing rough wooden tables and benches. "We are on the pampas," said Ricardo, as we seated ourselves. The place was filled with large family parties. Waiters were hurrying back and forth. "Things have changed so radically in this country that one can no longer get waited on without a long interval of sitting," said Señora Kelly. She pointed to a slim, dark waiter who was peering at us from behind a booth and pulling at his mustache. "You see," she said, lowering her voice, "he perceives us, and knows that we are people of some elegance and breeding, and thus we will be kept waiting forever." Señor Kelly rapped on the table and looked quite severe. The waiter finally came over, took our order, and brought us some thick black coffee and some little sweet cakes.

We went back to the car, and there was an interminable delay while Señor Kelly waited in a long line to get some gasoline. Then we were off again. I insisted upon sitting up front with my companions, claiming that riding in the backseat made me carsick. I figured that when Ricardo turned to talk to me, his eyes would be at least at right angles to the road. We scooted along the flat road until, at about twelve-thirty, we skidded around a curve and came in sight of the Atlantic Ocean and the roofs of Mar del Plata, far below. The town was brilliantly white in the sun and splashed with bright red roofs. The broad sands, the pounding surf, and the crowds packing the beach under multicolored beach umbrellas gave the panorama an unnatural quality, as though it were a theatrical scene, carefully prepared and rehearsed, with every property and every member of the cast in its place. There was none of the ragged gentility of an Italian beach or the endemic democracy of Coney Island. It was simply a beach *scene* and, like much else that I saw in Argentina, an example of life's mirroring art.

"Observe the long quay—there," said Ricardo, taking both hands off the wheel and leaning out the window. I told Ricardo that I had already spotted it. He put his hands back on the wheel. "The U-boats landed there—the ones Hitler and his group are said to have come on," he said.

"I think there is something to the story," said his wife. "Do you remember *The Great Dictator*, with Charles Chaplin? Well, we met Charles Chaplin once when we were in the States. Rather unpleasant, face-to-face, I thought, but he was magnificent as Hitler."

"They tell me he is in Patagonia," said her husband. "Mad as a hatter. One of Mussolini's sons races around Mar del Plata in a roadster, Fritz Mandl can be seen eating barbecued baby beef at the Plaza Grill in Buenos Aires, and there is said to be quite a shipping trade in Nazis heading this way, sent by a ring in Denmark, so why not Hitler?"

"You didn't mean that Charles Chaplin was in Patagonia, did you?" asked his wife.

Her husband again took both hands off the wheel. "I did not," he said. "I meant Hitler."

Not far from the beach, we stopped in the driveway of a large wooden country house of English architecture. I had noticed a number of similar houses on the streets along which we had been driving. It had a porch running three-quarters of the way around and a trellis to the second story, covered with the largest chrysanthemums I have ever seen, all delicate pink and violet. Formal gardens stretched away from the house for some distance. They had carefully gravelled walks, bright green grass, evenly trimmed hedges, and, scattered under clumps of trees, small white cast-iron benches. This, too, was a scene so meticulously designed, so nearly perfect, that I had the illusion that the curtain had fallen on my view of the beach and, after our entr'acte conversation about Hitler, had risen upon another set. Señor and Señora Kelly bade me a brisk farewell and sped off. I stood alone for a minute, until the front door opened and a middle-aged woman, in the starched white dress one would expect of an English nanny, bustled out. "You are expected," she said to me. "I will show you to your room. What will you have for breakfast tomorrow morning, and at what time? There is a bell behind the bed, in the event that you desire something during the night. Leave out your trousers and tie to be pressed. The bath adjoining your room is shared; therefore test the door before attempting the tub. Lunch will be served within the hour. All are presently at the beach or otherwise occupied. Follow, please."

I told her that I would have orange juice, toast, and coffee, at nine o'-clock, followed her into the house, and found myself in a broad white entrance hall, which had a number of doors in it, all closed. Massive bell jars filled with artistically arranged pink-and-white coral shells stood on small tables against the walls. From one wall hung a turtle-green relief map of South America; there were tiny gashes for the minor rivers and long, deep wounds for the Amazon, the Orinoco, and the broad estuary of the Río de la Plata. Argentina, colored a light yellow, far down toward the bottom of the map—and toward the bottom of the world—seemed distant and vestigial, as though it were the fragmentary remains of some ancient creature's tail. It came as a shock to realize that I was standing somewhere along that tail and had come from far above the limits of that map.

"Your room is down this corridor," said the lady who looked like a nanny. It was large and comfortable, with gaily flowered chintz draperies, a big bed, several chairs, and an extremely high wardrobe. I took a bath, first having made certain that no one was in the tub. When I had dressed,

I stuck my head out into the corridor. There was not a sound anywhere. I picked up a *Life of Picasso* that was lying on my bedside table. I read a few pages, began to feel lonely, and decided to take a walk. I went down the corridor to the entrance hall and there noticed a door that was slightly ajar. Exhilarated beyond prudence at the prospect of human company, I peeked in. Half hidden by a grand piano topped by a big bowl of chrysanthemums, a very tall, thin, distinguished-looking woman with gray hair was playing solitaire at a card table near a window. I stood in the doorway for a solid half minute before I inadvertently coughed, but she did not look up—whether she was absorbed in the game or merely a firm believer in no interruptions while playing, I shall never know—and I quickly backed out.

Nobody and nothing beckoned but the formal gardens, so I strolled among them along a circular gravel walk. I made the circuit several times, past the flower beds, the white benches, the clumps of trees, and the evenly trimmed hedges. On my fourth or fifth round, I noticed a man in a butler's short white jacket standing on the porch, trying to attract my attention. He announced that lunch was ready, and I followed him to the room where I had seen the solitaire player. She was still there, but the card table and the deck of cards had been put away, and she had moved to a long sofa. In the room there were now also two women in white sports clothes and a middle-aged man wearing brown-and-white shoes, spotless white flannel trousers, and a striking brown jacket of a soft material resembling doeskin. They had evidently been talking, but at the sight of me conversation ceased, and for a moment or two before the man rose to greet me they sat in formal, erect, consciously pleasant poses, as though they were about to be photographed. They were like a group snapshot of well-to-do summer people in one of those big old wooden houses, all porch and sunlight, at a place like Sea Girt, New Jersey, circa 1908. Introductions were now made. The solitaire player turned out to be the sister of my hostess, who she said was due any moment, and the others were a young female cousin and a husband and wife who were friends of the hostess. An attractive, deeply tanned young woman entered the room, nodded to everyone, and sat down. After an embarrassing pause, she was introduced. Another cousin. My hostess arrived, tall and preoccupied, shook hands with me, and spoke earnestly and privately with her sister for several minutes. Then, at exactly two-thirty, the double doors leading to the dining room were opened by the butler, who was now wearing white gloves. He had changed to another jacket, even whiter and more starched. We moved into the dining room slowly, with the exception of the hostess, who preceded us at a fast clip, sat down at one end of the table, and instantly began to eat. Her lunch—a tremendous salad of mixed greens and tomatoes and a platter of boiled chicken—had already been put on the table. The rest of us were served a vast number of courses: soup, chicken, salad, vegetables (a separate course), beef, more vegetables, lush melons, grapes and peaches, and coffee, very thick and black. The butler was assisted by a footman, similarly gloved and coated. Throughout the meal, we drank a delicate Bordeaux-like wine, from the excellent vineyards near Mendoza, in west Argentina.

Except for a few modulated family exchanges, there was no conversation until the hostess had finished her lunch, which she did as the rest of us were still somewhere between the first vegetable course and the beef course. She then assumed the role of discussion leader and moderator, successfully encouraged conversation, firmly steered it down prescribed channels, and never permitted it to get out of hand. The man and wife were planning, I learned, to build a summer home in Mar del Plata, and a suitable period of time was devoted to a discussion of the materials to be used in its construction (mostly stone and concrete), the high cost of these materials, and the petty annoyances and irritating delays incidental to building. Almost as though she were turning the pages of a lesson book, the hostess shifted the conversation to the Mar del Plata beach. Everyone but me had been at the beach that morning, and was therefore able to contribute to the discussion. All agreed that the water had been cool and invigorating. The sunburned young lady ventured that she had been troubled by a recurring thought of late. "One seems to see so many ugly faces there," she said. "This is strange. I do not think this was so in other years." All of us automatically looked to the hostess for a reply, accepting the fact that a difficulty of this nature—its diagnosis, perhaps even the moral to be drawn from it—lay within her bailiwick. She was quite equal to the occasion. "It is not so much that the faces are *ugly*, my dear," she said, "as that there are so many *new* ones. There are hundreds of thousands of people who have never *been* on that beach before. Formerly, if one did not personally know everyone on the beach, one knew the family, or who he was. The faces were familiar, hence never questioned or examined for their varying degrees of beauty. The issue never arose. But the strange is unfortunately often ugly to us, partially because we are frightened by it. The point you have raised," she continued, rising and walking slowly up and down behind her chair, "brings into focus the entire problem of Mar del Plata today. Witness the Casino—the throngs at the roulette tables night and day, the millions of pesos crossing the board, the *anonymity* of the crowds. When Father and his circle founded the Casino, such crowds would have been considered scandalous. Even the shops on the ocean side of the Casino have changed in character. Señora Perón's favorite jeweller now occupies the place of honor—the store in the very center of the arcade—and fills his windows with glittering and worthless baubles. The crowds press against the windows and cannot tell real gems from spurious ones."

Our hostess sat down and drummed on the table with her fruit knife. The others seemed to be absorbing her remarks, and for a minute or two the silence was unbroken except for the hushed and genteel sound of crumbs being deftly swept off the table by the footman. The hostess turned toward me. "After lunch," she said, "I would be pleased to walk with you to the beach. There are things in Mar del Plata that should interest a visitor to our country. We will observe the city from the Tower, and visit the Casino and the Golf Club. I think that you should walk along the beach itself. I will show you the spot where the German U-boats are said to have landed. Has anyone told you the tale of the U-boats' landing here?" I said yes, I had heard the story, and added that I wondered whether she placed any credence in it.

"I can say only this," interrupted the gentleman who was going to build a house. "Just this morning, I heard once again the story of the chauffeur." He said this with more emotion than I had thought him capable of. Two or three people nodded and sighed, the way one does when a bit of disagreeable knowledge is aired for the enlightenment of a stranger. "A gentleman who owns a large *estancia* near Buenos Aires had in his employ a trusted chauffeur," he went on. "One day, while being driven to his office by the chauffeur, his man related to him a most disturbing incident. He was certain of nothing—the incident had been fleeting, he was embarrassed even to mention it—but he could swear that while he was vacationing the week before with his wife's people in the south of Argentina, Hitler had driven past in a big closed car. It was a silly thought, too ridiculous, but he was haunted by the vision of that man speeding past. His employer laughed carelessly, thanked him for the intelligence, and returned to reading *La Prensa*. However, on the way home that evening he told the chauffeur that the story had nagged at him all day and that he felt that it might be worth some thought, perhaps even some investigation. Would the chauffeur be willing, he asked, to repeat the story, insubstantial as it might appear to be, to a trusted friend of his in one of the government offices? The man said that although this friend worked for the government, he was extremely anti-Perón and in a position to conduct a discreet inquiry into the matter. After all, one never knew these days, did one? The chauffeur agreed that one never knew these days, and he further agreed to relate the tale to his employer's friend."

The gentleman telling the story pushed his chair back an inch or two and paused for dramatic effect. "My melancholy narrative comes to an abrupt conclusion," he continued. "The chauffeur did not appear for work the morning after he had related the tale to his employer, or the morning after that. The employer had, in the meantime, arranged an interview for him with his friend in the government—without telling his friend the purpose of the interview—but this appointment was never kept. Several days passed. The chauffeur's wife telephoned the employer's office. Her husband had not been home. Where was he? Was he driving his employer to some distant place? No one knew where he was. No one yet knows. To this day, no trace—a complete and total disappearance. Naturally, the question that arose was: Had anyone other than the employer—who had told the tale to no one—been told the story by the chauffeur? Yes, the wife of the chauffeur had heard it. Her husband had mentioned the incident while they were still on vacation. Had others been present at the time? Yes, some members of the family, but they had joked about the story. Under what circumstances had the story been told? Why, at a restaurant, during a family party, while there was much gaiety and singing. Had others over-heard the tale? Yes, yes, come to think of it, people at the adjoining table had heard what her husband was saying. They had leaned over intently to listen. They did not seem amused. . . ."

Some time later, the Führer again broke through the thin crust of conversation. I was spending an afternoon at a celebrated *estancia*. I had gone once again to my friend's villa at Mar del Plata and had expressed to her my desire to see such a place, and she had promptly and graciously arranged it for me. The *estancia*, which was owned by a cousin of hers, had been visited a quarter of a century before by the then Prince of Wales, who had spent several days around the place, admiring the high-spirited horses and riding polo ponies. During his stay in Argentina, the prince had visited many celebrated *estancias*, and those at which he had fallen from polo ponies were thenceforth considered to be Very Distinguished. He had tumbled off a pony—no harm done—at the one I visited.

I was driven to the *estancia*, which was an hour or two away, in a chartreuse-colored limousine by one of my hostess's men, who wore a tight-fitting livery the precise color of the car. We bounced and jiggled across the dusty pampas, and along orange dirt roads, in swirls of dust. The day was painfully close, and the dust seeped in around the windows of the car and caught in my throat. Ahead of us were threatening black clouds. Before long, day turned into night, and storybook thunder and lightning boomed and crackled. Still there was no rain. Suddenly, there was a nasty, jagged flash, and the car swerved and then came to a halt before a big and forbidding log gate. The stop and the flash were so close together that for an instant I thought we had been struck. To my left, just inside the gate, was a structure that was pure Humperdinck, with a slanted, colorful tile roof that might have been gingerbread trimmed with sequins. Out of the house, as in a dream, ran a little girl with long blonde curls, wearing a calico dress. She swung open the big gate and we drove on. We had passed the gatekeeper's cottage, the driver said. For at least a mile, the road twisted under an archway of great oaks. We seemed to be passing through a deep forest, and yet, until we had got to the gate, there had been scarcely a tree. Soon there were breaks in the forest wall, and I could see pastureland stretching to the horizon, with cattle grazing in the distance. Then the forest closed around us again. Then more views of pasture, more forest; then the road widened, and curved gracefully past a park of lush lawn bordered with box hedges to an ivy-covered Tudor castle, complete with turrets, casement windows, a massive oak door, and a broad flagstone terrace with steps leading up to it.

At the top of the steps, where I half expected to see Henry VIII, stood an El Greco in modern dress, a singularly tall and lugubrious gentleman with a long, dark face, sunken cheeks, and a thin, high-bridged nose. He had on a brown-and-white sports jacket, gray flannel trousers, and heavy brown sandals. I got out of the car, and he descended the steps, one hand in his pocket, the other outstretched. He was the owner of the *estancia*, and he had been expecting me. The imminence of the rain, he said, had upset some of his plans for showing me around. He told me that I was about to have an encounter with a *pampero*, one of the famous southwest winds of Argentina, which blow with a cold and awesome violence, often accompanied not only by rain but by hailstones large enough to crush a man's skull. He thought that we should make a rapid tour of the grounds and then repair to the house. There was another crackle of lightning and another boom of thunder, and he said we had better get going. He dismissed my car, telling the driver to take it off to the garage behind the house. Then he pointed to a beautiful, serene willow at one end of the terrace. I noticed a maze of roots curling over the ground near it, running every which way. My host suddenly said, "Yes, it's become a troublesome tree. It is one of the first I planted here. It has always stood at the foot of the terrace, almost like a flagstaff. When I built here in 1902, not a tree. Now, as you can see, hundreds of thousands of trees. I imported the seeds from all over the world—from England, from North America, from Java and the Indies—and set my trees out in little pots. I set out oak and pine, blue spruce, chestnut, maple, hickory, hawthorn, Lombardy poplar, black acacia, plum, cherry, peach, paradise. I landscaped everywhere, set banks of small trees below balconies of large ones, grouped them here in a semicircular design, there in full squares of green. It took time and imagination, and, I fancy, some artistry. The small rocks directly ahead"—my host thrust out a hand—"are a perfect prospect from the terrace of my house. Those small rocks were there when I came, standing oddly among the grasses, and it was here I decided to build. Then I put the willow in its pot and it grew, and now these roots have broken through the earth around the tree and crept under the terrace, and perhaps under the house. I walked out of the house one morning several months ago and saw these roots coming out of the ground, and decided to cut down my trees, all my trees, every tree on the place." He looked at me—somewhat desperately, I thought—for some slight sign of agreement with his decision. "If I do not destroy them, they will destroy me. The willow roots are a portent. I must cut down the trees. We are at the business now. Every day, the men are out chopping them down." I have rarely seen a man look as sad as this man looked then.

We walked briskly behind the castle, crossed a rustic bridge over a small lake, and reached a wooden dock with several swan boats tied to it. "A park without a lake is no park, and I wanted my park to be complete," said my host. We skirted the lake on a path lined with trees, which led to a quadrangle of low farm buildings of stucco, with red tile roofs. Beyond stretched a broad field alive with potatoes in flower. My host stopped in the middle of the quadrangle, surveyed his buildings, and then suddenly pointed skyward at a bird. "Blackbird," he said. "Many blackbirds all over the place. Came from England. On one trip back from England, I brought a whole Noah's Ark with me. My boxwood is from Holland." We walked under an archway into another courtyard, where a farmhand was exercising a handsome chestnut-brown horse. The farmhand was short and squat. He was wearing the traditional balloonlike trousers of the Argentine farmhand, and the bottom of each trouser leg was wrapped around his ankle in the manner of a cyclist's. My host nodded to the man, patted the horse, and told me that the animal was twenty-four years old and had made a distinguished record on Argentine racetracks. "This is the twilight of a life," he said. "Dotage. There is a little lamb that usually plays at the horse's feet. Together, they are two children. Our cattle are superior—best in show year after year. Once, we raised practically nothing but sheep here, but the sheep are in Patagonia now. This soil is much too good to waste on sheep. I have a bird park nearby—some rare wild specimens—but it is too much to see today. And anyway I'm weary of all the screeching. Come along."

We entered one of the farm buildings and walked through a low-ceilinged room and out a door at the other end. I had time to see only a group of farmhands huddled over a black metal pot of some bubbling gruel. My host led me to a new Chevrolet sedan parked in another courtyard, and we started off, down tree-lined roads and around tree-lined turns. After a silence of several minutes, I asked whether the contents of the black metal pot were being prepared for human or animal consumption. "Porridge soup for the stock," he said. "A thick, nourishing brew.

We have oats and dirt for the chickens but thick porridge soup for the stock. See the fences. Chicken wire of the highest quality. I was laughed at when I put up my fences and strung chicken wire between the posts. Using quebracho wood from our north for the posts was quite orthodox, but chicken wire was considered extravagant. Today, one can buy it nowhere, and the wire is as good as the day it came." The road now passed through a deep, or apparently deep, forest, much like the one through which the road leading to the castle passed. At one point, we crossed a small clearing, and I saw a pile of timber and several workmen operating a power saw. And now my host began to unburden himself of some pressing thoughts.

The Perón government, it seemed, had been eying the large estates for quite a while and had come forth with a scheme for buying up some of their acreage. My host felt that the scheme had its merits, since its purpose, so the government said, was the construction of houses and schools for those who lived and worked on the land, but if a man did not wish to sell at the price proposed, or to sell as much land as was wanted, the government set about expropriating the land on its own terms. In some cases, land had been taken from friends of his and then used not for the desirable purposes so widely advertised but for military rest homes and pleasure resorts for Perónist favorites. "The note of vengeance is the disturbing element," he said. "I and my kind understand the land and its use and power, and to a large extent the country was built up and has prospered through our skill and daring. I think the present government is misreading the history of the country. It does not know the nation's real source of wealth. My personal problem is something else again. This place is my lifework. I *am* this place. Had I been a painter, I could have done as I wished with my paintings at the close of my life. I am doing as I wish with my trees."

We drove to the clubhouse of my host's private nine-hole golf course. He said that he rarely used either the clubhouse or the course now—that he was in no mood for golf. The building consisted of a single large, damp room, with a bleak stone fireplace in the center. A long table was covered with English sporting magazines, some of them two or three years old. On the walls were hanging a few old golf clubs and several silver plaques. As we climbed back into the car, the rain came, in a thick, almost impenetrable sheet, and we drove to the castle cautiously and in silence. We went through the massive oak door into an immense great hall, panelled in dark wood and hung with portraits of my host's ancestors, and walked to the huge dining room, which had a huge table that was dwarfed by a huger sideboard. Both articles of furniture were laden with glasses, bottles of wine and whiskey, bowls of ice, platters of cold meat and sandwiches, cakes, cookies, candies, and sides of beef. Tea had been set out, my host observed. Far down at the other end of the sideboard I saw a finely wrought silver tea set. "Before tea, the trophies," my host said, and we went into a room whose walls were covered with photographs of quite obviously superior bulls, mostly shorthorns, with short, stout legs. Scattered on side tables were sixty or seventy trophies: tall, thin silver cups; low, fat silver cups; silver bowls the size of washtubs; and urns, medallions, and plaques. "Today, we breed for meat," he said. "Our stock is heavier, with less bone. These trophies go back to the second decade of the century. There's one from the Sociedad Rural of 1921." He swept me on into a third room, a combination salon-and-study. Books bound in red morocco filled ceiling-high bookcases. There were many Currier and Ives prints along the walls. A Renaissance table in the center of the room was piled with orderly stacks of magazines—*Punch*, the *Illustrated London News*, *Life*, the *Ladies' Home Journal*, and *Promenade*, the magazine that is presented to the guests of several New York hotels. I picked up a copy of *Promenade*, and my host said, "Ah, *that*. It fascinates my mother-in-law. She visited New York last year for the first time—it was always Europe in other years—and returned with a passion for ice water at every meal, and *Promenade*. Each morning while in New York, she would leave the Ritz-Carlton after breakfast and toddle over to Mark Cross's. She would remain there until lunch, ordering leather goods. After lunch, she would spend several hours more in Mark Cross's. My Currier and Iveses were all bought in Paris. Please sign the guestbook." The guestbook was lying on a desk beside an assortment of family snapshots in silver frames, paperweights, letter openers, cigarette boxes, and an imitation bronze key that bore the inscription "Welcome to Washington, D.C." I signed the book, and my host showed me the signature, many pages back, of the Prince of Wales. The sight of it seemed to make him even sadder.

We returned to the dining room for tea and found my host's wife, an ample, stately woman in her middle sixties, sitting at the head of the table. She was distressed. In the middle of the morning, she said, she had rung for a servant and asked him to bring the teacart to her room. The message had been passed along downstairs. By the time it reached the kitchen, it had become an order to hitch up the pony cart for the Señora so that she could ride about the estate. The pony cart had been instantly made ready, and a man had stood alongside it for several hours, waiting to help the Señora in. He had gone without lunch. In fact, he had stood beside the cart until an hour before, when the Señora's mother had gone out for her regular afternoon ride. The servant was understandably indignant, the other servants had discussed the matter, and, all in all, the help, from top to bottom, were behaving peculiarly. She had spent the past half hour trying to patch things up. "These days, our inside people are mostly Central Europeans—Czechs and Poles," she told me. "One never knows whether the orders are misunderstood or deliberately twisted. Incidents like this, whatever the reason, are unpleasant." She was further distressed because her mother had not yet returned from her ride and had unquestionably been caught in the downpour. She had dispatched a man in a car to get her, but she was afraid that her mother would catch cold.

We chatted for several minutes. I had a glass of dark sherry and some small cucumber-and-watercress sandwiches and had just asked for another glass of sherry when through the door from the great hall came a stooped, tiny-boned woman of advanced age, dressed in black lace. Her face was a torment of wrinkles—so numerous and running in so many directions that the effect was one of cynical good humor rather than of antiquity.

"Mother!" my hostess cried. "You are soaking!"

"A Scotch-and-water, please," said the old lady. We shook hands and she sat down beside me.

"Mother," her daughter said, "you must not sit in those wet clothes."

"First my Scotch-and-water, then my story, and then I will go upstairs, like a good girl," the old lady said. Her son-in-law handed her a highball and she took a sip.

"You are a stranger here," she said to me, "and perhaps you do not know what troubles us. Many of us think Hitler is here."

Her daughter got up and quickly walked around the table to the mother's chair. "Not that again," she said.

"It is *not* nonsense," the mother said. She patted my knee. "The old often know a great deal. They say I dwell on this, but they all feel something, too. It's only that I am willing to speak out. Just now, I was riding in my pony cart. It is my daily custom, and I went quite far with my pony today. The light was interesting and the shadows led me on, and I reached one edge of our place, far down at the end of the woods, close on the village, and I saw him."

"Saw whom?" asked her son-in-law.

"Hitler, of course," she said. "He went past in a car."

I looked at my host. His face had the expression I had noted when he glanced down at the roots of the willow tree beside the terrace.

"If it was not Hitler, then it was a man who looked very, very much like him," said the old lady. She patted my knee again and rose. "I have had some Scotch-and-water, I have told my story, and now I will go upstairs."

The conversation petered out, so I finished my sherry and a few minutes later was on my way back to Mar del Plata. The storm was over, but for the entire distance we ploughed through ugly thick mud.

Buenos Aires provided small relief from the odd sense of doom I encountered on my trips to the country. It seemed an extraordinarily gloomy city. The *porteños*, as the residents of Buenos Aires call themselves (the term means "people of the port"), try anxiously to convince visitors that the city is gaiety incarnate. I had the feeling that they were trying to convince themselves, too, and not entirely succeeding. They refer to Buenos Aires, when talking to a stranger, as the Paris of South America, and then look at him wistfully, as though awaiting corroboration. The city may not be gay, but it is something of a miracle. It has a population of three and a half million, and is the seventh-largest city on earth, and the third-largest in the Western Hemisphere. Its layout is strikingly defiant. Here is no huddling along a narrow stretch beside the water, no fear of moving inland. The original settlers and successive waves of later immigrants faced broad spaces on which they could build, and they built. The city stretches back into the pampas from the brown waters of the Río de la Plata for many miles. It is wonderfully loose and uncramped. Its boulevards are long, wide, and lined with trees. The city is still growing, since there are no barriers. One can travel by subway to the counterpart of New Lots Avenue and see an occasional gaucho of the pampas buying his evening newspaper and then riding home on horseback. Hundreds of thousands of the *porteños* live in the suburbs and travel on fast and frequent railway trains to the city. Five subway lines crisscross the city. The New York subways are barbaric in comparison. Their subway trains are not as fast as ours, but also they are nowhere near as noisy. The cars have fluorescent lights of various colors. The stations are spotless and are decorated with mosaics depicting familiar scenes from Argentine history. Parks are plentiful and, to a North American, unnaturally clean; the red-dirt paths are never littered with paper and debris, and look as though the groundkeeper of the West Side Tennis Club were on hand twenty-four hours a day. Even in the heart of the city the streets are so clean that they make a visitor from New York envious.

The *porteños* take an elaborate pride in their fine, clean city, but they seem to be reaching for something more. Their constant emphasis on a gaiety that does not exist gives them away. I had the impression that, having settled down and grimly and studiously created a city—again, much as one would build a stage set—they are lonely and confused in it, and dubious about the drama being enacted upon the stage. Practically all Argentines are of European stock, and Buenos Aires derives from European cities. It has the sidewalk cafés of Paris, the drawn shutters of Madrid, and the polite suburbs of London. Europe was the model, and Europe is far away. One has the feeling that, having turned their backs upon Europe, the *porteños* feel a disturbing sense of remoteness from it. I took long walks through the city at night and fancied that I *saw* their loneliness. A great deal of it is inarticulate. Argentine husbands have a habit of going out after supper and heading for a *confitería*. One sees them sitting by themselves at tiny tables on warm nights, toying with glasses of beer or vermouth, motionless and abstracted. By the act of leaving the house, they have asserted their manhood, and yet such self-conscious posturings of independence appear to bespeak a deep uncertainty. Evenings when they go forth with their families to cabarets, the sense of collective loneliness is almost unbearable, and suddenly someone will raise his voice in song. Others will join in, and a sad melody will momentarily bring them together. The professional entertainers themselves seem to be victims of the prevailing gloom. They leap to the bandstand and, in voices so sorrowful they are almost ludicrous, begin to chant the lyrics of popular tangos. One evening when I was making the rounds of some cabarets, I collected the words of three of these tangos. They translate, roughly:

All my life, I have been a good friend to everyone. I have given away everything I own and now I am alone, ill, in my dirty and gloomy small room in my neighborhood slum, coughing blood. No one comes to see me now except my dear mother. Ah, now I realize my cruelty to her. I am at the point of death and I recognize my love for her. She is the only one who really cares for me.

Do you recall, loved one, that sable coat I bought for you when we were both poor and I loved you in our neighborhood slum? Do you remember how I went without cigarettes for months and borrowed from all my friends? I even went to the usurer. Do you remember? And just last night I saw you leave a nightclub with a fashion plate, and I could not help but think that our love is a dead thing, but I am still paying for the sable coat.

Ah, beloved, do you recall when you were a poor seamstress, trying hard to eat every day and dodging poverty in our neighborhood slum, and you bestowed upon me tenderness and love such as you will never give another? And now you have been deceived by some stupid playboy, and you have all the money one could desire, and you play with him as a cat plays with a poor mouse. But the day will come when you will be just an old, worn-out piece of furniture. On that day, dearly beloved, should you need a friend, advice, or any kind of help, remember that you can come to me, there will always be an old friend willing to risk even his skin for you, should the occasion present itself.

The streets at night are crowded with people shuffling back and forth under bright neon signs, window-shopping, pushing into movie palaces, or stopping to drink cups of *caffè espresso* with great solemnity, in gleaming Nedick-like coffee shops. There is every sign of prosperity, even an air of aggressive superiority, and yet the air is filled with melancholy and unrest. It did not seem like the traditional melancholy of the Spanish peoples. I felt this particularly one evening when I was invited to have dinner with a group of young people, all in their twenties. They were mostly students and office workers, and their wives and girlfriends, and they were all passionately, philosophically anti-Perón. They had a keen sense of the value of civil liberties and felt that to destroy them in the name of social welfare was a crime of unthinkable proportions. They were equally anti-Communist, on clearly defined humanist grounds, and resented the game the Communist party was playing in Argentina. For example, all the newspapers of Buenos Aires, with the exception of *La Hora*, the Communist paper, and *La Prensa* and *La Nación*, two honored conservative journals, have willingly or unwillingly been stridently pro-Perón. Both *La Prensa* and *La Nación* have been constantly harassed by Perón, been forced to cut down the size of their issues, turn over newsprint to pro-Perón papers, and so on. But *La Hora* is published without interference. Perón allows it to continue, my friends feel, in order to give the impression that he is, after all, a truly liberal fellow. *La Hora* takes full advantage of this situation. For one thing, it scrupulously avoids personal attacks on Señor and Señora Perón and it pays lip service to the Peróns' social program. The second did not deceive my friends. One should expect this of the Communists, they said. Their thesis was that the Peróns were worth years of propaganda to the Communists, who could ask for nothing better than a regime that softens up the people and slowly destroys their capacity to think for themselves and the means by which they can redress whatever grievances they are still conscious of. My friends were disillusioned about the rich landowning families, who, they said, though often well-intentioned, had governed arrogantly for decades, had become divorced from the people and their needs, and had lost their power and their prestige. These young people were as confused as liberals the world over are today. They were, however, more aware than any group I have encountered anywhere of the struggle in which they are engaged—warding off the constant inroads on what they held dear by the extreme Right and the extreme Left.

But there was something else that disturbed these people. During the early part of the evening, they seemed unable to express what it was. After dinner, the way was cleared for an explanation. It was suggested that one of the group take me to a street-corner political meeting in an outlying part of the city, a workmen's section in the slaughterhouse district. Some local elections were coming up, and a prominent anti-Perón politician was to speak. Such meetings were not easy to arrange. The police, several days in advance, required a complete list of the expected speakers, and no substitutions were permitted. There was always the possibility that some of Perón's bullyboys would attack the speakers or, as had actually happened, run a streetcar or bus into the crowd, pretending that it had got out of control.

My guide and I took a taxi to the corner where the meeting was being held. It had already started, and a short, sturdy, dynamic young man, standing in front of a microphone connected to a sound truck, was haranguing the crowd. The audience was grouped in an odd manner. Some ten or fifteen persons, all obviously quite agitated, were standing close to the speaker, forming a tight semicircle in front of him. They wildly applauded every statement he made. Directly behind them, sitting haughtily erect on restive horses, were four or five mounted policemen. Behind them, at a discreet distance of some fifty or sixty yards, across the street and up on the sidewalk, stood the main body of onlookers, a straggly group of perhaps a hundred and fifty people. These listened to the speaker in ostentatious silence. Every once in a while, one among them would spontaneously make the first gestures of applause, but he would quickly look around and, with feigned casualness, slip his hands in his pockets. More mounted police rode back and forth between the big clump of spectators and the little clump. The latter, my friend explained, were all hotheads, with a streak of martyrdom. They were willing to take a chance on having the cops behind them. The larger group was playing it more cautiously; in the event of trouble, they had a good chance of getting away.

A minute or two after we arrived, the featured speaker of the evening was introduced. He was a tall, thin, tense man. My friend whispered to me that he was known for his moral and physical courage and for his pungent criticisms of the Perón regime. He lost no time getting under way. He tore into the regime with controlled fervor and mock politeness, but he spared few aspects of the government. The president, he said, paid far too much tribute to the constitutional provision forbidding him to succeed himself at the end of his six-year term, in 1952. "Just wait and see what happens," he said. "Señor Perón will find a way to answer the call of his beloved people. He will find a way to remain among us for another six years." This brought forth shouts from the inner group. From across the street, silence. He called attention to the fact that one-third of the budget was devoted to military expenditures; that since 1943 the army had played a major role in Argentine life; that this was a new and disquieting development, foreign to the country's traditions. He spoke of a Father Filippo, who he said had many Nazi ideas, and the evils of permitting him to advise the president and his inner circle. He asked why the president, who was so ardently pro-Franco, never dared make a speech praising Franco. He reminded his listeners that it was almost impossible for opposition parties to obtain radio time, so involved were the regulations, so limited the time available, and so prohibitive the cost. "We must submit every word ahead of time," he said, "pay plenty, and then *may* be granted five minutes every other day. We are forbidden to speak in full sentences. Only slogans are permitted." Even this minute concession to freedom was a rude joke, he declared, since it was in effect for only a week or two before an election, and was forbidden as soon as the election was over. Meanwhile, the government had spent during the previous year a hundred million pesos for propaganda and fifty million on cider, cakes, and small gifts to be bestowed upon the populace by the Señor and the Señora. He went on to say that the unions had lost their freedom and that the courts and universities were being brought under rigid Perónist control. "Oh, suddenly everything has become big and strange for our Argentina," he said.

"I want you to meet the speaker," whispered my friend. "Leave things to me." He ducked around behind the speaker, who was in the midst of his peroration. The veins stood out on the speaker's neck as he shouted, "My prayer is that Señor Perón will live long enough to witness with his own eyes the ruin to which he is leading our great country." The inner circle shrieked its approval, the police cantered up and down the street on their horses, and the outer crowd melted into the night.

I felt a tug on my arm. It was my friend. "Come," he said, and before I knew what was happening, I was shoved into the backseat of a small black automobile, which instantly drove off. On one side of me was my friend, on the other the man who had just finished speaking. He was leaning forward in a tense, half-crouching position. No one said anything. The car plunged ahead at something more than the usual frenetic rate of Argentine speed. We raced down a wide boulevard, swerved around a dark corner, and then around another. The driver manipulated the car as though we were being pursued by a posse, but when I turned and glanced out the back window, I saw no one following us. I asked the speaker what the speed and anxiety signified. He grunted and said that discretion was the better part of valor—one never knew what might happen these days. It was safer to make a swift getaway and avoid the possibility of an "accident."

I told him that I had enjoyed his speech, and he seemed pleased. My friend had apparently explained to him that I was a North American. "What I was doing this evening was an educational exercise," he said.

"One must keep talking wherever one can and articulate the dark undercurrents that none of us fully understand." He glanced out the back window, as I had done a moment before. Then he sat back against the seat, in a semirelaxed fashion. He pounded his knee with one hand. "We are obsessed with an idea," he said. "Somewhere in this government there is an evil master plan of foreign origin. One pernicious step after another is taken, each seemingly unrelated to the others. Examine them and you will find that they have been tried in another country first. I feel that the men with the plan are determined that it will not fail. They will take a roundabout route, as we are doing now in this car, but always I sense a determination to force their ideas upon us. All this is alien to us." He stiffened, and I noticed in the dim light that his face had a drawn and pained expression. "I have felt this to be true since those first stories of the German U-boats' landing at Mar del Plata," he said. "And one keeps hearing of strange arrivals of boatloads of Nazis, of elaborate undergrounds operating between Spain and Argentina. One hears and hears and hears, and yet there is no sound!" The car stopped before an apartment house on a dark side street. The three of us got out. The windows of the building were all shuttered. The speaker looked up and down the street, shook my hand, and disappeared through the front door.

It was not yet midnight. I had arranged to turn up that night at the Plaza, one of the big hotels, to meet a friend of Señora Perón, a man who had said that perhaps he could put me in touch with her. He thought very highly of her, and was said to be associated with the foreign and domestic adventurers and speculators in her entourage. I was as suspicious of this man as he was of me, but I had decided that the game was worth playing. I explained all this to my young Argentine friend, who rolled his eyes, walked me to the corner, got me a taxi, wished me well, and bade me good night.

I went directly to the Plaza Grill, a sumptuous, brilliantly lighted, and exceedingly comfortable eating place. The room was filled when I arrived. The tables were covered with food—big steaks, large bowls of vegetables, mounds of cheese. I spotted the man I was looking for across the room. He was sitting with a man in his fifties with a bull neck and iron gray hair, a beautiful, willowy young woman with hennaed hair, and a dumpy fellow with matted jet-black hair, a little black mustache, and outsize French cuffs. As I arrived at the table, I heard the man with the mustache snarl at a waiter, "Beast! You have brought the wrong cigarettes!" The waiter made an obsequious gesture, turned to a side table, and handed the man another pack of cigarettes, on a small silver tray. "All waiters are beasts," the man said to his companions. There were four lamb chops on his plate. I was introduced. The lady was the wife of the bullnecked gentleman; the man who had called for the cigarettes was a man I will call Count R.

I sat down beside the lady, who was eating a thick and juicy filet mignon. "Papa," she said to her husband, "what time does the yacht sail tomorrow?"

Her husband poured himself a glass of wine. "Pet," he said, with a thick German accent, "I have told you several times today that the yacht sails at eleven."

"Oh," she said. She asked him for some wine and drank it down in one gulp. "My husband is Swiss," she whispered to me, answering a question that was in my mind. "Such fine people. The count here is remarkable. He has been telling us of Mussolini's last days. He was with the Duce toward the end." I looked at the count, who bowed slightly over his four lamb chops and shot his cuffs.

"Life on the yacht is such fun!" said the friend of Señora Perón. "What gay sailing! So many friends of the Peróns!"

"They are charming people indeed," said the supposed Swiss.

I asked him what part of Switzerland he came from. He twisted his glass, blinked, and said, "Zurich." He turned toward the count. "You were saying . . ."

The count again shot his cuffs and swallowed a large chunk of chop. "The problem of Europe——" he began.

"*Ach, ja,*" said the Swiss.

The count beamed. "Someday," he said, "the true story, without the propaganda, will be told, and all the world will know the real greatness of those men. I saw the Duce over the years—always a figure of stature and magnificence." There was a buzz of approval.

The lady now poured herself a glass of wine. "The count here knew Hitler, too," she said to me. "Personally."

"Someday," the count was saying, "*he* will assume his rightful place among the crusaders and geniuses of the world." He raised his eyebrows.

"What a vision, what a program! The great unifier of Europe. A savior! How the world needs him today!" He went back to his chops.

The lady poured herself another glass of wine, drank it right down, leaned toward me, and said, "My husband is what you call an international banker, a financier. Millions! Billions! Money's corrupt, so I say what's the difference how you make it? He makes so much money that he sleeps most of the day. Naps all the time. Swiss!" She began to laugh.

Her husband banged the table with his fist. "Pet!" he said. "You drink too much and talk too much!"

My friend suggested that he and I step outside the Grill for a moment, and he walked as far as the door with me. He had wanted very much for me to meet Señora Perón, he said; it would have been an educational experience; he had tried his best; she was so difficult to pin down; he must go back to the others; thank you; good night.

At five the next afternoon, a North American friend, in Argentina on business, telephoned me to say that if I would join him right away at the Casa Rosada—the government house—I stood a chance of meeting Perón. He expected to be closeted with the president and several other North Americans for half an hour, and then he would ask the president to greet me. I walked the short distance across the broad Plaza de Mayo to the Casa Rosada, a graceful, elegant pink brick Spanish structure. My friend and his group were just arriving as I got there. We all went in together, past several soldiers with sabres who were standing at attention. An attendant whisked us into an elevator. When we got out, he led the way down a long, wide corridor, through several salons, and into a cream-colored anteroom with brocaded sofas and chairs. My friend and his party were ushered down another long corridor, to the president's office. A middle-aged colonel, whom I took to be some sort of protocol officer, requested that I wait in the anteroom until summoned. There were four other colonels in the room, all drinking black coffee from demitasses. I wandered into the corridor leading to the president's office. The corridor ran half the length of the building, had many big windows overlooking the waterfront, and was lined on both sides with stiff little Empire chairs and tables. Some fifteen bright landscapes hanging along the walls gave it the air of a dignified private gallery. On one small table was a framed quotation from the Argentine epic poem *Martin Fierro*: "If you make a great deal of money, be modest about it—don't show off. Just be quiet and don't act like a rich man; this is a virtue." Obviously, the president was conscious of the role he felt he should play in these surroundings.

My turn came quickly. A door at the other end of the corridor swung open, and a blue-uniformed majordomo beckoned. As I crossed the threshold of the president's office, I saw Perón standing at the far end of a very long and impressive table, at which my friend and his party were seated. Perón bounded toward me and embraced me in typical South American fashion; he put one arm around my shoulder and squeezed, then pounded my back, then drew me toward him and squeezed again. Not until he had led me to a seat at the table did I have a chance to really get a look at him. He is a bit above normal height, and has thick shoulders and a red and slightly pudgy face, somewhat disfigured by what appears to be some form of acne. His eyes are small and very active. He was wearing a brown Palm Beach suit. He seemed ill at ease, and his smile seemed mechanical. Five white telephones and a small bottle of pills were at his side, and behind him, on a desk, I saw a photograph of Señora Perón, etched on glass. At one side of the room was an enormous do-or-die picture of some of Peron's *descamisados*, or "shirtless ones," in revolt. With nervous movements, Perón sat down at the head of the table, took a Chesterfield from a pack in front of him, tapped it several times, lighted it, and took several quick puffs. Someone asked him what he felt were his greatest accomplishments. He did not have to grope for a reply. "My social and economic reforms," he said immediately. "Close behind them are my judicial reforms. Of what use would the other reforms be without accompanying judicial reforms? Our judicial system needed overhauling. We require new laws, new judges. After all"—he paused and winked—"we are in the age of the stratosphere." He added that there was much work yet to be done before his term of office was over. He sighed. "One must have plans for all phases of life," he said. "This takes time." He told us that he was working harder than any other president of Argentina had ever worked, and that it was not all fun. Most other presidents, he said, had come down to the office for an hour or two to sign papers and then gone back home. "Education is our next great step," he said, almost angrily. He leaned forward. Now the president of Argentina seemed about to unburden himself. "I have gone from one university to another and seen no scientific spirit of inquiry. The old professors just walk into a classroom, sit down, read from a book, and walk out. Education must mold and apply." He began to clasp and unclasp his hands. "This is not a matter of putting my own people into the universities. It is a matter of getting politics out of the universities. I am accused of dismissing professors from the universities. This is not true. A group of professors addressed insolent messages to the revolutionary government and resigned, and that was a fortunate thing, since it saved me the trouble of getting rid of them."

The president then stood up, to signify that the meeting was over. "Of what use is it to develop just the arm?" he asked. "One must mold and develop the *entire* organism." He reached behind him to his desk, picked up a jar of sour balls, and held it out to us. Several of us helped ourselves. I passed by his desk and saw that Señora Perón's photograph showed her in a long white "Gone with the Wind" dress, while another picture of her, ingeniously etched on the opposite side of the glass, showed her with a bandanna tied gaily around her head. The president stood fondly in front of the picture for a few moments, popped a sour ball into his mouth, led us to the door, and opened it.

There, outside, surrounded by a hushed group of officials, was Señora Perón, in a fluffy pink dress with a large bustle. Her hair was arranged in a series of golden quoits, one above another. Her skin was strikingly pale, and her eyes were heavy-lidded and lowered. I noticed that, without raising her eyes, she was glancing rapidly from one of us to another. She stood there, a figure in a pageant, as though she had just made her entrance as a young, hard, fanatical queen, poised, supremely confident, all-powerful. She played the role to perfection. She began to shake hands with us, one by one. Her expression never changed. She held out her hand to me, and I took it for an instant. It was stone cold.

(*1948*)

Natchez, Mississippi

Alt., 202. Pop., 23,791. No one in Natchez is entirely certain how many of Natchez's antebellum houses are haunted. "Some white folks put the figure as high as 97, 98 percent," an elderly white Natchez resident said recently. "The colored say it's higher." Admittedly, ghosts are all over town, are white, have a tendency to bump graciously into one another and to call each other "honey" as they float around the old houses, are a harmless lot, and live in the past. Otherwise sane people who have overheard conversations between ghosts report that the ghosts take special pleasure in working the word "old" into their speech. For instance, they refer to the Mississippi, which flows past the high bluffs of the city, as "Ol' Man River," and do so without embarrassment. They leave the impression that they are on speaking terms with the old man. No house, of course, is referred to by ghosts as anything but old. As far as a Natchez ghost is concerned, a house isn't a house unless it's old. Oaks are old oaks, magnolias are old magnolias, moonlight is old moonlight, and the South is the Old South. Every once in a while, a ghost refers to the New Old South, but the ghost's heart obviously isn't in it.

The pleasures of a Natchez ghost are relatively simple, and, for the most part, nocturnal. At Dunleith, for example, an enormous, square three-story house with gleaming white pillars on all four sides, the resident ghost is a Miss Percy, who once did part-time work as a lady-in-waiting at the court of Louis Philippe. Miss Percy was pretty, and had a sad and fetching voice, which she often raised in song. She also played the harp. The years do not seem to have dampened her talents, for, it is said, quite often at night, especially when there is a moon, she can be heard singing her plaintive dirges and plucking the strings of her harp. Her voice carries all through the house. She is said to be still in good voice, and also to have retained her good looks. Not all ghosts are as pretty as Miss Percy, or as musical. Many of them, it is reported, are quite vain, and spend a good deal of time, when nobody is supposed to be looking, standing around in front of petticoat mirrors, which rest on wooden frames and rise a few feet from the floor. Without a petticoat mirror, a ghost has no way of knowing if her petticoat is showing. Over at Elmscourt, a house whose graceful exterior ironwork has a lacy grape design, the ghosts are both sporting and scholarly. They hang around the big library, it is said, reading *Chivalric Days* and *Caesar's Interlinear*, and discussing the bloodlines of the thoroughbred horses owned by old Frank Surget, who built the old house.

Natchez ghosts love to ring old bells, and Natchez houses are filled with old bells—bells of all sizes and shapes, clustered together on a lower floor and connected with rooms throughout the house. In the old days, a slave could instantly distinguish by the mere tone of a bell what room he was being summoned to, and by whom. It might have been Ol' Massa himself, waiting for his julep, or it might have been an emergency call from Granny's room, Granny having fallen out of her big bed with the tufted red canopy. Ghosts also love to gossip. Over at Arlington, for instance, the ghosts are reported to sweep through the center hall, with its fine paintings by Maratti and Castiglione, or whisk through the damask-lined drawing room—the Gold Room—gossiping about Jane Surget White. Jane was the bride of J. H. White, an architect, who more than two hundred years ago built Arlington for her pleasure, and celebrated its completion with a gay and lavish fête. Natchez attended and joy abounded. Next morning, Miss Jane was found dead. Nobody has ever been able to figure out what happened to her, but the ghosts are still working on it. She herself returns periodically, it is said, but she has kept mum for many years and departs as swiftly as she materializes. In some houses, the ghosts just sit around and chew the fat about Henry Clay and Jefferson Davis; in others, they wait until everybody is asleep and then slip downstairs to the dining rooms and noiselessly swing the punkahs—huge, heavy wooden objects that hang from the ceilings above the dining-room tables and used to serve as fans. Properly manipulated, by ropes, a punkah can kick up quite a blow, even in Mississippi. In the old days, there was always a pickaninny, or a couple of pickaninnies, conveniently available to pull the ropes and send breezes across the tables where the gentry ate their meals and discussed the fine points of Sir Walter Scott. The pickaninnies were considered to be as cute as buttons. When a pickaninny grew up, he became a niggra, and was no longer considered as cute as a button.

The ghosts in the old Natchez houses are, of course, self-employed; they set their own hours, and come and go pretty much as they please. Old Natchez hands claim that the ghosts work the year round, except during Pilgrimage, which generally takes place in March, and during which thirty of the old houses are thrown open to the public for regularly conducted tours. Ghosts duck out during Pilgrimage. They hate crowds. The only ghost in evidence during Pilgrimage is the ubiquitous ghost of the Old South, and he nowhere shows himself to better advantage than during performances of the Confederate Pageant, a nighttime feature of Pilgrimage. Two garden clubs participate in Pilgrimage—the Pilgrimage Garden Club, which shows twenty-six old houses, and the Natchez Garden Club, which shows four old houses—and although there is a certain amount of genteel hostility between the two groups ("We *suffer* them," a Pilgrimage Garden Club lady said not long ago of the Natchez Garden Club ladies. "We really do not know who they *are*"), they maintain impeccable relations throughout the Confederate Pageant. To avoid hurt feelings, two sets of Kings, Queens, Pages, Mascots to the King, and other Court Flunkies are selected, one set from one club, the other set from the other. Each set reigns for two weeks, and invests considerable sums in court raiment. The Pageant itself takes the form of an established series of what the program calls "living pictures from our treasured past, a past not merely filled with moonlight and magnolias but one made up of adventure and lusty action." The life of the Old South slowly, inexorably unfolds before the eyes of the audience. In front of a set depicting Dunleith, happy, carefree, white children dance around a Maypole, tangling and untangling its bright-colored ribbons. The scene shifts to the Briers, where Jefferson Davis marries Varina Howell (The Rose of Mississippi), and the bride bids farewell to her guests, little knowing that the man she has married is destined to lead the government of the Old South in the War Between the States. The scene shifts to the garden of a Big House with pillars. The happy, carefree children of the wellborn attend classes in the garden, with countless cousins, cousins of cousins, and cousins of cousins of cousins. Occasionally, an unruly child, or an ill-prepared one, interrupts the easy rhythm of the class, and is ordered by Schoolmaster to sit on a high stool and don a dunce's cap. This always brings down the house. The living pictures move on. Spirituals are heard being sung in the fields. The happy slaves are picking happy cotton. Polkas are danced in a Big House. Jefferson Military College holds its annual spring dance. (The Southern belles are ravishing.) Stirrup cups are raised before the start of the Hunt, in which pink-coated, aristocratic planters ride to hounds, and the hounds bay and strain at their leashes. Suddenly, war clouds rise. Sumter has been fired on. A way of life is threatened as the King and Queen and all their court hold a glittering farewell ball and, to the tune of "Dixie," speed the Confederate officers off to battle. To a great many Natchez white people, the Pageant does not represent a dead past. "They got themselves so confused," a Negro Natchez resident said recently, "that when they lookin' at the Pageant they think they're watchin' a newsreel, and that we're still in the fields pickin' cotton."

When Pilgrimage is over, the ghosts return to their houses and take up, ectoplasmically, where they left off. Sixteen antebellum houses keep open to tourists the year round, on a haphazard basis, and people visit them at a dollar a head. (Owners of Pilgrimage houses have a considerable stake in the Pilgrimage; their homes are virtually free of assessments.) Thousands visit Connolly's Tavern, the pride of the Natchez Garden Club, to admire its downstairs taproom, where rough rivermen once gathered to drink, tell gory tales, and sleep on the floor. Thousands more visit Stanton Hall, the pride of the Pilgrimage Garden Club, and often stop at the adjoining Carriage House for fried chicken with rice and giblet gravy. You can't beat the Carriage House for giblet gravy.

In the eleven months between Pilgrimages, Natchez settles down, stowing away its petticoats and swords. Once again, people become aware, on certain days and with the wind blowing in a certain direction, of the presence in town of the International Paper Company, for its acid fumes descend on the city. The automobiles of all the company's employees are sprayed with water as they leave the plant each day, so that no acid will be carried around town. "You must remember that the International Paper Company brings eight million dollars' worth of revenue into the city each year," a Natchez resident said not long ago, "and that a city such as Natchez will suffer a heap of chemicals in the air for eight million dollars." Natchez people become conscious again of the Mississippi, especially since a portion of the city slips into the river each year, owing to the looseness of the soil. "We keep losing bits and pieces of Natchez," a Natchez hostess remarked recently. "From time to time, some fine old family has to leave some fine old house that is teetering just a bit too close to the edge for comfort." Occasionally, a traveller passing through town will inquire about Natchez Under the Hill, a section below the bluffs, which is now largely washed away but was once reported to be the most murderous spot along the Mississippi. Brigands lay in wait for rivermen who had floated down the river on flatboats to New Orleans and then worked their way back up the river to Natchez, their pockets full, prior to heading north over the Natchez Trace, a leafy road that led from Natchez to Nashville. Natchez Under the Hill created its own species of criminal, not content with mere robbery but devoted to dismemberment, with special attention paid to the removal of the victims' eyes, ears, and tongues. Natchez Under the Hill once had a straightaway racetrack and countless taverns and houses of pleasure. Today, few people take the steep black road down to Natchez Under the Hill. Broken shutters rattle on the windows of dilapidated old brick houses there. Small Negro children dart in and out among the shacks. "Keep Off," reads a sign near a wharf; "Cream of Kentucky," reads a faded sign on the side of a building. The Mississippi, year in and year out, laps at the shores and makes inroads. Meanwhile, on top of the bluffs, the pecan factory moves briskly along. Trim Negro girls stand in clumps along a pecan production line, down which pieces of pecan jiggle on a moving belt, to move out, finally, upon a jiggling metal tray, where they shimmy and jump. Hour after hour, the girls cull the dark meat from the white meat. The dark meat is considered less desirable. "I pay my girls a dollar-fifteen an hour, or forty-six dollars a week," a man at the pecan factory said the other day. "Good pay, but I have my troubles, with girls havin' babies, or fixin' to have babies." The good pay has a tendency to divert strong, healthy young women from dusting off old chandeliers and horse prints. As one white matron recently expressed it, "Ah don't see how you can be expected to get good colored to come in and help when they're up in the pecan factory earning big wages." Pilgrimage comes and Pilgrimage goes, pecan factories open and pecan factories close, but what Natchez residents think about most and talk about most (an outsider might even call it an obsession) is the Situation. They think and talk about it all the time, winter and summer, morning and night. As a topic of conversation, ghosts run a poor second to the Situation. The Situation is terrible.

The Natchez residents who claim to know the most about the ghosts of Natchez agree that the ghosts at Longwood are the most inscrutable. Those ghosts never let a man know where they stand. The house they inhabit is a mysterious pink octagonal structure, rimmed with filigreed balconies and topped by a silvery turret. The construction of Longwood was interrupted by the start of the War Between the States. When the bugles began to blow, the workmen dropped their ladders, threw their hammers and saws into odd corners, abandoned their sandpaper, and marched off to battle. Today, the house stands incomplete, cobwebbed, and cavernous, and visitors often climb up and up to the top, startling birds and sending mice scampering. Everybody knows that the place is haunted, but nobody has ever heard a Longwood ghost make so much as a rustling sound. The ghosts are said to just hang around the place, ruminating. "When you come right down to it," a Natchez man who has familiarized himself with Natchez ghosts said not long ago, "Ah think the Longwood ghosts may be the smartest ghosts of all. They just stare, silently stare, at Natchez, sitting on the bluffs, slipping softly into the Mississippi."

(1963)

Omaha, Nebraska

Alt., 1,040. Pop., 301,598. Steaks mean a great deal to the people of Omaha. The people of Omaha not only hold them in considerable esteem but feel a deep and abiding affection for them. "Man and boy, rare, medium rare, medium, medium well, and well done, I have always loved a good steak," a long-time Omaha resident said the other day, his voice breaking. When an Omaha man (or boy) speaks of a steak, one expects him to pull from his pocket a series of treasured snapshots of steaks. Omaha is crowded with steakhouses, and the steakhouses are crowded with steaks. The steakhouses are crowded with natives, too, a good many of them distressed and perplexed, and often wounded in spirit, by the ordeal of ordering a steak. They have no trouble eating the steak, but they have never become reconciled to the ordeal of ordering it. The problem is one of terminology. Sometime during lunch, the average Omaha citizen will begin to think about the steak he is going to eat for dinner. Business worries, small irritations, jingling telephones—all these are sloughed off or submerged as he contemplates the vision of the steak that awaits him at the close of day. When the great moment finally arrives and he is seated in the steakhouse of his choice, the ritual begins. In a steakhouse, salad is served as a first course, and the waitress (waitresses outnumber waiters in the steakhouses of Omaha) must start out by determining what type of dressing he would like—Thousand Island, Roquefort, or Italian (a euphemism for a dressing that contains an ingredient unmentionable in the

Middle West; namely, garlic). Then, and only then, is it time to order the steak itself.

"And what kind of a steak will it be tonight?" asks the waitress.

The Omaha customer falls into the trap every time. "An Omaha steak," he says.

"You mean a Kansas City sirloin?" asks the waitress.

"No, an Omaha steak," says the customer, but the fight has already gone out of him.

"How about a nice strip sirloin, New York cut?" asks the waitress.

"I want an Omaha steak," says the customer.

"There just isn't any steak by that name," says the waitress. And there isn't.

The customer settles for a steak labelled something other than Omaha, but he has come close to snapping. "We know deep in our hearts that an Omaha steak is the Rolls-Royce of steaks, but try and find one," an Omaha steak addict recently remarked. "I've got nothing against a Kansas City sirloin, you understand, but it annoys me to think that Kansas City has something we don't have. Kansas City *always* seems to have something we don't have. As for a New York cut, I don't know what that is, really, and I don't care. I want an Omaha steak!" It's an unsettling situation.

Omaha bills itself as the World's Largest Livestock Market and Meat-Packing Center. Statistically, this is a fact. Omaha residents see no particular reason to keep the fact a secret, but the moment they pass the information along to the uninitiated they run into a dispiriting wall of skepticism. The situation, like that of the Omaha steaks, is enough to make a strong man weep. An Omaha livestock and meat-packing enthusiast—and the term is applicable to most of the literate population—is an encyclopedia of statistics: number of hogs slaughtered, number of sheep slaughtered, number of cattle slaughtered, total receipts of livestock on the hoof. These statistics trip off the tongue, and are generally greeted with some such remark from strangers as "What about Chicago?" or "Always thought Chicago had the largest stockyards" or "Isn't Chicago 'hog butcher for the world'?" "It's a kind of cultural lag," an Omaha man who works with hogs, and whose father before him worked with hogs, said not long ago. "Nothing much you can do except sit around and wait for the truth to catch up with the people." Actually, Chicago is fourth in livestock "receipts," with South St. Paul, Minnesota, and Sioux City, Iowa, second and third.

The Omaha Union Stockyards are models of gracious living quarters— more than a hundred acres of pens and buildings dedicated to making the last days of a sheep or steer or hog relaxed and comfortable. "We try to make the animals as happy as possible during their brief stay with us," one stockyard executive has said. "Really, we go about as far as we can go. We run a sort of hotel, you know, with nothing but quality food and plenty of it, and we are fanatical, almost, about keeping the stalls clean. The vast majority of our guests, of course, never get back for a return visit." The man was unable to continue speaking, and it was clear that the image of an Omaha steak had taken possession of his mind. More than six million head of livestock passed through the yards last year. They hailed from twenty-eight states. On Sunday nights, when the largest shipments arrive, trucks loaded with livestock are backed up for miles. The traffic jam is a fierce one, and noisy. The vast majority of these doomed transients end up in one of the nineteen packing plants in Omaha itself (all four of the largest packers—Cudahy, Armour, Swift, and Wilson—have plants adjoining the yards), but more than a million head are snapped up in Omaha by buyers and sent along to cities in thirty-six states. And more than six hundred thousand head of "feeder" stock are sent along to buyers in twenty-one states and Canada. Travel is broadening.

Omaha does not confine the comfort of its facilities to livestock. There are almost as many small hotels around town as there are steakhouses. They are cozy small hotels, and they are occupied, for the most part, by cattlemen. One of these cattlemen, stopping by a steakhouse, never makes the mistake of asking for an Omaha steak; he not only is satisfied with a Kansas City sirloin or a New York cut but generally orders a second one. Cattlemen cannot be distinguished from anybody else on the streets, however. "There is no cowboy theme on our streets," an Omaha man said recently. "No Western motif." Cattlemen have a habit of coming into town with their wives and dropping them off there. The cattlemen themselves waste little time in town. They head for the stockyards and find their pleasure in the yards proper (round the clock, hog calls fill the air), in the lobby of the Livestock Exchange Building, where livestock quotations are posted

("Trading moderate, active prices for butchers, and sows mostly steady"), and in the barbershop, the bank, the bar, the dining room, and the cafeteria (with steers-and-scenery murals) that are scattered through the building. Downtown Omaha is laid out like a grid, and the ladies walk up and down its streets shopping, many of them in Brandeis, a large store, or in the Thomas Kilpatrick and Co. Department Store, which up to a few years ago still sent out handwritten bills to its charge customers. It is all very well for the men to be at the yards, deep in butchers, barrows, and gilts, but they are missing many of the sights of a city that calls itself not only the World's Largest Livestock Market and Meat-Packing Center but the Crossroads of the Nation, the Agricultural Capital of the World, the Insurance and Finance Center of the Plains, the Nation's Largest Producer of Quick-Frozen Meat and Fruit Pies, the Gateway to the West, and the Gateway to the East. If one faces west, Omaha is the Gateway to the West. If one faces east, Omaha is the Gateway to the East.

Due east, across the Missouri, in Iowa, lies Council Bluffs. The bluffs themselves are high, brown, dusty, treeless, ominous palisades. Nothing seems to grow on them, and although real-estate developers keep eying them, they are uninhabited. Indians liked to powwow, chowchow, and blow smoke rings on Council Bluffs in the old days. The old days are gone. A cattleman's wife—or anybody else, for that matter—can stand gazing at Council Bluffs for so long that she will forget to turn west and see the tall headquarters of Mutual of Omaha and United of Omaha, or the fourteen-story home office of the Northern Natural Gas Company. Northern's chairman of the board, John F. Merriam, is a patron of the arts, a crusader for natural gas, a friend of pipelines, the chief designer of a unique circular conference table with moveable parts for his directors' room, and the sixty-sixth king of Ak-Sar-Ben, a powerful civic organization that engages in good works and operates a pari-mutuel track, an annual rodeo, and the celebrated 4-H Baby Beef Show. Ak-Sar-Ben is Nebraska spelled backward. The people of Omaha like the word Ak-Sar-Ben almost as much as the word Nebraska, and a bridge called the Ak-Sar-Ben connects Ahamo and Licnuoc Sffulb.

In Omaha, the land sweeps gently to the west, ever rising. Winds blow in from the plains, steaks are broiled, Ak-Sar-Ben crowns its kings, hospitals

are built, bulldozers churn up entire neighborhoods for interstate high-
ways. Life, as they say, goes on. Life goes on, too, at the headquarters of
the Strategic Air Command, several miles south of the city. "Don't Be
Alarmed at Sudden Jet-Engine Noises," reads a sign on the highway near
the approach to S.A.C. Headquarters. When visitors read the sign, they
jump. It is the first indication that there is something other than the smell
of pig in the Omaha air. Directly outside the huge headquarters of
S.A.C.—off the highway and up a wide drive—is a huge sign reading
"Peace Is Our Profession," and hard by it, amid neatly tended grass, stands
a huge, silvery Atlas Intercontinental Ballistic Missile. It is a striking
lawn ornament. The nerve center of S.A.C.—a retaliatory force, with
planes in the air at all times—lies forty-five feet below ground, in the command post. Visitors reach it by descending concrete ramps and passing
along fortresslike corridors, while being scrutinized by impassive guards
who wear sidearms, black boots with thick white laces, and dark blue berets. The berets have the intercontinental touch. Giant maps on rollers
stretch the length of a hundred-and-forty-foot-long room, which is
thirty-nine feet wide and twenty-one feet high. Heavy beige hangings
hide many of the maps. A two-story glass-enclosed observation post,
about fifty feet long, faces this room, which is the operations map room,
and a desk runs the length of the observation post. At intervals along the
desk are markers indicating which officer is to sit where and when: Chief
Disaster Evaluation, Disaster Control Operations, and so on. Weather
maps are everywhere. Facing the post, above the maps, are red clocks, blue
clocks, green clocks, telling the time in Moscow, Omsk, Thule, Alaska,
Tokyo, Guam, London, and Omaha. There is an Alert Hour clock. There
is an Execution Hour clock. "Emergency plans would be revealed by pulling back the curtains covering the maps," a colonel remarks. Behind the
observation post are thousands of red boxes, radar screens, switchboards,
and colored lights on control boards. A quiet buzz fills the air.

"Time is the important element in the entire operation," the colonel
says softly, but there is excitement in his voice. "To talk with Guam," he
says, "all I have to do is pick up a phone." He picks up a phone and talks
with Guam. "Can pick up a phone and talk anywhere in the free world
instantly," he says softly, but there is excitement in his voice. He draws in
his breath. "That's the gold phone," he says, pointing to a gold phone.

"The vital message would come in over the gold phone. And *that's* the red phone." He points to a red phone. "*The red phone!* The vital message would go out over the red phone. In fact, we have two red phones. *Can't take any chances on anything happening to the red phone!* Time is the important element in the entire operation. When Mr. K. wakes up in the morning in Moscow, we want him to know we are here. He doesn't forget we are here."

The bereted, white-laced guards are armed, the colonel says, in case someone should go crazy. That's the question most people ask him, the colonel says: What would happen if someone went crazy?

(1961)

Honolulu, Hawaii

Alt., 951. Pop., 294,194. "*Aloha*" is a powerful word in Honolulu. Say "*Aloha*," and doors open. "Believe me, you not only *can* say '*Aloha*' at all times of the day and night, and for practically all purposes, but you find that you *do* say '*Aloha*' at all times of the day and night," a resident of Honolulu recently told a visitor.

"*Aloha*," said the visitor, and a door opened.

The visitor found himself walking into the lobby of an old-fashioned high-ceilinged, white-pillared, Maugham-type hotel. "*Aloha*," said a young lady wearing a dazzling red muumuu. A three-ring *lei* of pastel orchids was draped around her neck. She draped a similar *lei* around the neck of the visitor. "I am to be your guide for this evening," said the young lady. "You are in beautiful Waikiki, a few miles from downtown Honolulu, on the beautiful island of Oahu, Honolulu County, U.S.A. The island of Oahu has about five-sixths of the population of the Hawaiian Islands and about 10 percent of the land area. All around you are glittering hotels, fine shops, and international restaurants, and *makai*—toward the sea—you can hear the soft sound of the turquoise combers breaking gently on beautiful Waikiki Beach. Behind us are the *maunas*—mountains—topped with swiftly moving gossamer rain clouds. Shiny white high-rise buildings have become the trademark of our progress on this volcanic island that rises from the sea: the twenty-seven-story condominium apartment house, the Ilikai, which is the largest ever built on fee-simple land, and the Ala Moana Building, twenty-five stories high, with a revolving restaurant on the top, which adjoins the Ala Moana Shopping Center—fifty acres, ninety stores, two levels, a parking area for five thousand cars, and trash baskets that read '*Mahalo*,' or 'Thank you.' " She drew a deep breath. "*Aloha*," she said.

"*Aloha*," said the visitor.

Someone in the lobby was languorously plucking a ukulele. The scent of suntan oil was overpowering. Swarms of men and women, many of them elderly and all of them arrayed in bright-colored sports costumes, flowed endlessly back and forth through the lobby, as though propelled by some strong tide. "Most of the people you see here are just happy visitors—businessmen and dentists, let us say, and schoolteachers, and people who have saved and know that Hawaii is just a wish away," said the young lady. "You find yourself in the heart of one of the most famous hotel strips on the face of the earth. We might be in the small, choice Waikikian, with its authentic Polynesian architecture and its hyperbolic paraboloid lobby and its Tahitian Lanai, or at the Princess Kaiulani, or at the Halekulani, or at the Royal Hawaiian, or at the Surfrider, or at the Hawaiian Village, but we are at the Moana, one of the older hotels. We might be about to attend a *puka puka*, an *otea*, a *poi* festival, or a Royal *Luau*, complete with *kalua* pig. We might be on the verge of eating *lomi-lomi* salmon or tidbits of *pupus*. Or we could be across the island at the Polynesian Cultural Center, with its representative dwellings of Tongans, Tahitians, Fijians, Samoans, and Maoris, drinking coconut milk and eating taro root, sweet potatoes, and Maori bread. But instead we are at the Moana, and we are about to attend a *Na Kapuna*."

"*Aloha*," said the visitor.

"Come with me," said the young lady, directing the visitor *makai*—toward the sea—through the lobby and into an open courtyard dominated by a large banyan tree. The sound of the ukulele followed them, as did the scent of suntan oil. Several hundred tables had been set up in the courtyard, and several hundred persons, counterparts of those milling through the lobby, were seated at the tables, eating. A small stage occupied one end of the courtyard. "First we will get our food," said the young lady, leading the visitor to a long buffet table covered with what before 1959 could certainly have been described as Stateside food: ham, corned beef, cold chicken, assorted cold cuts, potato salad, coleslaw, celery, olives, pickles, radishes, and so on. The visitor and his guide filled their plates and took seats at one of the long tables. *"Na Kapuna* really means an Old-Timers' Night, a night for the old folks, something out of the Gay Nineties, the days of the monarchy, shades of Kalakaua and Liliuokalani," she said.

"*Aloha*," said the visitor.

"*Aloha*," said his guide. "Hear the surf," she went on, holding aloft a drumstick. "Diamond Head twinkles beyond us, but we can't see it from here. Above us is the clear Pacific sky. Our days are balmy and our nights tempered by the caresses of the trade winds. But we can get *kona* weather, too—two or three days of hot, damp winds from the Big Island, known as Hawaii, when people sulk and become short-tempered and depressed. But tonight we have the spirit of *aloha*, the spirit of friendliness. You can say '*Aloha*' for hello or good-bye, or when inquiring into the health of your uncle or asking for the loan of a surfboard, or even at a wake. It is OK to say '*Aloha*' at a wake. The guests here tonight are, of course, *haoles*, or Caucasians, but Honolulu is made up of Portuguese, Puerto Ricans, Negroes, Filipinos, Hawaiians, Chinese, and Japanese as well. They are all said to live together in a spirit of great harmony, in a spirit of *aloha*, but the Japanese and the Chinese do not always get along, and many people do not seem to like the Portuguese. Right now our population is about one-third Caucasian and one-third Japanese. The stars are out. *Aloha*."

"*Aloha*," said the visitor.

The entertainment was about to begin. On the small stage, several grass-skirted girls performed the hula. Ukuleles tinkled. The *haoles* applauded wildly. Hawaii had been only a wish away, and the wish was being fulfilled. The guide whispered into the visitor's ear. "Now you will watch an authentic hula lesson," she said. "This always brings down the house at a *Na Kapuna*." An enormous elderly woman, who appeared to be a cross between Sophie Tucker and Bloody Mary, mounted the stage. She wore a grass skirt, and her face was covered with wrinkles. She was surrounded by a group of young men with ukuleles. A hush fell over the vast throng of *haoles* eating potato salad. The elderly woman suddenly began to sing, fervently and throatily, in a voice that could easily have been heard over the *maunas*. Her grass skirt rustled slightly. The song had a seductive, hypnotic cadence. The guide translated for the visitor. "She is singing of a love most precious," the guide whispered. "She says, 'It is like an appealing perfume in the heart; your eyes are flirtatious, and I feel that you are adequate to fulfill our joy.'"

"*Na na lea lea*," sang the old woman.

"She is coming to the end of her song," whispered the guide. "She is saying, 'This is the end of my story,' and she is talking of *aloha*, or love." When the old woman had finished singing, the *haoles* were silent for a moment, and then burst into applause. The wish had been fulfilled; they had heard a song of love under the stars on the island of their dreams.

The old woman had not even begun to fight. "Now we will have the hula lesson," she said, in English, and called upon half a dozen male members of the audience to join her on the stage. Some coaxing was required, but not much, and an assorted group of middle-aged men, with an assortment of middle-aged paunches, mounted the stage. They stood facing the audience, their faces wearing oddly simple expressions. The old woman revolved her stomach and hips, and fluttered her hands. "I am bumping the apple," she said, setting her hips in sidewise motion. "I am bumping the orange [hips again sidewise], hitting the coffee bean [stomach forward], grinding the coffee [stomach revolving], then taking a trip around the island and going downhill [all motions at once]." She asked the volunteers to follow suit. Sweat poured from their brows, their hips swayed, their paunches rose and fell. "Come on! Come on!" cried the old lady. "Bump the apple, bump the orange, hit the coffee bean, grind the coffee, take a trip around the island, and GO DOWNHILL!" The volunteers shook and quivered, and the other *haoles* screamed with delight.

"It is easy to see why our *Na Kapuna* evenings are so popular," said the guide. "And now I must say 'Aloha.' Our evening is over." She disappeared as mysteriously as she had arrived.

The visitor returned to his hotel room, overlooking the turquoise combers breaking gently on Waikiki Beach. On his bed, which had been neatly turned down, he found a tiny pink orchid. "*Aloha*," he said to himself as he drifted into slumber.

The hula is almost as powerful as the "*Aloha*." Strangers to the island who drive through the dense traffic of Honolulu are constantly surprised to see hands fluttering from the windows of cars in front of them and alongside them. "All those people waving their hands out the windows of all those cars are practicing the hula," a man who has lived a long time in Honolulu recently told a visitor. "The motions of the hands describe the motions of the sun and the moon and the planets, and emotions too numerous to enumerate. Everybody is doing the hula all the time. Why, they play the song 'Lovely Hula Hands' so often on the big white Matson liners that arrive every ten days that it has become known as the Matson national anthem." At Sea Life Park, just beyond Diamond Head, where showmanship is combined with scholarly marine research, the dolphins have been taught to perform the hula. It is one of the least of their attainments. Sea Life dolphins are trilingual—they respond to commands in English, Hawaiian, and Japanese. They are spotted, spinning porpoises, and they are an extraordinarily gifted lot. Within twenty-four hours of being removed from the ocean, they have learned to press levers, and within a month they can hula. They love to hula. They hula in a small lagoon called Whaler's Cove—near a replica of the New England whaling ship *Essex*—accompanied by a native girl called Puanani. Puanani is something of a dolphin herself. She swims back and forth across the lagoon, occasionally climbing onto a small man-made island at one end to call out "*Aloha.*" The dolphins leap into the air and smile their strange smiles. The smiles mean "*Aloha.*" Puanani and the dolphins then swim together around the lagoon. "Makua, jump high!" cries Puanani, and Makua, a dolphin with an IQ of a hundred and seventy-four, jumps high. Makua can jump as high as seventeen feet. "Good porpoise, Makua!" cries Puanani. She urges Makua to jump even higher, and Makua jumps even higher. "*Very* good porpoise!" cries Puanani. Puanani then calls for the hula, and the dolphins rise from the water, bump the apple, bump the orange, hit the coffee bean, grind the coffee, and splash back into the water. Then all hands take a trip around the island.

Every day, hundreds of people board small sightseeing boats docked in Kewalo Basin, near central Honolulu, and head for Pearl Harbor. They are the same people who sit on the beach at Waikiki, visit the pineapple canneries, shop for wooden bowls, put on funny shirts and funny hats, and learn to eat thick *poi* with their fingers. A recent visitor boarded one of the small sightseeing boats, which sailed past the breakwater and headed into the open sea. From the deck of the boat he could enjoy a broad panorama of the leeward side of peaceful Oahu—Diamond Head far behind, the beach at Waikiki, the high-rise buildings, the volcanic mountains, the tall Aloha Tower guarding the harbor, the pineapple-shaped tower of the Dole Company, and the International Airport. During the first part of the boat ride, Oahu seemed an unreal island in an unreal sea, but then, as the boat approached Pearl Harbor, it suddenly became a pinpoint target—a tiny volcanic mass of brown, green, and yellow earth. When the boat entered Pearl Harbor itself, the ship's passengers became hushed. An announcer briskly declared through a loudspeaker that within a few minutes all cameras must be temporarily stowed amidships. The boat passed Bishops Point, to starboard, and Iroquois Point, to port, and stopped briefly at Drydock No. 4. Naval Police came aboard, briefly. It was a perfunctory boarding—part of the haunting past and the instinctive precaution. The businessmen and dentists and schoolteachers wore puzzled looks. Cameras were gathered up. Ahead lay giant cranes and huge drydocks, submarines and destroyers, parade grounds and the neatly tended lawns of barracks. A giant troopship swung by, heading out to sea. In the distance were fields of sugarcane, and the ever-present clouds of rain hung over the mountains. The announcer was a controlled man. It was not in him lightly to hurt the sensibilities of anyone aboard, Caucasian or Oriental. At one moment, he spoke softly of a Japanese decision not to bomb a hospital ship lying in Pearl Harbor, but then he lowered his voice slightly, and it took on a metallic tone, as he mentioned the harbor entrance, guarded by nets, through which Japanese submarines made their way in December 1941. The boat chugged slowly past Ford Island, in the middle of Pearl Harbor. The announcer's voice became chillier, more impersonal. History, he seemed to be saying, is history, and history is worth remembering. "Streaking in over Oahu from the west at 7:40 A.M., Japanese planes struck at Schofield Barracks. . . . At 8:00 A.M., another flight of torpedo planes attacked from the east. . . . The second attack came at 8:40 A.M. from the northeast, the attacking groups consisting of dive-bombers, high-level bombers, and fighter aircraft, which flew offshore of Waikiki in a circuitous route to strike at their targets out of the sun." The tiny vessel swung into Battleship Row and came alongside the *Utah*, crippled in the water. Perhaps a fifth of the *Utah*'s decks were still visible, the water washing up and down and across their rusted surfaces. "The bodies of fifty-eight navy men who lost their lives aboard the *Utah* still remain in the battered hulk," the announcer said. The little boat rounded the northern tip of Ford Island, turned east, and then turned south, gliding almost noiselessly now past hunks and chunks and pieces of other submerged vessels—bits of bulkhead, bits of deck, scraps of superstructures lying quietly in the water. There was rust and sea and memory in this strange graveyard, where the grotesque shapes of silent ships lay on their sides. "These ships didn't want to go down," said the announcer. The boat paused briefly alongside the *Arizona*, her fore and aft still showing, her midships covered with a memorial concrete canopy. "The *Arizona* is still honored as an active ship by the navy; she is still in commission, and the flag still flies aboard her, and her crew of eleven hundred and two men still sleep below," said the announcer. There was nothing for anybody aboard the tiny vessel to say, and nobody said anything. The vessel slid past the remains of the *West Virginia*, the *Tennessee*, and the *Oklahoma*, and headed back into the open sea, turning in the direction of Waikiki and the gleaming high-rise buildings. Children sat quietly along the upper deck, enjoying the Pacific breezes, and nobody said, "*Aloha*."

(1965)

Exchange

This morning, I walked beside a freshwater pond on Cape Cod, and, somewhat to my surprise, I didn't see the pond. I saw, in my mind's eye, a pond by Monet—a glimmering, glistening, unforgettable pond, filled with dazzling reflections and unfathomable depths. And now, back in my house and looking out at masses of trees, I do not see *these* trees but trees of varying shades of blue and green by Cézanne—trees that, although merely paint on canvas (and not in front of me), seem to move and sway with a power all their own. The mundane facts can be simply stated: I recently visited the National Gallery, in Washington, to view an exhibit titled "Impressionist to Early Modern Paintings from the U.S.S.R."—paintings from the Hermitage Museum, in Leningrad, and the Pushkin Museum of Fine Arts, in Moscow. (The exhibit has moved on to Los Angeles, and will be at the Metropolitan Museum from late August to early October.) I am now remembering that visit, and I find that, as so often happens when one is in the presence, or the afterglow, of great art, it is difficult to deal with so-called reality. I find it hard to determine what is more real: the Cézanne trees I saw in Washington or the stately locusts (in full bloom) just outside my window.

Fantasies aside, my visit to the National Gallery began at eight-thirty on a gray and sultry morning, when, an hour and a half before opening time, I arrived in front of I. M. Pei's stark white vaulting triangles, known as the East Building. J. Carter Brown, the gallery's director, had suggested that I spend a quiet hour and a half alone in the galleries, before they opened to the public, and before visiting with him and some of his associates involved in the preparation of this important exchange show. Almost all the pictures from Russia are from two pioneering collections—that of Sergei Ivanovich Shchukin, a bold and farseeing lover of art, who, in addition to myriad other paintings, collected some thirty-seven Matisses and fifty-one Picassos, and that of Ivan Abramovich Morozov. Both Shchukin and Morozov were wealthy textile merchants. Many of the paintings had hung in the elaborate, heavily chandeliered dining room of Trubetskoy Palace, Shchukin's home in Moscow. After the Revolution, his collection was nationalized; the palace was no longer his. His life was, of course, in jeopardy. He was allowed to occupy a small room off the kitchen, and—in what must have produced for him unimaginably poignant moments—to act as official guide, explaining the paintings to visitors. Shchukin, a generous man, truly believed that his paintings belonged to the Russian people. Eventually, though, he moved to Paris, and he died there, in 1936. (Morozov, also a Muscovite, died in Carlsbad in 1921.)

I was met at the door to the new wing of the National Gallery by two uniformed guards, who viewed me with grave suspicion. I was rescued by the arrival of Randall Kremer, a personable young man from the gallery's information office. "We're expecting you," he said. "Come with me." We walked by the guards and through the high area that is the main open space on the ground floor. "People have been pouring through," said Mr. Kremer. "Great lines—thirty-three thousand the first ten days alone. Great excitement."

Suddenly, all the grayness of the Washington morning was transformed into a world of deep red. I was facing, just outside the entrance to the exhibit proper, Matisse's huge *Harmony in Red*, a nearly six-foot-by-seven-foot painting that had been one of the centerpieces of the Shchukin home and now belongs to the Hermitage. "Somehow or other, J. Carter Brown managed to get this one for us," Mr. Kremer said. "It had been promised to an exhibit in France, and at first was not to travel to any other American city. Fortunately, the Russians changed their minds, and the picture will be seen in the other two cities." The picture is unforgettable. There is a table, chairs, fruit on the table, fluted glass plates holding more fruit, carafes, and an austere, possessive woman with a tall orangy-red coiffure who is arranging the fruit. The wild pattern of the wallpaper—blue baskets, and what seem to be antic branches of trees—drops without perspective to encompass the table itself. Beyond a window are three small white trees: Snow? Blossoms? Memories? I stood silently in front of the painting. "I will leave you alone now," Mr. Kremer said, "and let you wander through the rest of the exhibit."

I had the galleries to myself, and for a moment this was hard to believe. I could stand back from the paintings, I could move up close to them. The exhibit had been divided among small rooms, with only a few pictures in each. There was a room of Cézannes: trees, bridges, an unforgettable self-portrait; a miracle of a woman in blue; a mountain deep in mystery, and a still life with a napkin shaped like a mountain, and equally mysterious. A tragic van Gogh of hopeless prisoners, walking hopelessly in an unbreakable circle—an utterly claustrophobic circular prison space. A room of exotic, warmly colored Gauguins, with titles such as *Aha Oe Feii?*, meaning, in Tahitian, "Are You Jealous?," and *Nave Nave Moe,* meaning "Reveries," both of these framed in elaborate gold with Russian legends: a room with ancient dreams of ancient gods, blue canoes, cigarette-smoking nude natives with sly eyes, and another piercing self-portrait—this one, of Gauguin, without the deceptive self-confidence of the Cézanne, and betraying Gauguin's dark troubles. A Matisse room. Goldfish in a bowl, atop a purple tabletop with slim green legs. And another huge Matisse, the size of *Harmony in Red*, titled *Conversation*. Two figures face one another: presumably Matisse, in blue pajamas with vertical white stripes, on the left, and, on the right, a woman in black, her neck bordered in green, who is presumably his wife. She is of stern visage. There is a window between them, and figuratively connecting the two is a curlicued metal window guard. Its design binds them together and at the same time separates them. It catalyzes. Perhaps they are being destroyed. Perhaps they are being restored. Beyond the grillwork, there is truce and a peace—a tree and three small pools of water. But the two figures are commanding and disturbing presences.

HE: But I don't see how you could possibly . . .
SHE: It is perfectly clear to me, and would be to you if you would be honest with yourself for just one single moment of our lives. . . .

Another room. Picassos. A still life with skull, a Cubist portrait of the dealer Ambroise Vollard (sly, sullen, imperious, pretending to be asleep), and, in the same room, three monumental women—massive, gigantic figures from some deep and unknown past. I think I could have stood in front of the picture of the three women for many hours, but guards had now begun to come into the room, and there was suddenly a great bustle, and the sound of hundreds of voices. The public was being admitted. The pictures were no longer mine, but there had been almost vocal communication between us. Now the dialogue was to be enlarged.

Mr. Kremer reappeared at my side and escorted me to the executive floor, on seven, and into the office of J. Carter Brown. Mr. Brown is fifty-one but looks like a man of forty. He is slim and enthusiastic. He has been the director of the gallery since 1969, when he was thirty-four. He was in blue—blue suit, blue tie. A Capitol somewhat shrouded in mist was visible through his large window, its dome forming a perfect centerpiece. On his walls were a lively Klee, a poetic Rothko, and a religious painting. "Rubens," Mr. Brown said. "Or school of. The painting comforts me. You will notice that St. Peter is holding the keys to heaven. I have no guarantee, but I like to think this may give me a certain advantage." He smiled a youthful smile. "This whole wonderful exchange of paintings has a somewhat long history," he said. "It derives from a visit I paid in 1983 to Lugano, Switzerland, and to the Villa Favorita, the villa and museum maintained there by Baron Heinrich Thyssen-Bornemisza. We know the baron quite well. He is on our Trustees Council. He has a wonderful collection. Well, in 1983 he had an exchange of paintings with the Soviet Union. The pictures were displayed in an inspired manner—in clusters, in small rooms. I instantly said to myself, 'If we ever have a show like this, we must exhibit in the same way, in clusters, never too much in one room—each room a feast.' The Picassos were in a stairwell, the Matisse *Harmony in Red* in a room with wallpaper of figurations much like those in the painting itself. The baron stayed home and bargained with the Soviets. They always require symmetry. They give you something, you give them something. One makes them a sporting proposition. Things seemed to be going well in June of 1983, when I saw the exhibit. The baron had given them some wonderful things, including a van Eyck. Noises from the U.S.S.R. were positive in those days. There hadn't been a chance of exchanging pictures back in 1980, for example, during the boycott of the Olympics following the invasion of Afghanistan. But in 1983 everybody seemed to be for it. Secretary Shultz; Arthur Hartman, our ambassador to the Soviet Union; Charles Wick, head of the United States Information Agency—they were all for it. I thought we were set, and got back here filled with hope.

"Then, in September, we heard of the downing of the Korean airliner. Flight 007. I knew that our hopes had gone down with that plane. But some instinct was at work in me, and I proceeded as though we would have an exhibit after all. We had the Swiss transparencies of the pictures from the Hermitage and the Pushkin. I had faith. I worked out a truce with Pei for proper spacing for the still imaginary exhibit. I wanted control of the space in our galleries. Space is the key to this exhibit. Cluster is the key to this exhibit. We have learned how to invoke space in our galleries—the long gallery, for instance, in our 'Treasure Houses of Britain' exhibit. One thing I knew was that if the moment of agreement came we had to assure the Soviets that the paintings would be immune from judicial seizure. Heirs whose works have been nationalized might complain. There was an instance once in Paris—perhaps apocryphal—of a truck driven by Russian exiles backing up to a gallery and removing a painting. Some people look upon a cultural exchange of this nature as a political thing. I fight that notion. I see this as being part of the history of painting. After all, great art always teaches you something new. In matters of this kind, the political angle is both possible and impossible, often at the same time. Politics in this sort of agreement is really a roll of the dice. A man like Armand Hammer, for instance, never leaves the Soviet Union without a signed agreement. Won't leave until he has a piece of paper in his hand. To go back for a moment, I went ahead and constructed the galleries you were in this morning. I had a hunch something would happen, and it paid off. First, though, there was a stagnant period. Everything was 'Nyet.' Not a chance. I said to myself, 'We will wait for a cultural agreement.' I had a strange confidence that *one* thing would come out of a summit—a cultural agreement. That would be the meeting of the minds. When the agreement finally came, in November of 1985, we were ready. We were all geared up. Cables went back and forth. Curators went back and forth. The Soviets agreed to send over forty pictures in eighty days. Quick movement was required. We live, after all, in the real world, and one never knows how long any of this harmony will last. I put great pressure on them for the magnificent *Harmony in Red*. It had been promised for a French exhibit, but I managed to get it for our museum.

"I want to talk for a moment about some of the paintings. That great Picasso of the three women; 1908. He is getting into African art. When you look at it, you realize he is in the midst of a search rather than a discovery. I am fascinated with this picture—its monumentality. There is a background for it—Cézanne bathers. The women have their arms over their heads as though drying themselves. Russet. Clay colors. Wonderful colors. But Picasso is putting his entire weight into the form rather than the color. The energy is palpable. The figures are *bursting* from the canvas. I see the picture as going back to Michelangelo's *Bound Slave*, in the Louvre, rather than to the Cézanne. Picasso knew his art history, and he was certainly familiar with that sculpture. As for the Picasso *Still Life with Skull*, perhaps 1907, that, too, grips me. Picasso made conundrums, and there are many in this painting. There is, of course, a long history of *vanitas* still lifes, and this picture has many objects reflecting pleasure. There are books, a pipe, a palette with brushes, perhaps a mirror reflecting death and the skull itself. But there is a mystery in the upper right of the picture. I can sense a nude woman in what may be a mirror or a picture frame, and she has a hysterical grimace. Perhaps her hands are over her head, as in the incomparable *Three Women*. We really don't know. There is a theory that while painting Picasso looked out his studio window and saw the body of a neighboring German painter, Vigels, who had hanged himself in his studio window. This may well be the basis of the picture." Mr. Brown looked out at the misty Capitol dome. "It is a gray day," he said.

When I left Mr. Brown's office, I ran into Charles Stuckey, the curator of modern painting. "Let's have a cup of coffee," he said, and he led me into a nearby employee cafeteria. Mr. Stuckey is in his early forties, with large eyes and, again, great enthusiasm. "As you know," he said, "this entire show is based on Carter Brown's visit to Lugano. There has been a true exchange with the Soviets. We have sent over forty paintings, including Courbets, Degas, Bonnards, Cézannes, Pissarros, Monets, Sisleys, and so on. There was hard bargaining on a high professional level over each painting. Each picture was carefully examined. Curiously, they had their hearts set on one picture, our Manet *Dead Toreador*. They had seen it reproduced, and they simply had to have it. They got it. Once the summit took place, last November, I promptly went to Leningrad and to Moscow, with David Bull, who is the head of painting conservation here. Bargaining, bargaining. I still don't know how Carter Brown managed the *Harmony in Red*. But there it is, downstairs. I must tell you that everybody was bending over backward to understand everybody else. The most touching thing is that the pictures we sent to Russia have been viewed by thousands of people, standing long hours in long lines at, for instance, twenty-eight degrees below zero. That says something about the needs of people everywhere. When you are dealing with the Russians, you are dealing with people who know what they are doing. We were always sizing one another up. To our surprise, at first they didn't want Monet's *Garden at Vetheuil*. It wasn't a haystack and it wasn't a water lily. But they changed their minds. They wanted, for instance, more Degas than Cézanne. They have, they feel, too many Corots. Funny thing, you might have a hard time interesting them in a show by David, for instance, but they would line up at all hours for Goya, El Greco, Picasso. All Spaniards. And they truly love Gauguin. I guess he represents sunshine and warmth in the long Russian winters. We had some trouble explaining that we couldn't lend our great Picasso *Family of Saltimbanques*. It's part of the Chester Dale Collection and, under the terms of the acquisition, never to be lent. Bull and I concentrated on obtaining the great Matisse *Conversation*. It has never been seen before in this country. I was so impressed by Matisse's blue striped pajamas that I went over to Woodward & Lothrop the other day and bought a pair that look very much like those pajamas. They are tight. While we were dealing with the staffs of the museums—with, for example, A. G. Kostenevich, of the Hermitage, and M. Bessonova, of the Pushkin (she is a woman, by the way)—Armand Hammer was dealing on another level, with the ministries, the political people. Incidentally, the director of the Hermitage has been there forty years, the director of the Pushkin thirty. One must bear in mind that the exchange process is just starting. There has been a quantum leap in the last three or four months between the two countries. We have experienced quite an education dealing with our Russian counterparts. After all, they have a longer museum tradition than we do. I don't know where these people were trained, but I do know that if there were Olympic prizes for museum skills these people would come up with gold medals."

After leaving Mr. Stuckey, I had a brief encounter with John Wilmerding, the gallery's deputy director. He, too, is immensely personable, knowledgeable, and outgoing. We talked for a few moments of the Shelburne Museum, in Vermont, which was founded by his grandmother, Mrs. J. Watson Webb. It happens to be one of my favorites—a potpourri of everything from farm implements to a side-wheeler and duck decoys. "That side-wheeler was a funny one," Mr. Wilmerding said. "My grandmother was intent on its being in the museum. 'Watson,' she said to my grandfather, 'we must have that side-wheeler brought in from Lake Champlain, and placed in the museum.' 'Electra,' said her husband, 'you are crazy, but I know I can't stop you.' So tracks were laid from Lake Champlain, and the side-wheeler somehow got to the museum, sinking many times into the spring mud. But, to get back to our wonderful Russian pictures, think for a moment of the mutual trust that has taken place: our treasures there, their treasures here. They have sent the equivalent of hard currency—millions of dollars' worth of pictures—right into our bastion of evil. The pictures could be held hostage, after all."

I asked how he accounted for the great public interest in the pictures.

"You know," he said slowly, "it has something to do with originals, the real thing. Almost everything these days is a replica. Television offers no nourishment. There are replicas of this, replicas of that. Even the human heart may now be synthetic—a reproduction. A most touching thing happened when our Russian friends, the curators, went through the exhibit here. The curator from the Pushkin walked through the final door, and there was Picasso's *Woman from Mallorca*, on loan from her museum. There was that beautiful woman with the white kerchief over her head. So quiet, so lovely. And then the curator walked a few steps farther, into a larger room with our pictures, and there was our great Picasso *Family of Saltimbanques*, and on the extreme right of the picture was that same woman from Mallorca. I could see how deeply moved the woman from Moscow was."

I went downstairs for a last look at the pictures. Crowds six and seven deep were now around each canvas. They were silent. They were engrossed. I stood a moment gazing at the incomparably quiet woman from

Mallorca, keeping her message proudly to herself. And then I, too, turned a corner into a larger room, and there the woman was again, seated, over the long years, in a Beckett landscape, in the company of Picasso's travelling carnival players, noble survivors in a hostile world. And I had a slim clue to the message of the pictures: there are no boundaries, no barriers, except those which we erect in our blindness.

(1986)

Indian Summer

There were some true Indian-summer days last week—midautumn days
of mild weather, following the first frost, with clear blue skies above and a
gray-orange haze hovering below. Indian-summer days have always delighted us (they are an unexpected premium, a last, grasping reminiscence), and on one of those eighty-odd-degree days we left our hat on a
wintry hook in the office and headed down toward the Battery. Don't ask
us why we headed down toward the Battery. It was Indian summer, and we
headed down toward the Battery. Water had something to do with it, we
suppose, and the sense of living on an island, and reaching out and back
on such a lovely day. It seemed as though the people we passed along the
street were abstracted in a happy, quiet way, as though they, too, were
thinking of far-off places and pleasant things done long ago. We collided
with a young man down near Bowling Green (he wasn't looking where he
was going), and he said, quite solemnly, "I beg your pardon." It had been
a long time since anybody had said, "I beg your pardon," to us on a New
York street. There was something in the air. Indian summer. The windows
of the Isbrandtsen Line, on lower Broadway, were filled with sleek models
of freighters, and the freighters looked as though they wanted to steam
right out through the windows and head for the sea. We walked into Bowling Green Park and looked at the statue of Abraham de Peyster, a plump
Dutch chap from the old, old days when Bowling Green was Rockefeller
Center. He sits placidly watching the Custom House. De Peyster was just

about everything one could be around Nieuw Amsterdam when there were Indians on hand for the Indian summers: alderman, mayor, comptroller, acting governor of the province—a sort of Robert de Moses. The Sara Woodard Memorial Chrysanthemum Planting in the park was still alive, and deceptively soft in color, since it was prepared to survive Indian summer, and Halloween, and Thanksgiving.

Our steps turned south again, to Cass Gilbert's lump of a Custom House, and up to the huge, buzzing rotunda on the second floor, where hundreds of exporters were having their export declarations declared, or checked, or scrutinized, or whatever one has done to an export declaration. The exporters stood in front of the clerks at an elliptical desk a city block long, and looking down on all of them were the harbor murals of Reginald Marsh: the giant three-stackers, the squat tugs, the cargo being unloaded, the celebrity (Greta Garbo) being interviewed on shipboard, the longshoremen, the smoke, the sea, *Ambrose Lightship*—the whole salty wonderworld of the Port of New York. How Marsh did it we will never know, but he did it, *a secco*, on a ceiling with concave surfaces that curve both horizontally and vertically. A clerk noticed us craning our neck. He was a romantic-looking fellow. A long line of exporters were awaiting his attention, but he forgot them. "Like the murals?" he asked.

We nodded.

"Marsh was very popular down here with everybody," he said. "He was willing to work for ninety cents an hour to do these murals for the Federal Arts project, because he wanted to perpetuate his work. He was an artist, all right. He lived on Fourteenth Street and he knew the city. New Yorkers hardly ever come in here, but out-of-towners do. Big shots come through once in a while on a tour, but I notice they don't linger. I love the one up there with the car being unloaded."

The line of exporters grew impatient.

The clerk sighed. "I love them all," he said, "but I especially love the one with the car being unloaded."

We thanked him, and left the Custom House, and walked along the sea wall near the old Battery. The old Battery is Clinton National Monument now, and rather forbidding, but there was Indian summer in the air, and haze, and the sun trying to beat its way through, and gulls just sitting and bobbing up and down on the water, and foghorns, and a Turner-like orange mist all over the harbor. We stopped by a souvenir stand and bought a rabbit-foot attached to a button that was also orange. The button read, "New York." The concessionaire was talking to a small man in a bowler hat. "You see my silvery models of the Statue of Liberty?" he was saying. "Well, they're not real silver, but do you remember a poem called 'The Midnight Ride of Paul Revere'?"

The man in the bowler hat said he did.

"Well, Revere was a silversmith," said the concessionaire, "and he put his mark on the bottom of his silverwork, and sometimes people come across one and it's worth a hundred dollars."

The man in the bowler hat nodded appreciatively and looked out across the harbor.

"I think I know the name of the period," the concessionaire said. He was looking out over the harbor, too. "It was Colonial. The Colonial period."

"Yeh, yeh, that's right," said the other man.

We walked along West Street, and at Liberty Street took a ferry (the *Wilkes-Barre*) to Jersey City. We wanted to be out on the water, if only for a few minutes. The city was meshed in haze. Indian summer. There was an autumn tinge in the air, a hint of what was coming, and the river had a swell to it. We walked around the terminal on the Jersey side for a few minutes, and came back to Manhattan on the ferry *Red Bank*, and it wasn't until we were out on West Street again that we realized nobody had asked us for any money. A beautiful ride, and a free one.

Nobody really knows how Indian summer got its name, but we like to think that it has something to do with the Indians' giving us summer back for a few restful, easy days and then taking it away again before people get too many notions.

(1956)

Design by David Bullen
Typeset in Mergenthaler Garamond #3
by Wilsted & Taylor
Printed by Malloy Lithographing
on acid-free paper